"Most consultants write about what they know; only a select few can write well about what they live. Ginny lives the material in this book, and anyone fortunate enough to participate in one of her leadership workshops will find this book to be a stimulating reminder of the key lessons learned there. For those who haven't participated in her workshops, this book will give a taste of what it looks and feels like to be a focused, grounded leader in an age of great speed and distraction. Highly recommended!"

—Eric Olson, PhD, Global Practice Managing Partner, Heidrick & Struggles

"**The Zen Leader** is an empowering guide for anyone in business or public service who wants to express an effective, inspired, full-bodied style of leadership that both engages humanity and preserves sanity."

—Lisa Sarasohn, author of *The Woman's Belly Book*

"This is a wonderful book—a great contribution to the field!"

—Dr. Stephen Rhinesmith, author of *A Manager's Guide to Globalization*

"Timely and relevant, **The Zen Leader** suggests a profound shift in our thinking. Whitelaw's paradigm shift transforms us from being proverbial hamsters in suits to actually thriving in the midst of chaos. This should be recommended reading for leaders in all categories!"

—Jane M. Stevenson, vice chairman, board & CEO services, Korn/Ferry International; author of *Breaking Away*

D0089688

"Dr. Whitelaw brings together her experience as a PhD biophysicist, a leader at NASA, and a Zen Master to provide a unique and practical perspective to the juggling act called leadership. In **The Zen Leader** Dr. Ginny Whitelaw shares with readers her passion and commitment to supporting leaders in achieving a balance between their doing and their being. With a very practical approach she interweaves theories and techniques that combine the challenges and realities of leadership with an understanding of Buddhist principles that allow one to step back and contemplate and seek higher levels of consciousness and awareness. Her explanations and acknowledgment of our physical bodies and sensations as stress barometers is of particular interest as one of the many examples of simple indicators of imbalances and extremes."

—Betty Shotton, CEO and founder of Liftoff Leadership, LLC, leadership speaker, and author of *Liftoff Leadership*

"...an incredible journey through soul-searching ideas, critical leadership issues, and practical exercises that embed the understanding and ability to make the flip at our very core. Fascinating!"

—Virginia McLaughlin, Oliver Wyman Leadership Development

"...craftsmanship of a high order. The writing is original, creative, penetrating, insightful, humane, and grounded in the body...it goes far beyond ordinary advice."

—Gordon Greene, Roshi, Chozen-ji Wisconsin Betsuin

The
Zen Leader

The
Zen Leader

10 Ways to go from Barely Managing to Leading Fearlessly

GINNY WHITELAW

The Career Press, Inc.

Pompton Plains, N.J.

THE ZEN LEADER
EDITED AND TYPESET BY KARA KUMPEL
Cover design by Wes Youssi/M80 Branding
Printed in the U.S.A.

To order this title, please call toll-free 1-800-CAREER-1 (NJ and Canada: 201-848-0310) to order using VISA or MasterCard, or for further information on books from Career Press.

The Career Press, Inc.
220 West Parkway, Unit 12
Pompton Plains, NJ 07444
www.careerpress.com

Library of Congress Cataloging-in-Publication Data
Whitelaw, Ginny.
    The Zen leader : 10 ways to go from barely managing to leading fearlessly / by Ginny Whitelaw.
        p. cm.
    Includes bibliographical references and index.
    ISBN 978-1-60163-211-1 -- ISBN 978-1-60163-604-1 (ebook) 1. Leadership--Psychological aspects. 2. Management--
    Psychological aspects. 3. Zen Buddhism. I. Title.

    HD57.7.W476 2012
    658.4'092--dc23

2012000055

to the old man in the woods
who has nowhere to go,
and to you
who are going somewhere

Acknowledgments

I AM SO grateful to the people who have made this book possible: to my teacher and friends, Gordon Greene Roshi, Pat Greene, Ken Kushner Roshi, Everett Ogawa, Alex Greene, and Ximena Prudencio: the fire of our shared training surely germinated the seed of this book. I am grateful to my earlier teachers, Tanouye Roshi, Hosokawa Roshi, and Toyoda Rokoji, whose compassionate edge sliced through the clay. Deep thanks also go to the Daihonzan Chozen-ji, and Yokoyama Roshi, Tsuha Roshi, and Honda Roshi, who inspire me again and again.

For the leadership learnings and inspiration of this book, I owe a great deal to my clients and a terrific group of colleagues: Stephen Rhinesmith, Yolanda Hofer, Gavin Wallbridge, Lars Cederholm, Alicia Dahill, Eric Olsen, Virginia McLaughlin, Agnes Mura, Susan Dunn, Carole France, Michael Hansen, Gyongyi Kallai, and Bob

Caron. For opening this entire path and paving it with enormous joy, I thank my remarkable husband and partner, Mark Kiefaber. I also thank Anthony Attan for the great growth he's bringing to our work at Focus Leadership, and Will Kiefaber for skillfully servicing it.

When this book started to sprout, I wrote to publisher Constance Kellough, who could have ignored me, but instead became a terrific guide. I thank her and the chain of catalysts who brought this book into being, from Holly Kerby to David Dotlich, Barbara Monteiro, Leah Spiro, Maryann Karinch, and finally, Michael Pye and the great publishing team at Career Press. Extra thanks to my multi-talented sister, Diane Chencharick, for her insightful reviews, clever illustrations, and website artistry. I further thank Diane, Barbara, Anthony, Mark, and the team now helping to get this book out to the world.

And finally, I so deeply appreciate the family that let me sprout: my parents—John and Betty Whitelaw—Mary Whitelaw, Jean Lane, and Larry Whitelaw.

Contents

Zen is to transcend life and death (all dualism),

to truly realize that the entire universe is the True Human Body

>*through the discipline of mind and body in oneness.*

>*Miyomoto Niten (Musashi) called it* Iwo no mi *(body of a*

>>*huge boulder—*

>>*going through life rolling and turning like a huge boulder);*

>*Yagyu Sekishusai named it* Marobashi no michi *(a bridge*

>>*like a round ball—*

>>*being in accord with the myriad changes of life).*

>*Besides this actual realization, there is nothing else.*

—from the Canon of Daihonzan Chozen-ji, Honolulu, Hawaii

Omori Sogen Rotaishi

October 1, 1979

Introduction

Reaching the Boiling Point

IT'S SUNDAY NIGHT, and I'm welcoming a group of high-potential leaders to a five-day executive leadership program. "How many of you seriously doubted that you had time to be here this week?" I ask. Every hand shoots into the air with a collective moan of acknowledgment. Any pause in the action and BlackBerrys pop from their holsters: scroll, scroll, check, scan, thumb, thumb a five-word response, hit Send, now back with you, didn't miss a thing. As I get to know these leaders I learn what's top of mind: *Where are we going? How can this company expect me to keep doing more with less? Why didn't I get the promotion I'd been promised? How much more of this can I take?* These are incredibly talented leaders—consummate multitaskers—yet they would tell you that keeping up with the pace is a relentless challenge and, most of the time, they're barely managing.

It's a week later and I'm holding a coaching session with a recently promoted VP, one of the success stories of her company. "If there were two of me, I couldn't get this job done," she says, giving me a rapid-fire rundown of her reality. "I'm being asked to double the book of business, innovate new products, develop my people—and oh, by the way, cut 20 percent of them—build this global brand team with people I've never met, and let's not forget the second job I go home to." My pulse has picked up five beats a minute just listening to her. A picture flashes in my mind of those flat, little tile puzzles I used to play with as a child that had 16 spaces and 15 tiles, and the game was to rearrange them into a picture. Except hers was a 16-tile life—no space whatsoever, no way to move. This is success? I sense the wonderful discipline and drive for achievement that has brought this woman so far. And yet she's now living a life that is more suffocating than rewarding. By her own account, she's barely managing.

Examples such as these are neither isolated nor unusual, but rather a product of our times and our state of development colliding in a seemingly unsolvable tension to *do more*. Technology has supercharged the pace of life and business, as evident in how quickly news, products, and jobs move around the world, and in the high-frequency electronic messaging that has us, on average, parsing 176 e-mails a day[1]—not to mention tweeting, streaming, and Linking In.

Moore's Law tells us technology is capable of doubling its capacity every few years. We, too, are increasing our capacity, especially the most achievement-driven among us who tend to land in lives of leadership. We're working faster, more efficiently, longer, and harder. All of which is reaching a boiling point evident in measures of workplace stress: 75 percent report their jobs are "very stressful"; 1 in 3 say that they're heading for burnout;[2] 61 percent say heavy workload has a significant impact on stress level, with executives and managers having the most stressful jobs.[3] The U.S. Bureau of Labor Statistics estimates job stress costs businesses more than $300 billion dollars a year.[4] As one leader put it to me,

"At first we responded to the pressure by working weekends. But what do you do when weekends are used up?" If speeding up is our answer, face it, we'll never keep up with Moore's Law.

For good reason: speed leads to more speed. As technologies accelerated the pace of business, for example, it was natural that leaders would speed up, maybe get a mobile device to read e-mails in the 13 seconds spent waiting for an elevator, and now—surprise!—everyone is doing the same thing, an order of magnitude more messages are flowing, and the cycle escalates. Businesses could use technology to replace customer service people with kiosks, setting new competitive standards that squeezed out entire industries, and now, even more has to be done with even less. *Leaner*, *smarter*, *faster*, *cheaper* have become common watchwords in the strategies of companies and the tactics of leaders.

As leaders, we might respond with one-minute management techniques, speedy tweets, and technology-turbocharged multitasking, which all work for a while, even as they thin out our life experience, as we flit from one thing to the next. What's more, we become remarkably unconscious of the price we're paying in attention span, health, relationships, and even intelligence. A study done at the Kings College of Psychiatry in London showed that when people multitasked, they firmly believed their performance wasn't affected at all, while objective measures showed their effective IQ dropped 10 points![5]

Yet like frogs in a pot of slowly heating water who never detect the trend and leap to safety, our tendency is to stay in the game, put up with the pressure, and find better ways to manage it. We try to manage our time, quiet our minds, control our tempers, dull the pressure with drink or drugs, escape from it temporarily on a trip or a weekend (still regularly checking our e-mail), and throw ourselves at it again on Monday morning. We might have even picked up *The Zen Leader* hoping it will show us how to be peaceful in all this churn. And in one sense, it will fulfill that promise. But if we take to this book as just another stress-reduction technique to cope with pressure, it will fail to serve us as fully as it could. Because if we're just trying to manage the pressure, no matter how well we do it, as it heads toward the boiling point, we head toward trouble.

Do we break down? Do we give up? Those may feel like the only choices, and surely many have made them.

Leaders for a Better World

But the life of leadership demands another choice. *The Zen Leader* opens up an entirely different possibility: to *use* the pressure, rather than be used by it. Yes, pressure can feel terrible. It is what "necessity" feels like, as in necessity being the mother of invention. You can bet that the first creatures to claw their way onto dry land weren't finding the ocean to be a perfectly comfortable place to live. But the upside of pressure is that it can propel breakthrough development and leaps to new consciousness. Einstein once said, "We cannot solve problems at the same level we were at when we created them." If our stage of development is not up to the challenges we have created, our only healthy alternative as leaders is to *break free and flip to the next stage.*

It is perhaps no accident that this pressure should show up heaviest on the shoulders of today's leaders, for the very word *leader* suggests one who goes first. Leaders who can *use* this pressure to propel their development create a better world, or what Eckhart Tolle calls "a new earth." They are leaders in whom a radically new consciousness begins to emerge—not all at once, but in waves of increasing effect and endurance—who lead beyond their own egos, who can attract the future with joy and enthusiasm, rather than exhausting themselves and their people. They are people who may not even consider themselves leaders, but through their authentic self-expression, they add value, create beauty, or set others free. They are those who have leapt from the proverbial frog's pot, only to find that even this leap doesn't "take" the first time it's tried. Yet neither is this development one safe, plodding step after another. Rather it's discontinuous, nonlinear, a phase shift from this to that, from not-seeing to seeing, from in-the-pot to free. Whereas this development may be supported by process and practice, it is not itself a process, but more of a radical reframing, an inversion: a *flip*. It is a flip that takes many forms; for example:

- ❧ from coping with pressure outside-in, to diving right in and transforming situations from the inside out.

- ❧ from exhausting oneself and others in the drive for results, to attracting the future and people who help create it.

- ❧ from *being* one's personality—playing only to strengths—to *seeing* one's personality and applying the right kind of energy to any situation.

These flips in consciousness are all grounded in the human body, where they manifest as various energy patterns, muscular tension, thoughts, emotions, body language, leadership presence, style, and behaviors. Each of these flips is an experience—not just a concept—and each flip unfolds more of the natural Zen leader in you.

In me? Yes. For here is the truth of it: The Zen leader is not some model "out there" for you to emulate. Rather, it is your own dynamic Being, leading beyond the ego, creatively adapting moment by moment—like a ball on fast-moving waters. To realize this leader, each chapter guides you through a flip that is both inwardly profound and outwardly practical. Not only will you find *your* energy and presence transformed by these flips, but the tools of leadership are transformed as well: how you set vision and strategy, create the future, develop and inspire others, and optimize hard choices. You'll learn how to reframe problems into opportunities, shift victims into players, and turn pressure into progress. Far from barely managing, you'll discover how to lead fearlessly, using joy and enthusiasm as your guides. If this sounds like some kind of nirvana, that's no coincidence; these flips build on one another and lead to the ultimate inversion in consciousness—the final chapter—from delusion to awakening.

The pressure will not go away. But here is a way beyond giving up or giving in. Rather, give way and reveal the Zen leader in you. Do we ever need it!

1

From Coping to Transforming

"CALM UNDER PRESSURE." "A quiet mind with wisdom."
"Peaceful, above it all." These are the answers I'm hearing from
a group of leaders who have joined me for a workshop on Zen and
Leadership, after I've asked them to describe a "Zen leader." They
have come here for perhaps the same reasons you picked up this
book: They want to be more successful in their work, happier in
their lives, and more peaceful in themselves. Do I have something
to give them—sort of the Zen equivalent to noise-canceling head-
phones—that will help them cope with their challenging days? No,
this is not about coping. Will I help them rise above it all? No, this
is not about becoming aloof. Will I give them anything?

"No," I tell them, as I tell you: You already have everything
you need. What I will help you do is clear out what you don't need.

Break free of the points where you're stuck. See beyond what boxes you in. I will show you how to flip to new levels in your development where the untenable problems of the last level become as easy as child's play. I call these "flips" because they invert ordinary ways of thinking, and radically reframe your sense of self and the world. These flips transform your leadership to truly serving others, and not your own needs for security, achievement, and so forth. Flip by flip, you unfold the dynamic, boundless capacity that is the Zen leader in you. Get out of your own way and what remains is—yes—calm, wise, and peaceful, and also agile, creative, and extremely powerful.

Are you in? That may seem like a rhetorical question, but it's really at the heart of our first flip from coping to transforming, and the foundation of leadership. It's a flip from standing on the sidelines to what Kevin Cashman calls "leading with character,"[1] in which we fully enter the situation with the best we've got, transforming it as we add our value. It is a felt shift in the body from outside-in to inside-out, from putting up with forces or people "out there," apart from ourselves, to diving right in, becoming a part of the chaotic dance, and extending our energy to create value. It is a flip from victim to player, from observer to participant.

This flip is the foundation of real leadership as we'll use the term in this book. Borrowing from Cashman, we define *leadership* not as occupying an elevated slot on an organization chart, but as extending one's authentic, transformative energy to create value for others. Whether at home or at work, even highly skilled leaders will recognize many times in which they cope, rather than transform. This chapter will help you recognize those coping minefields, and feel into the flip that is your own energy for transformation.

Not Just Words

"Okay, rest the blade of your hand on my shoulder," I say to the student, facing her maybe a foot away. This isn't a martial arts class, though I taught Aikido for many years. This is a leadership program in which I'm introducing a simple exercise—"unbendable arm"—that embodies the flip that is essential to Aikido, and also in moving from coping to transforming. I cup both of my hands over the crook of her arm and demonstrate that I mean to press down, bending the arm. "At first, just resist the pressure," I tell her. Two arms against one, if we're of reasonably the same size, eventually her arm gives way. "How did that feel?" I ask, and hear answers such as:

"Pretty awful."

"Tense; wondering how much I could take."

"Feeling like I lost."

That's what coping feels like: a sense that forces are bearing down on us. Even if we're holding up for now, we're struggling with the pressure, and what we're doing can hardly be called leadership.

"Shake that out," I tell her, and ask her to replace her hand in the same position. "But this time, don't resist," I say. "Instead, imagine a fire on that opposite wall and your arm is the firehose. Water—or energy—flows from your fingers. Or imagine your vision is on that wall and you are extending toward it." To her amazement, she finds she is much stronger. "How did that feel?" I ask, and now hear things like:

"Effortless!"

"Stronger, more integrated."

"I can't believe it—what kind of trick is this?"

That's what extending energy into a situation feels like, which is how we transform situations. *That*, we can rightfully call leadership.

This flip is so simple that my partner in the exercise I just described— and you, if you had a partner right now—could do it instantly, and yet it can be so subtle that we miss it. It is more than words, more tangible than a concept: it is a felt shift in the body from defensive resistance to relaxed extension. You can get a feel for it if you stubbornly fold your arms for moment and take on the most defensive, hunkered-down posture you can imagine. Now shake that out, extend a relaxed arm, palm up and open, and imagine a line of energy (or water, if you prefer) running through your arm and out your fingers. Comparing these two postures, notice which one feels more ready to listen, engage, or help another person.

Although not quite at these extremes, moment by moment, we do make a choice that favors either coping or transforming in our posture to the world.

The Coping Trap

I'm 14 years old, playing the old family piano. My 7-year-old brother has snuck up behind me and—gitch!—jabs me in the ribs. I freeze as every muscle contracts with being startled. This is my coping reaction, and, as you might imagine, the music gets pretty awful.

Fast-forward 20 years and I'm a shiny, up-and-coming manager on the Space Station Program at NASA, trying to influence the 20-year veteran in front of me to get his part of the communication system to work with the part I represent. "No, we can't do that," he says to my proposed interface. "Our design is fixed." Mind you, these are early days in the design process; the station won't fly for another 12 years. But his defenses are up, shields in place: "No, the answer is no," he says. I had no idea how to influence him, and I recall the frustration to this day.

Whether a momentary startle or a long-term defense, coping is our way of registering a *no* vote: no, I don't like this; no, I don't want to do this; no, this isn't really happening. Whining, worrying, complaining, defending, denying, resisting, tolerating, storming out, blowing up, folding our arms in defiance—coping takes many forms. It can be loud and dramatic or passively resistant. It can be justified—someone has just stolen our wallet, trashed our cherished project, or hired away our best employee—and we often take great pains to explain just how justified we are in our coping. Yet this mode is fundamentally defensive, reactive, and negatively tinged, as in, "How much of this can I take?" At its root is a simple protest: Something is happening *to* me and I don't accept it.

Outside-in. That's what we could call the energetic direction of this mode: a force out there is impinging on me in here, sticking me to the spot, or, as we say in Zen, "stopping the mind." If you closely observe yourself or anyone in coping mode, you'll see signs of this stopping or stuckness (try the Gotcha! exercise). Physically it might register as freezing—if only for a moment—or a tightly held posture, a frozen jaw, or repeating the same animated gestures again and again. In thought, it's a storyline that keeps replaying, a neurotic loop—"...after all I've done for this company..."—that re-justifies itself. I've come to recognize mental replay as an early warning sign of coping mode. If that little voice in my head replays the same tape twice—as in why someone's behavior has every right to anger me—I know I'm in coping mode.

"Get over it," we might say to shake ourselves out of coping mode. Or even more truthfully, "Get over yourself," as we sense that coping has us stuck in a self that is small and out of sync with what's going on. Coping pins us to a spot—however uncomfortable, at least we know where we stand. As we play out our various coping dramas—being overworked, underappreciated, double-crossed, undercut, cut off on the freeway—we increasingly identify with them (in other words, the ego

Gotcha!

Imagine you're in a play, asked to depict a character suddenly startled by very bad news. How do you show the audience you're startled? What's the first thing your body does? What's your facial expression? What happens to your breath?

Now shake that out, rewind the play, and imagine your character is startled by news that turns out to be good. After your initial startle reaction, how do you show your transition to realizing the news is good?

You may notice that the startle reaction in both cases has a quality of frozenness, indicative of coping. When the news turns out to be good in the second case, notice how acceptance melts or relaxes the body. One's sense of whether the news is good or bad can have a great deal to do with how quickly we move to acceptance—or whether we get there at all.

identifies itself with the spot they stick us to), making them more likely to repeat again. Which is why, even though coping feels somewhere between neutral and awful, we do it so much. Even if it drastically limits our life, we're still drawing a sense of identity from it, however twisted. A story I heard early in my coaching career illustrates this point.

I'm in a five-day leadership program with Gary, one of the handful of people with whom I'll be having several one-on-one coaching sessions. The point of these sessions is to help people make sense of all the feedback they're getting in the program and figure out how to use it. Gary's feedback is terrible. His people don't know where they're going, he's not helping them develop, and he's negative and complaining all the time. If coping were an occupation, he'd be fulltime. In my second coaching session with him, when we're supposed to be connecting the dots in the data, he's mentally somewhere else. Arms crossed, report closed, he doesn't even want to look at the data. I don't know what to say, so I toss in a question and listen. He wanders around in his answer. I listen. He wanders more. I listen more. The session ends in what I judge to be complete failure. I have no idea how to be useful.

The next day we have our third and final coaching session. Gary strides into the room, slaps his report down on the table in front of us, and announces, "My mother died when I was 4 years old. Everyone felt sorry for me. I learned very quickly that if I played victim, I could get what I wanted. Well, my people are telling me that I can't lead as a victim. And they're right." My jaw drops with the sudden insight coming from this man. I can sense his newfound freedom; it's as though he's expanded into a larger version of himself.

This experience taught me so much as a coach about the power of listening and not trying to be so useful with all my answers. But it also taught me how coping mode can become an insidious habit that weaves its way into our sense of who we are. For years, Gary had stopped his mind on being the little boy whose mother had died, and he'd found all the ways to be a victim. He got something out of it, to be sure—including a sense of identity—but it was too small an identity for the role of a leader. In a flip, he saw it.

Likewise, if you reflect on the coping modes or moments in your life, you'll see that coping arises from and reinforces a freeze-frame identity—a *self* that something is happening *to. But aren't we selves that stuff happens to?* you might ask. The answer, which we'll play with through every flip of this book, and which you must not take my word for but rather experience for yourself, is yes and no, and neither yes nor no. The insidious trap of coping mode is that it makes us think this dot of ego is *all* that we are. Stuck to this dot, we cannot lead effectively because we're not going anywhere. We're stuck defending the dot. Worse yet, mistaking a dot to be our self, we miss our boundless, flowing nature that can enter circumstances and forever transform them.

The Challenge of Transformation

I don't know exactly what Gary went through between our second and third coaching sessions, but I imagine it went something like this: He's trying to ignore the data, but it keeps haunting him. It makes him mad; how dare they say all those bad things about him, blah, blah, blah. He gets all tight and anxious, and then a tiny voice within clears its metaphorical throat and says, "Excuse me. Haven't you heard some of this before?" At some point a wall of defense crumbles, and the light of acceptance shines over the rubble. The tiny voice gets bolder: "They may have a point...they know I'm not helping them...they're right!"

Acceptance is always the first light of transformative energy. Acceptance doesn't mean we have to *like* what we're dealing with. It means we don't get stuck in whether we like it or not, we simply work with it. Gary certainly didn't like the feedback he was reading. But he got to the place of accepting "It is what it is," or "This is what's true for my people." As soon as acceptance starts working, it opens up the possibility of further transformation, as it did for Gary when accepting the feedback let him see a deeper truth about his own life.

Acceptance marks the flip between coping and transforming (see Figure 1.1 on the next page).

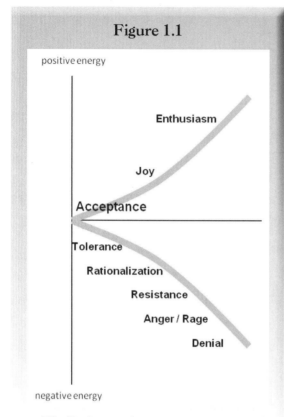

Figure 1.1

positive energy

Enthusiasm

Joy

Acceptance

Tolerance

Rationalization

Resistance

Anger / Rage

Denial

negative energy

The flip from coping to transforming.

It differs from tolerating, which is as good as coping gets, still holding the situation at arm's length as something we have to put up with. Acceptance ceases to resist. By setting aside its opinions, agenda, likes, and dislikes, acceptance is able to channel our full energy into working with the situation. The less energy gets siphoned off in reaction, the more energy is available for proaction.

But it gets better yet, for the energy of transformation is fundamentally positive, joyful, and enthusiastic, which is highly contagious and readily amplified. I'm sure that positive emotion is why I remember the conversation with Gary like it was yesterday. When he walked into that third coaching session, he was positively triumphant. As I felt the relief in him register in my own body, the sensation was sheer joy.

This joy is no accident, but rather a reliable indicator of transformative energy acting through us. When we flip into transforming, we feel more alive, present, connected, and conscious. No longer stuck to one point, we're free to maneuver, create, and explore. What happens to the self we were defending (and defining) in coping mode? Suddenly it flips from being a black hole of worry to a source of possibility as we tap, however briefly, our infinite nature. The Zen leader in us pours forth as we flip into being a generative hub, radiating from inside out the best we have to offer to the person, the problem, the situation. We may not register this flip consciously or have words to express it, but we will feel the joy transcending our smallness.

This joy tells us something beyond a self-serving ego is at work. Eckhart Tolle calls joy "the dynamic aspect of Being."² As we experience and express our universal Being, joy naturally arises. Enthusiasm follows, attracting others; when our inspired acts line up toward a vision or purpose, this we can call Zen leading. Acceptance, joy, and enthusiasm are the hallmarks of the Zen leader functioning in us. They're so essential to adding real value in the world that, as Tolle advises, if we're doing something *not* in one of these states, we should just stop. *Stop*. For otherwise, we're acting in coping mode, creating problems for ourselves and others, whether we know it or not.

Acceptance, joy, and enthusiasm may seem like tall orders—especially amidst the cacophony most leaders face every day. Yet most of us have tasted this possibility, and some make a steady diet of it. I often ask leaders what gives them joy in their work—not the big ego-stroking moments, but intrinsic, day-to-day enjoyment—and routinely hear answers like, "the work itself," "getting stuff done," "seeing the team succeed," or "watching my people grow." Doing work we enjoy, we may slip into a sort of "work *Samadhi*," or flow state; when we lose ourselves in the task, time disappears, and we only recognize we've been in this state once we leave it. Working with people we care about, toward meaningful goals, we may find it easy for our energy to flow from inside out, adding value to those relationships, making progress toward those goals. Any concerns for self seemingly disappear.

Until something happens.

An irritating e-mail, a financial setback, an unrealistic demand, or all of these at once, and suddenly we can find ourselves in a pit of worry, anger, or indignation—that is, coping. How long do we stay here before we can flip back into transformation and re-enter the situation with acceptance? Given that coping feels bad and transforming feels great, you'd think we'd make the flip instantly. But many of us don't, and most of us take our time about it. Because to flip, we have to let go—let go of the one who is worried, angry, indignant or self-berating. Even if we want to let go at a conscious level, we're working against a body of habits that has been trained by the cycles of drama we've lived up 'til now. Which is why to make this flip, like all flips, we have to engage the body. We can't just think our way there. The clear intent of thought can help, but grasping is deep in our muscle memory—starting with our grasp for life or survival instinct—and right before we let go, even if experience tells us it will feel great on the other side, it feels as though we're losing something: a little death.

Good news: The more we practice flipping from coping to transforming, the easier it gets, and the more confident we become that it will lead to something good. This transformative flip takes us down the path of transcending "I"-centered consciousness, which is a huge leap in human development as well as leadership development. Like plants growing toward the sun, our very nature pulls us toward the possibility of this transcendence, even as the impossibility of coping with ever more pressure pushes us out of old ways of thinking. Enough push, enough pull, and we're ready to flip.

How to do it?

The Zen Leader
Flip 1
Coping to Transforming

- ❧ Relax
- ❧ Enter
- ❧ Add value

The Zen Leader Flip 1: Coping to Transforming

Perhaps you've made this flip thousands of times—unwittingly, unconsciously. But let's tease apart what makes it work, so that you can make it a ready companion: a conscious competence. We'll break it into three parts, though in practice these flow seamlessly together and arise almost at once: relax, enter, add value.

Relax. You can simulate coping mode instantly by raising your shoulders up toward your ears (the way tense people look all the time). If you do that for a moment and then drop that tension—try it—you instantly feel less tight, less stuck. You might also notice that you simultaneously exhale, and you feel a sense of dropping down in the body toward your center, or lower abdomen. What's harder to do is relax the residual tension you unconsciously carry all the time, but breathing deeply to and from your center is a great way to approach this. The key to centering is to get out of your head, and allow tension in the upper body to drop away—as in a sigh of relief: ahhh! As an image, you might think of a big thermometer in which the bulb is your belly, filled by each breath (see Figure 1.2).

Figure 1.2

Relax

Enter

Add Value

The more centered and relaxed you are, the more completely you can take the next step, which is to enter.

Enter. To enter is to become one with whatever is going on, to merge with it in a completely relaxed state. It is not a tentative dipping of one's toe into the water, but instead a complete immersion. It is not being buffeted by the frayed edges of a situational hurricane, but rather moving right into the eye of the storm. Fear, anger, confusion, and other coping reactions may arise, but if you can feel into whatever resistance arises with a willingness to acknowledge it, and not let it stop you, you've found the door to entering.

To enter is to become the entire picture; an image for this stage is that of an all-embracing circle that is both you and the situation—subject and object—at once. If you imagine the flow state you enter when doing one of your favorite activities, you can get a sense of how total entering lets one disappear into an activity. Entering is like a child playing in a sandbox, or a kayaker deftly paddling in whitewater—no self stands apart. To get a firsthand experience of centering and entering, try the Chapter 1 exercises downloadable from our Website (*www.thezenleader. com*). The more completely you enter, the more completely you can add your value.

Add value. At the eye of the storm, the only direction for your energy is *out*. Having fully entered, your energy can flow from inside out, adding your value to the situation, transforming it through your presence as much as through anything you might do. You can feel this extension of energy by imagining—as my partner in the Aikido exercise did earlier—your arms as fire hoses, and the water (your energy) pouring forth to put out flames. An image for this stage is the radiant sun, extending its energy, transforming everything that basks in its light.

If you have a sense of this flip, you know how empowering it is. If you don't quite feel it yet, you surely can with practice, and the Website exercises will help. You may find this flip becomes even more clear and useful to you in actual application, which we turn to now.

Putting It to Work: Leadership that Transforms

One of the greatest challenges facing leaders every day is, well, reframing challenges. Is it a challenge or an opportunity? This is more than rhetoric, for this flip has to happen first in the mind of the leader. To find the opportunities in problems is a quality of can-do optimism that characterizes the most motivating leaders. While others are standing on the sidelines caught up in their fault-finding and blame-placing, the leader who can make this flip shows a way forward. Accepting "it is what it is," the Zen leader in us flips from defensiveness to curiosity, from resistance to creative engagement. What can we learn from it? How do we use it? How do we fix the damage, change the game, or leverage larger forces at work?

To see how this flip might apply to you, think of a problem that has been troubling you or keeping you up at night, and try this exercise:

1. Write down a statement of the problem starting with the words "The Problem is..."

   For example: *The problem is we lost a key customer and we may not make our revenue number this quarter.*

2. "Hold" this problem statement and notice what tightens in your body, and what thoughts and feelings arise. Jot down whatever reactions you notice. These are the signatures of coping, and the more you can get to know them in yourself, the easier they become to work with. Notice one place of tightness in your body and breathe into it, releasing it, relaxing it.

3. Go back to your problem statement and invite a bit of brain-storming. Starting with the phrase "The *real* problem is...," restate your problem six to 10 different ways from inside out—that is, using only "I"- or "we"-based statements (no blaming others!).

   For example: *The real problem is we aren't sure that our people are properly trained...we don't have enough customers in the pipeline...we don't know if our customers are happy...we're not reaching customers the way we used to...we're not solving our customers' real problems.*

   You may notice that as answers tumble out, new themes emerge and your initial story gives way to submerged insights. Keep restating the *real* problem until you sense that you've hit upon something important; something new.

4. Relax. Let go of the problem. Let go of the self the problem is happening to. You might imagine that self-who-has-the-problem as a player on a board game and now you want to become the one playing the game. You might think of this as stepping back

from a problem to gain perspective, or entering beyond the problem, where you become the entire picture, and can see the entire board, now with wisdom for your little board-playing self.

5. With this relaxed sense of bigness, look over your restatements with an eye for what the opportunities are here. Again speaking from inside out, starting with the phrase "I (or we) have a real opportunity here to...." Fill in the end of the sentence with as many opportunities as you can spot.

    For example: *We have a real opportunity here to get closer to our customers...learn what's not working for them...help them move forward... hone our coaching skills...find people who need us on social media... give them something useful for free....*

6. Look over your opportunities and pick one or two that seem most promising to pursue.

This is one empowering flip. It reframes everything from a focus on the self-having-a-problem to the creative agent who learns from what's going on and often changes the game. This flip won't supply all the answers, but it will get your energy going in the right direction, which is from inside out—adding the best value you have to offer.

Problems repeat when we respond to them by coping. When we respond in the spirit of transformation and pick one or two promising ways to do that, we're no longer in the same place that allowed the old problem to appear. Even if what we try doesn't work exactly as planned, we've learned something. Even if a comparable problem arises again, we won't be in the same place we once were for dealing with it. Our transformational leadership has transformed us.

If this flip still feels elusive, or you find you can't stay here for long, have patience. The next chapter will guide you deeper into the underlying physical flip that makes transformation possible. If coping mode is a ready companion, at least now you have more insight into what's holding it in place. If you find it hard to let go of the anger, indignation, blaming, or self-righteousness that makes acceptance impossible, you're in good company. Coping makes for good drama, and we're surrounded by it, from "not our fault" finger-pointing to "it's good for the ratings" political talk shows with their endless stream of attack and counter-attack. Or maybe for you, coping mode takes the form of self flagellation, as in, "I'm not good enough," "I'm a screw-up," or "Everyone's right and I'm wrong." This, too, is good drama, and no less than self-righteousness, it sticks us to the dot of self.

What we know with certainty is that although coping may make life interesting, it doesn't make for good leadership. Neither does it lead to joy, enthusiasm, nor anyplace that truly serves us. For that, we need to flip.

The Zen Leader

Flip 1 Takeaways

Coping to Transforming

Coping is stuck. Transforming creates movement. Acceptance is the turning point. This flip is the **beginning of real leadership.**

Acceptance allows you to **relax,** engage, or **enter** a situation, and **add value** where you can.

Apply this flip using **5 steps to convert problems to opportunities:**

1. **Problem statement.** "The problem is...[state your issue]."

2. **Hold.** Notice what tightens or tenses as you "hold" this problem.

3. **Restatements.** "The *real* problem is...[brainstorm six to 10 "I"- or "we"-based answers]."

4. **Relax.** Let go of the problem, let go of your self having it; come up a level.

5. **Opportunities.** Reframe your restatements: "I (we) have a real opportunity to...[choose one or two that are promising].

2

From Tension to Extension

"I'M NOT TENSE," Rob protested at my suggestion that he seemed about ready to explode. He was edged forward in his chair during our coaching session, right leg vibrating six beats a second, shoulders up around his ears. I pulled out my cell phone and snapped a quick picture of him, setting it down on the table between us (love that technology!). "Take a look at this picture and tell me what vibe you get from that leader," I say to him. "Intense," he responds. I encourage him to keep looking. "Has his mind made up...not listening...nervous...a time bomb." Exactly.

That's what tension does: it makes us small, edgy, and nervous. What's more, most of us don't even recognize how much tension we're carrying, and how much that tension locks us into a cell of our own making. Try this experiment: Sit forward in your chair, press your feet into the ground, make fists of your hands, tense your forearms, and bore your eyes into this paper is if they were burning lasers. What do you notice? Almost certainly you notice the paper. But do you notice what's happening out the window? Probably not. Do you notice how tension spreads through the whole front of your body, making everything tight? Is the feeling expansive or small? Connected or separate? Experiences vary, but most of us find this is a fast track to our most isolated, tense, and defended self.

Now flip that around. Let out a deep sigh of relief and sit back in your chair. Let your eyes drift into peripheral, 180-degree vision by extending your arms to your sides, palms up and open, and seeing both hands and everything in between. Let your arms drift down comfortably, and imagine a line of energy flowing down the backs of your arms, and out through the backs of your fingertips. Check out the feeling: Is it larger than before? More flowing? More connected? Yes, you may say, but it also feels less sharply focused and...well...less *productive*. And therein lies a key tension in leadership: it's easier to trust what we can control and get done using tension than it is to trust what comes when we let go, and let extension operate.

This simple flip between tension and extension shows up not only in the body, but also in emotions, thought processes, and everyday leadership behaviors. In this chapter, we explore how sustained tension can lead to barely managing, career derailment, and burnout, whereas extension is based in the much more sustainable rhythm of drive and recovery. Extension enables the awareness and sensitivity that lets us transform situations, rather than crashing into them with unsustainable change efforts. Extension gives rise to natural durability in our energy, and in all that it creates. Building on the flip of Chapter 1, we look at three "laws" of energy management that flip tension into extension and allow the transformational Zen leader in us to spring forth.

Tension Produces Movement—Until it Doesn't

Tension is not all bad. The truth is, we couldn't move a single muscle without it. In its simplest form, in the simplest animals (and even a few plants), tension is a contraction: fibers sliding past one another, like the closing of a fan. When the ends of those fibers are connected to different parts of a body, tension pulls those parts closer together. Relaxation, like opening a fan, lets them return to full length. Alternating tension and relaxation, a body can start to wiggle and move, from the simplest, squirming paramecium, to the complex human body. Every muscle in our body linking every bone of our skeleton operates on this principle: When it tenses, things contract; when it relaxes, things move further apart. We also have muscles, such as the heart, that oscillate with their cycles of tension and relaxation to move our blood. Tension produces movement; that's not a bad thing.

The start of trouble is when tension doesn't let go—when it "forgets" how to relax. This happens in muscle fibers when the little tracks that allow fibers to slide past one another get stuck. These tracks require energy (like lubrication) to operate, and without it, they simply freeze, like a sliding glass door stuck slightly off its track. As a muscle gets more fibers stuck in this condition, its starts to feel harder, less supple, and it takes more energy to get it moving at all. As one of my Zen teachers, Tanouye Roshi, used to say, "The body of a baby is soft and pliable. The body of a corpse is stiff and rigid. We're somewhere in between."

Just where we are "in between" has a great deal to do with our energy. The more we are like a baby, the more energy flows smoothly through our body, the easier we move, and the more energy we have available to add value in the world. The tighter we are, the more that tightness traps energy, keeping it from getting to all the muscles that need it, leading to a vicious cycle of more tightness that requires more effort to overcome in order to make movement possible. Think how much energy it takes to open a slightly stuck sliding glass door. In effect, when our muscles are somewhat stuck we have to do the same thing—put a lot of energy into overcoming our own resistance!

Worse yet, we're not even aware of it until symptoms are acute, and we don't know why. We only notice how tired we are by the end of a day, how persistent certain aches and pains have become, or how we don't have the energy for another project, a difficult conversation, or patience with our children. This tension doesn't affect merely moving our bodies through space. It affects everything: our emotions, thoughts, and behaviors. Coping mode exactly expresses this stuckness, registering its voice of *no*. Not moving. Blaming others. Remaining the victim.

Stuck tension in the body weighs into every decision regarding whether we have the energy to act freely in the situation and add our value. So when we talk about tension as something to flip out of, we're not talking about the healthy cycle of tension and release that's at the heart of life's movement. We're talking about habitual tension that doesn't release fully and, in time, ossifies body and mind.

This habitual tension can reside anywhere in the body, but if we were to locate a fundamental source—the primal contraction—it would be in the deep muscles lining the front side of the spine. You can see this primal contraction in the simplest sea creatures that curl up when provoked, or little inchworms that become instant circles when they sense a threat. This biological version of "circling the wagons," be they segments of an inchworm or our own vertebrae, is a coping mechanism of animals large and small. In humans, we see it in the extremes among the most downtrodden and depressed, hence phrases like "huddled masses" and "curled up into a fetal position." But in more subtle ways, we all carry some of this tension, which you can experience (not that you'd want to, but to make the point) if you feel into your body's response to deflating news or an emotional sock to the gut. In fact, these deep, frontal muscles are great at storing pain and difficult emotions, as anyone who has experienced deep bodywork to release these muscles could tell you. Body therapists call these muscles "core" for good reason.

It doesn't stop there. Because tension contracts muscles, held tension distorts the body, and then the opposing muscles have to start working harder to compensate. Generally what we experience as back pain originates from over-taxed muscles in our back compensating for over-tight muscles in our core. Tension begets more tension, most of which passes beneath our conscious awareness—until it painfully doesn't. The early warning signs are mostly benign: headaches, stiff necks, sore backs, achy shoulders, gastrointestinal discomfort, elevated pulse, higher blood pressure. But most busy people (including myself for a good deal of my life) power through those signals with an aspirin here, an antacid there, so of course the symptoms have to get worse to get our attention. And why are we putting all this tension into our body? Because it's the natural companion of coping mode. Whenever we're in the grip (even the phrase suggests a contraction!) of anger, indignation, worry, or any of the faces of coping mode, tension is both the byproduct and exactly what holds it in place.

The Price of Tension for Leaders

"Contain the vein!" laughs one of the more vocal team members when asked what it's like to work for Elliot, a senior vice president of product development known for his angry outbursts. I've been Elliot's coach for a couple of months, and I'm meeting with the people who report to him to see how they handle his volatility. "We watch him closely," the person went on, and when the vein in his forehead starts to pulsate, we know he's about to blow." They've made it something of a joke— "Contain the vein!"—and when the vein is well-contained, Elliot laughs along with them. He knows he has "a temper problem"; it was why the company suggested he work with a coach in the first place. What he doesn't know is how much the team members shade what they tell him, protect themselves in partial truths, and carefully pick when to feed him information so as not to set off the vein. The more I talk to the team, the more I see how they're managing Elliot, rather than him leading them.

Energy is contagious in general, but a leader's volatility is doubly so, first because it signals danger and fear and, second, because it comes from the very person to whom others look for safety. At a deep, brainstem level, a question we're always asking about leaders is, "Do I want to follow you?" A leader's volatility quickly spreads tension in the land and raises doubts.

In addition to volatility, there is a host of ways leaders pay the price of tension, perhaps best characterized by psychologist Robert Hogan, and applied to leaders by David Dotlich and Peter Cairo.[1] They identify 11 ways that leaders under stress sabotage their effectiveness or derail their careers—a catalogue of coping mechanisms. For example:

- ☯ The cynic who's always trying to find fault and cast blame
- ☯ The worrier, who agonizes over every decision or plays it safe
- ☯ The center of attention whose insecurity demands the spotlight
- ☯ The arrogant one who must be right and long ago stopped listening
- ☯ The perfectionist determined to get reality under control

Charades

In the game of Charades, we use only gestures or movements to wordlessly portray something.

Take a few seconds to portray each of the five "derailing" characters described in the list, enough so that someone could guess what attitude you're depicting.

Notice what tenses in your body and how your posture changes to create each impression. Notice what tension patterns are common to all characters and what changes going from, say, the worrier to the arrogant.

If you were playing a game of Charades and were asked to portray any of these characters (try the exercise to the left) you would instantly find that to act it out, you would start tensing your body in specific ways: a furtive, eye-darting look for the cynic, a puffed up chest for the arrogant person, and so on. These gestures are not accidental; in the game of Charades we might exaggerate them to make them more visible, but even when held inside, these same subtle tensions are at work.

From the research that Hogan and others have done, we know that everyone has potential derailers that are more likely to surface when we're under stress or low on energy. In other words, these coping mechanisms function at a macro level much the way our muscles function at a micro level: like sliding glass doors that can get stuck or derail when energy is scarce. The cost to the human being is a vicious, energy-draining cycle. The cost to leadership is that it stops doing anything productive.

Unfortunately, that doesn't mean we stop doing. If we simply paused when we sensed our tension or tiredness, we would do less damage and return to a relaxed state more readily. But, no, we tend to keep on going—we're so busy, after all, and there's so much to do. Besides, the first thing lost in our spun-up tension is the clear-flowing awareness that could see we're digging our hole deeper. Spun up in tension, our mind can lock onto a particular goal and lock out the bigger picture: *Hit this target, catch this flight, get through this agenda item.* Or, if we're less focused, before we get through one item, our mind has daisy-chained onto another and we leave a frenetic trail of half-doneness. In our tension, people can become objects to use, a means to our ends: *Get this person to do what I want, ignore that person who doesn't serve me.* We listen less and push more, focusing on tasks, numbers, and speed. We may find ourselves taking whatever we can get, spewing anger, shading the truth to an oversight committee, or turning a blind eye to corruption. In the grip, our awareness shrinks to a fear-driven dot of self, and we feel somehow separate from the chain reactions we're setting off. Leaders in the grip create small, brutish worlds.

Leading With Extension

If tension makes us smaller, extension makes us larger, or, more accurately, returns us to our natural state. Extension doesn't mean we're always reaching for something. Rather it is the absence of contraction and the presence of openness, sometimes simply called presence itself, which plugs us into the free-flowing energy of the earth, of the universe. This may seem like wishful, woo-woo thinking to the pragmatic leader, yet throughout the story of humanity, this profound connectedness has been the wondrous skill of great warriors, the compassion of saints, the insight of mystics, the wisdom of shamans, the genius of great artists, the gift of healers, and the prescient intuition of great leaders. It is the Zen leader in you, rolling through life like a huge boulder, according the myriad changes—acting with gravitas and complete agility with whatever is going on. This agile gravitas is *you* leading with extension.

Extension is the opposite of being stuck. It is a mind and body flowing naturally with the circumstances. Our self-in-our-skin is not so much the source of that energy as an open conduit for it, adding our unique value as it passes through. Far from being some kind of miraculous channeling, this state of openness is our most natural, unstuck self. In the absence of tension, there is simply nothing to block the flow.

Having said that, it is also inevitable that we get stuck on things, big and little: a song we can't get out of our head, a replayed snippet of conversation, a recurring fear—the mind is easily trapped in eddies of thought. Thoughts whir around like blades of a fan, and if the same thing isn't repeating, one thing leads to another. "Have to follow up with Jane...she never got back with me...I hate it when people don't get back with me...what's this other irritating e-mail about?...oh, I'm late for a meeting...where did I leave my notes?..." Add some emotion to the mix, as in a dollop of fear about making our budget, or a sprinkling of nervousness about speaking in front of a group, and we get even more tense, more stuck.

So to say extension is our most natural state is not to say tension is somehow unnatural. It is part of how we're put together, and accepting the whole picture of who we are—coping and transforming, tense and extended—allows us to more easily relax into our transformative, extended selves. For if we berate ourselves for getting stuck in tension, all we do is create more tension, plunging ourselves into our own civil war. Just as acceptance is at the cusp where coping turns to transforming, it also flips tension to extension. The actions that flow through extension come out "clean": They don't leave a scent of ego or smallness. As free expressions of the Zen leader in us, they create openings in the world and free up others as well.

If you need an image of a leader who has exemplified this contagious openness, Nelson Mandela would certainly be a good one. In smallness, he could have sought revenge for 27 years spent in prison. But instead he extended forgiveness and opened a spirit of forgiveness throughout South Africa. He could have appropriated his power to the needs of his ego, as so many political leaders have done. But instead he applied it in the spirit of service, inspiring a similar spirit in everyone from rugby players to businesspeople. Writer John Simpson, attending a banquet in honor of Mandela some years ago, watched how this openness irresistibly drew people to Mandela: "It was the way he looked you straight in the eye and spoke just to you—to the person you wanted to be, perhaps, rather than the one you actually were."[2] John saw the contagious spirit of service when his South African wife spontaneously greeted Mandela. Mandela stopped and listened as though no one else mattered and time stood still. After she finished he said, "We need you back in South Africa. When are you coming home?" Who could resist such a leader?

Openness begets openness, freeing others to be more of who they are. Leading with extension extends our value into the world.

The Zen Leader Flip 2: Tension to Extension

You can make a mini version of this flip in any moment—as you had a chance to do at the start of this chapter. But to make it a way of life and leadership, you need energy. So here are what I've come to call the "3 Laws of Energy Management." If you follow them, you'll have energy to burn.

Rhythm, not relentless. Waking and sleeping, inhaling and exhaling, even the beat of our heart reminds us: as biological systems, we're made to operate with rhythm. Stretch and release. Drive and recover. From the work of Yerkes Dodson in the early 1900s, extended by Jim Loehr and Tony Schwartz,[3] we know the best way to manage our energy is on and *off*, not on and *on*. I often ask leaders, "What do you do when your iPhone shows a low battery?"

"Plug it in. Recharge it," they say.

The Zen Leader

Flip 2

Tension to Extension

☯ Rhythm, not relentless
☯ Down, not up
☯ Out, not in

"What do you do for yourself when you're at low charge?"

"Keep going!" they laugh.

But they get the point. We often take better care of our iPhones—a little piece of technology that will be in the trash heap in a few years—than we take care of our priceless, irreplaceable selves.

As Loehr and Schwartz emphasize in their work with "corporate athletes," this pulse of drive and recovery is also the key to full engagement.[4] Steady stress pushes a system to habituate and run down over time. Pulsing it keeps the system in a state of fresh activation. What's our equivalent to plugging in or recharging? What we do may vary, but invariably, energy comes through the body: we have to do something physically renewing. A best practice combines brief (two-minute) breaks every 90 minutes or so, with longer breaks (30 minutes) for meditation or exercise once or twice a day. You may already know of the perfect pulse practice for you, but if you'd like a good suggestion, see the Centering mini-break at the end of this chapter. You can also download further ideas for mini-breaks and renewing activities from *www.thezenleader.com*.

In addition to creating this macro pulse in our day, there is another kind of rhythm we can sense in the day itself. This is more subtle, and requires a good deal of sensitivity. If you'd like to try it, stand outside for a couple of minutes, open your senses, and take in the day. Slowly clap your hands at about a walking pace, making the pace faster and slower until you come to a rhythm that somehow takes less effort to maintain.[5] This is the energy or rhythm of the day. If you pace yourself to it, you will find your energy going much further.

As I said, this rhythm is subtle, and I, myself, missed it for many years because of my hurry-up habits. I thought if something is done in half the time, that's twice as good. I see this habit in leaders who move through their day so quickly that others can't keep up. People get into a refractory state to protect themselves from a whirlwind leader, while the leader gets frustrated that messages aren't being heard, delegation isn't working, and people aren't following. "Slow down," I now tell these leaders. "Find the rhythm where people can move with you, or you're going to be stuck doing everything yourself." The easiest rhythm to find with a group is the rhythm of the day we're all experiencing together. If you can sense this subtle pulse and let it be a soundless drumbeat underlying your actions, you will notice your energy is better supported, and others are more able to move with you. But don't take my word for it; sense it yourself.

Down, not up. The second law of energy management is already deeply embedded in our language and common sense. We have numerous expressions for what happens when we're tense, and the image is always of energy rising up: *spun up, upset, uptight, hotheaded.* Flip that around and you find expressions like *settle down, calm down, pipe down, ground yourself,* and the image is always of energy dropping down.

In our physical bodies, this principle plays out when we let energy drop down into our lower abdomen, rather than rise up into our heads, as in Figure 2.1. Even as you read these words, notice your breath and relax any tension in your shoulders and ribcage. Invite your breath energy to drop more deeply into the lower abdomen. This area, what the Japanese call *"hara"* and what we likened to the bulb of a large thermometer, is the center of our most powerful actions,

Figure 2.1

Down, not up; develops energy in the hara.

our nucleus for balance and natural control. "Natural control" is not a forced, taking-matters-into-my-own-hands kind of control, but rather a confident centeredness that reads the situation, senses the openings for change, and uses them appropriately. This deeper-than-conscious intu-ition that appropriately and spontaneously extends our energy comes from *hara* more readily than from the head, because in the head it can get second-guessed and caught up in all the whirling fan blades. Developing the *hara* gives more opportunity for this spontaneous Zen leader to arise. The Centering mini-break at the end of this chapter is a great practice for developing your breath and *hara*.

Breathe deeply to and from your *hara*, and energy will naturally de-velop in this center, along with the intuition to use it well.

Out, not in. You know the importance of this energy direction from Chapter 1, but now you can experience the physical essence of how to send your energy out, not in. Try this: Raise your left arm out to your side. The front of your arm—the flexor side—is what tightens when you make a fist (see Figure 2.2a).

Relax your hand and feel a line of energy running along the back of your arm—on the extensor side—running through the back of your hand and out through your fingers (Figure 2.2b). Similarly extend your right arm, and make the same flip to a line of energy running along the back, exten-sor side. Feel into your spine and similarly relax the muscles along the front of the spine and extend slightly along the back of the spine, feeling a lift through the back of your neck, the rims of your ears, and out the top of your

Figure 2.2

Energy extends along the backside.

head. Sense this line of energy extending down through your legs, gently extending the balls of your feet into the earth.[6] Now dial back the gain on all of this until you just barely feel these lines of extension and you have the idea of this third law of energy management: out, not in. This extension manifests physically by relaxing of the front, flexor side of the body and extending through the back, extensor side.

"Out, not in" gives a natural direction to our energy. It aligns our actions along a vector emanating from inside out, and directed toward where we want to go. As we'll see, leadership vision, mission, and goals are but practical expressions of this sense of direction. In combination with a sustainable rhythm and centeredness, this flip into extension gives us more energy, better aligned. Who wouldn't want that?

Putting It to Work: More Energy, Better Aligned

Applying this flip in your life and leadership makes everything else possible, for it is the fuel you run on and the authentic extension of that energy into the world. The reflection questions that follow, which I often ask leaders in development programs or coaching sessions, will help you connect with your own wisdom regarding what best practices will support you in building energy, and what you know about the vision or purpose to which you'd apply it. Before starting, you might take a moment to relax, open your senses, center your breath, and ever so slightly open the back-side extensor channels. Once you're centered, even if you're not sure what to write, read the questions and start writing without hesitation:

1. What is an early warning sign for you that your energy is low?

2. What could you do in a two-minute recovery break that would help you most?

3. To better pace yourself in the rhythm of the day, which of these do you generally need to do most? (A) slow down, (B) speed up, (C) stabilize, or (D) better focus your energy.

4. If you could prescribe an energy-renewing activity you could do maybe 30 minutes per day that would help you in whatever

way you just identified, what would be your best prescription to yourself?

5. Write down six things you do—inside or outside of work—that make you feel most energized, satisfied, and "on purpose."

6. Write down six things you know about what you're creating and wanting to create through your presence and leadership.

7. Looking over the previous two lists, craft a statement that captures your leadership vision or purpose. Write a second sentence that captures a key way you will go about it (for example, an important strategy).

We know that vision, purpose, and strategy are important for inspiring and aligning followership. But perhaps now you can also appreciate that only transformation-grade energy (as opposed to coping) gives rise to a vision, purpose, or strategy worth following. Even within us, more energy, better aligned, feeds a virtuous cycle. With more energy, it's easier to remain unstuck; there's more lubrication for the tracks of our internal sliding glass doors. When we're unstuck, energy naturally flows to rejuvenate us. When that energy is aligned toward a vision and way of working, it's better focused and less drained by distractions and irritations. Finally, when our vision and way of working arise from what we find intrinsically energizing, we get more energy as we go.

The flip from tension to extension is the physical realization of moving from coping to transforming. Being able to build and align energy is also the foundational tool for sustainable leadership and all the flips to follow. If you're ever stuck, drained, frustrated, tormented, indignant, frightened, defensive, dull, or depressed, come back here.

Flush with energy, we're ready to dive deeper into the complexities of leadership today, most of which can be characterized by a single word: *paradox*.

The Zen Leader
Flip 2 Takeaways
Tension to Extension

The Three Laws of Energy Management:

1. **Rhythm, not relentless.** Build a rhythm into your day, including practices that stretch and renew. Sense and match the rhythm of the day.

2. **Down, not up.** Settle down and breathe deeply to and from your center.

3. **Out, not in.** Extend your energy through the extensor side of the body, relaxing the front flexor-side.

Apply this flip to:

- ☯ Build energy through **physical practice**. Mindful practice frees up energy.

- ☯ Align energy on a **vision or purpose**, and a **way of working** that is intrinsically satisfying.

The Zen Leader
Core Practice: Centering Mini-Break

Tension flips into extension when we have enough awareness and energy to let go of what's stuck. We can do this by punctuating work activities with mini-recovery breaks and, once or twice a day, engaging in a physically renewing practice. You can use the Centering Mini-Break whenever you need to get unstuck from your head and centered in *hara*. Other mini-break ideas are available online (at *www.thezenleader.com*), as well as a host of longer-term practices that may become part of your personal prescription for building and sustaining your energy over time.

Figure 2.3

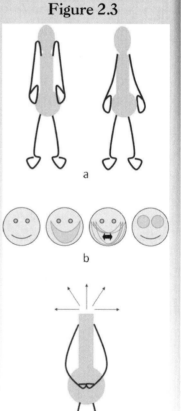

1. Stand comfortably, feet shoulder-width apart. Shrug your **shoulders** as high up toward your ears as possible, and then drop them, as in Figure 2.3a. Repeat several times; notice that you automatically exhale as you drop your shoulders.

2. Loosen up your **face.** Do this by opening your jaw as wide as possible and closing it a few times, moving your lower jaw laterally back and forth a few times, opening your eyes as wide as possible and closing them a few times; make a few crazy faces (Figure 2.3b).

3. Loosen up your **neck.** Stretching your neck long, lay your left ear over toward your left shoulder. Roll your head forward and around like a free-swinging pendulum

until your right ear is toward your right shoulder. Stretch your neck long, and roll back the other way. Repeat a few times.

4. Stand comfortably, with the weight on the balls of your feet. Let your eyes soften, using peripheral vision to see 180 degrees around you—all at once and nothing in particular. Picture your torso in the shape of a thermometer bulb, clear and relaxed in the shoulders and ribcage, with your belly free to expand with each breath. Place your hands on your lower belly and breathe slowly in and out through your nose, letting tension drop away with every exhale until you can feel your breath move under your hands (Figure 2.3c).

5. On your next inhale, let your hands rise, palms up, to your solar plexus, allowing the breath to fill your belly from the bottom (Figure 2.3d).

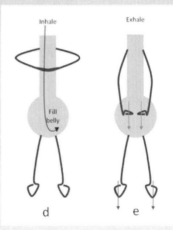

6. As you exhale, turn your palms to the ground and gently push them down, along with your breath. At the same time, imagine tiny rockets firing out of the heels of both feet and notice how this extends the backs of the legs, bringing the weight to the balls of the feet (Figure 2.3e).

7. Release and relax on the inhale as hands rise up. Extend through the balls of the feet on the exhale as hands press down. (Figure 2.3d and e alternating). Repeat, ever slower, for five to 10 breaths.

3

From *Or* to *And*

JOIN ME AT NASA for a moment, as we go back a few years and a new Administrator, Dan Goldin, has entered with a storm of challenges to the space agency. "Faster, better, cheaper!" he extols the troops at the Johnson Space Center auditorium, repeating his mantra for how our programs need to improve on all fronts. The frustration in the room grows, as the collective engineering mindset grapples with this apparent contradiction. "I can give you two out of three," mutters the engineer next to me. He's stuck in this seemingly unsolvable puzzle. "Which one don't you want?" he asks under his breath, looking for the indignant, head-nod agreement around him. Nothing can throw us into coping mode faster than being asked to do the seemingly impossible.

And yet, isn't that what leaders are increasingly being asked to do? Technology accelerates, and competition raises the bar, even as it drives prices down. "Faster, better, cheaper" is hardly a pressure unique to NASA. And while NASA never fully realized Goldin's charge, that's not to say it's impossible. Only that it requires a flip to a different mindset: from *Or* to *And*.

Cost or quality? A similar choice reigned in the auto industry for years. If you wanted low cost, you had to accept that your car windows would leak, or your transmission would seize up in a few years. If you wanted good quality, you had to pay Cadillac prices. Consumers, not unlike Dan Goldin, wanted both. So when the Japanese car manufacturers figured out how to give it to them by combining low cost and mass production from the quality movement, those companies soared in market share and set a new standard. Cost *and* quality became a reality.

Figure 3.1

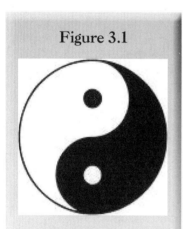

The paradoxical nature of reality is depicted in the yin-yang symbol of Taoism, in which emptiness (black) gives rise to form (white), form to emptiness, and each contains the other (the dots within). Imagine this symbol in constant transition of white into black and black into white, and you have a feel for the unending movement of paradox.

"Only paradox comes anywhere near to comprehending the fullness of life," Carl Jung once said. He wasn't a teenager when he said it, though, for even Carl Jung had to develop to a stage where he could flip from *Or* to *And*. Do we focus on the short term or the long term? Yes. Do we focus on growth or reduce costs? Yes. When we teach paradox management in our leadership programs, we still come upon leaders locked onto the rightness of *one* perspective—something the nervous system is very good at doing: lock on, lock out, that is, lock on one thing, lock out everything else. Or, if they admit to multiple perspectives, they're still convinced a single, static solution exists—a "happy medium"—rather than an endless dynamism between forces, neither complete without its apparent opposite.

Our collective consciousness is barely at the cusp of "getting" paradox. You can see us falling short whenever a politician tries to lay out both sides of an issue and gets attacked for "flip-flopping" or "speaking out of both sides of his mouth." We prefer the simple clarity of: "Here's the truth. Are you with me or against me?" It's a developmental leap to be able to dynamically optimize multiple truths—or, put in businessspeak, to dynamically optimize multiple truths. Yet this is what leaders are increasingly called to do in trading off cost and quality, short-term and long-term, pushing for results and taking time to develop people. Although there may still be a place for simple answers to complex problems, the Zen leader in us knows they are solutions for the moment, not places to dwell. In accord to the myriad changes, the Zen leader plays in paradox.

That said, not every decision has to be treated as a paradox. There are still some garden-variety problems that have point solutions and can be checked off the list: responding to a power failure, or deciding whether to hire Jane. Once I decide on Jane, I probably don't have to keep coming back to it. Try that with something like work-life balance ("Oh, I fixed that on Tuesday") and you'll see it's a different kind of animal. Yet, once we have an eye for paradox, we often see that even simple problems are a part of a larger picture that is paradoxical. For example, I can make a hiring decision about Jane and check it off my list. But I may be basing my decision on broader considerations about my overall talent pool: Is it right for the short term and the long term? Does it create the right balance of technical skills and people skills? I may recognize that the decision on Jane has broader implications for the type of person I hire next time.

In this chapter, you're invited into the psychological and physical flip from "lock on, lock out" to a way of seeing paradox. We draw on the work of Barry Johnson to show a simple framework for managing paradox, and understanding when a leader needs to shift focus. Like putting on a pair of 3D glasses, once you have an eye for paradox, the movie of life will never be the same.

Lock On, Lock Out

What makes paradox difficult to grasp? Well, let's start with the fact that it's ungraspable. It has no single answer for all time. And here we are, wired with a nervous system that searches for a single answer to lock onto, because then it can stop searching. Our schooling as children reinforced this habit: getting the right answer for 5 + 7, the proper spelling of *hippopotamus*, or the correct date of the Norman Conquest (1066, in case you're wondering).

Figure 3.2

a

b

Lock On, Lock Out. What's figure, what's ground?

Even our schooling is but a mirror of how our nervous system likes to seize upon a single, "right" answer and cannot hold two different answers at exactly the same moment. This "lock on, lock out" phenomenon has been studied many ways, including through ambiguous pictures such as those in Figure 3.2.

As you look at Figure 3.2a, your mind will flip back and forth between seeing two faces and seeing a vase. You might think you're seeing them at the same time, but actually, your mind is alternating what it locks on to (which is why this picture is more visually fatiguing than a regular picture of a vase).

If we make the flip a little harder to do, you can catch your mind in the act. Look now at Figure 3.2b. If you see an old woman looking out of the page, that is correct, but not complete. Do you also see the young woman looking into the page? Because you need to rearrange more lines and change scale, this flip in perception takes longer, and it's easier to notice that locking on to "old woman" locks out "young woman."

Added to our "lock on, lock out" tendency is the complication that what we lock on to comes from our own particular perspective. It may, in no way, represent the whole picture, as in the old anecdote of eight blind people feeling and describing the contours of an elephant: Each one has a completely different experience and each one can be correct without being complete. Or take a look at Figure 3.3.

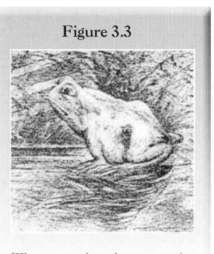

Figure 3.3

If you see a frog, that is correct, and not complete. What else is in the picture? I've heard leaders make up all kinds of secondary images, so perhaps this is a Rorschach test. But every so often, someone changes his perspective, tips his head to the side, and sees it instantly: a horse!

What you see depends on your point of view.

The importance of perspective also plays out in business and organizations all the time. One leader at headquarters sees what's right from a perspective of cost control and standardization, while another leader in the field sees what's right from the perspective of meeting unique customer needs and beating local competitors. Which one is right? Or one day a leader is besieged by shareholders who want greater profits, and the next day faces a relief organization that wants a product donated across Africa for the common good. Which is right? Both; neither; you can't split the difference, and yet you have to act. This is a hefty challenge for a mind that gravitates to finding right answers, and grew up with absolute certainty that right answers exist.

Step back in time to when we were young children learning to count. You might recall how literal and physical we make the process: touching each finger as we count—1, 2, 3—being happily certain when we named the right number. These primitive, literal thought patterns that we all had as children—and carry vestiges of into adulthood—work against comprehending paradox. The fact that we do grow *up* (in other words, become more mature) means that only gradually are we able to think in more empathetic, abstract, and relative terms, and we're always able to regress. Moreover, by the time our mind has developed enough to comprehend paradox, we already have some pretty strong "lock on, lock out" habits built up from all those years of checking our arithmetic, correcting our spelling, and knowing when the Magna Carta was written (1215, for the record).

Paradox takes us into the realm of not knowing, of not solving a problem once and for all, but rather managing an ongoing dynamic between two (or more) "right" answers, neither of which is sufficient by itself. To embrace and work with paradox, we have to suspend our mind's pull to nail down an answer. We have to accept the more complex dynamism of *And*, while relinquishing our grasp on the simple stasis of *Or*.

A Paradox You're Getting Right Without Even Knowing It

The good news is we do this all the time—without even thinking about it—and can call upon a ready example of how to make this flip from *Or* to *And*. Consider "inhale and exhale": which is right? Okay, stupid question. We know our very life is supported by a healthy oscillation between these two, neither of which would support us by itself. In truth, this is the nature of all paradox: a greater good is served through a healthy tension between the poles. From our perspective, purpose, or personality, however, we may be highly partial to only one side. But play along with this example, and it will guide you through much tougher ones.

Let's say we're on the side of inhale: it's our favorite part of breathing. Take in a deep breath and all that oxygen rushes in, filling the lungs, replenishing the blood—obviously inhale is where it's at. Keep holding that inhale, inhale, inhale, and, after enough stubborn persistence, you may notice a buzz of lightheadedness and other physiological signals that are saying, "Enough already!" And naturally, all you want to do is let go of all that holding...

And breathe out...exhale. What were we thinking? Exhale is the most excellent part of the breath cycle. It lets out all that carbon dioxide and toxins, and relaxes the mind and body. Recalling the unpleasantness we just left, of course, *this* is what we should keep doing: exhaling on and on and on, until a sense of utter depletion is now filling our body. We can no longer speak or move as a grasping gasp begins to form deep within us, and all we want to do is...

Breathe in, at last!

Of course we don't normally drive our breath to such extremes, because we know both sides are equally "right" and not sufficient by themselves. Moreover, we're tuned to subtle, physiological signals for when to make a switch from inhale to exhale, exhale to inhale, without driving to unnatural extremes. Recognizing that both sides are valuable (and problematic if held too long), and having a way to sense when it's time to switch: these are two principles for making the flip from *Or* to *And*.

Barry Johnson, in his groundbreaking book, *Polarity Management*,[1] offers a simple way to diagram the And-ness of paradox and get a handle on managing it. We can depict a paradox as opposite poles on a graph, as in Figure 3.4a on the next page.

On each side, we can identify a few things that are "right" about attending to this side, as well as potential concerns if we overdo it. Figure 3.4b fills in this diagram for our simple breathing example.

For inhale vs. exhale, this picture may seem banal and obvious. But for the more complex paradoxes leaders are forever facing in business

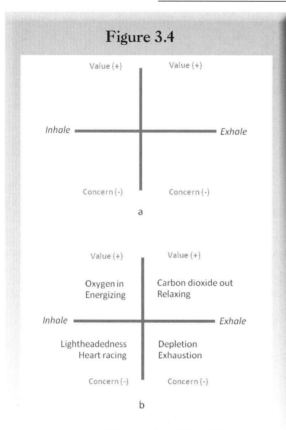

Figure 3.4

A map of the paradox of breathing.

(for example, short-term vs. long-term, global vs. local), in politics (national interests vs. local interests, rallying the base vs. non-partisan pragmatism), or between work and home life, even drawing this picture can be a breakthrough in understanding. Think of the Israeli-Palestinian conflict and still, as of this writing, what a breakthrough it would be to get to a diagram like this, or have each side acknowledge the rightness of the other! Yet, in this politically charged debate, if you see only one side as "right" you'll be back in "lock on, lock out" simplicity. Stir in plenty of fiery emotion, attacks and counter-attacks, and you have what has been appropriately called the "tyranny of the *Or*." It tears apart families, companies, countries, and large swaths of our world. The leader who is big enough to hold both sides, see what's valuable and concerning about each, and optimize the two toward a greater good, is the leader who can build bridges of understanding and heal the wounds of the world. The Zen leader who can flip *Or* to *And* helps everyone breathe a little easier.

Healthy Tension *Is* the Point

As we saw in Chapter 2, tension can be healthy or not. A healthy alternation of tension and release is the principle of all muscle movement. On the other hand, unhealthy, stuck tension is the seed of trouble. Likewise in making the flip from *Or* to *And*, we're not trying to find some static compromise where no tension exists. If the tension between inhale and exhale did not exist, that would be the equivalent of not breathing at all! Rather, it's the healthy tension or tug of war between inhale and exhale that serves a greater good—namely, keeping us alive.

That same principle applies to all paradox. In almost all cases of navigating paradox, at any moment we are favoring one side or the other, just as when we breathe, we are either inhaling *or* exhaling. But in time, if we balance our attention to both sides appropriately, we can maintain a healthy tension between the two. Similar to healthy tension in our muscles, the healthy tension between poles of a paradox is exactly what propels movement toward a greater good.

Now what constitutes *appropriate* balance? That's the question. It's answered pretty simply for inhale and exhale, being wired into our nervous system. Moreover, we own both sides of the inhale-exhale debate: We don't have to influence the Department of Inhale that it's time to free up some inhale resources for our breathing project; we don't have to scamper over to the Ministry of Exhale—those sluggards—and persuade them to get back on the job. Yet in organizational life, most paradoxes have sides with different owners, often operating with different incentives, in different subcultures, with little understanding between them. In business, we might have a sales organization pushing for growth across the globe, and a finance organization putting the brakes on growth in unprofitable markets. Or an organization could have marketing teams pushing a new product, while safety teams are clamoring to be heard on the risks.

Good minds can and will disagree on what constitutes an appropriate balance when a paradox spreads across people. Even in managing our own paradoxes—for example, in work-life balance—the people around us would rarely agree on how we should manage it, and even we second guess ourselves! Yet surfacing the trade-offs through genuine dialogue or reflection is part of what keeps paradoxical tension healthy. Once we let go of the idea of *one* appropriate balance or *one* right answer, we can harness this healthy tension toward a greater good, navigating instead by listening to signals or reading measures from both sides that tell us when to shift.

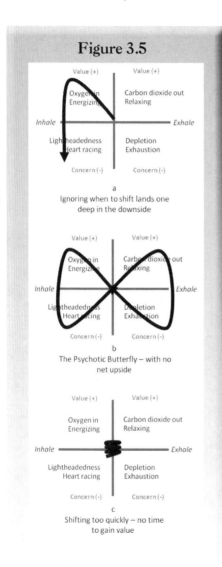

The pitfalls of paradox.

In the case of breathing, subtle, physiological signals tell us when to switch sides. If we ignore these signals, more dramatic alarms start firing off, as in a racing heart or lightheadedness, and we fall deep into the downside of overdoing inhale. We could depict this on our paradox drawing as in Figure 3.5a.

Deep into the concerns of inhale, it's easy to overreact, race to the other side, and overdo it until we're deep into the downside drama of exhale. Figure 3.5b depicts this driving to extremes in what is known as the "psychotic butterfly." One would have to work hard to make breathing this difficult, but unmanaged paradoxes in business and organizational life tend to go to extremes, simply because the benefits of one side gain momentum, and those in power ignore the subtle signals to shift. As one of my clients describes the value-destroying management style in her company, "We go guardrail to guardrail."

Back to our breathing example, we can also err on the side of shifting too quickly. If we go back and forth between inhale and exhale too quickly, we don't get much benefit from either one (see Figure 3.5c). This, too, will start signaling that something is wrong, as we find ourselves panting or hyperventilating. And this, too, happens in organizational life. As another client described it, "We change so often, people are numb and confused. They've learned they can wait out any change they don't like, and we aren't getting traction on much of anything." This, too, is a waste.

The healthy alternative for any paradox we're navigating is to look for signals, measures, and thresholds that tell us when to shift. We can identify the minimal upside we'll settle for, the downside we'll tolerate, the edges of the envelope we'll push, and then fly our paradox like a plane between two altitudes (Figure 3.6).

Johnson calls these signals or thresholds "flags": green flags when they measure what's good enough, red flags when they mark downside concerns we don't want to fall below. To conclude our breathing example, a green flag to switch from inhale to exhale might be a threshold of "enough oxygen." A red flag to switch from exhale back to inhale might be a threshold for "need oxygen."

In breathing, we might not be aware that these signals are operating, but you can appreciate the importance of having signals on both sides to make the whole

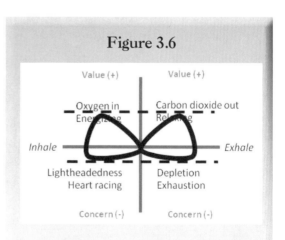

The Figure-8 of artful "And-ness": navigating between the thresholds, with more upside than down.

cycle function well. The biggest mistake leaders make in managing the healthy tension of *And* is they measure only one side—whichever *Or* they are partial to. So a sales organization might have measures of revenue against their sales targets, but not pay attention to profit margins. Or a finance organization may be closely tracking profits, but miss important flags around growth, such as market share. Bring these two organizations into a dialogue around an optimal way to manage a healthy tension between growth and profit, identifying upsides, downsides, and measures on both sides, and one can move beyond choosing between growth *Or* profits toward the greater good of sustainable, profitable growth.

Enemies of *And*: Overreaction and Under-reaction

A roomful of leaders in the pharmaceutical industry have had the same introduction to paradox you've just had. Now we want to apply their learning to a real situation facing their company: namely, the tension to be well run, safe, and reliable—undeniably necessary in their high-risk, highly regulated industry—and the need to be more innovative, not only in new drugs, but also in all aspects of their business. We've talked about how innovation itself is a paradox between creating ideas and having the discipline to move the best ideas through a resisting bureaucracy; that it requires a healthy tension between flexibility and control. Wanting to explore how this paradox is currently playing out in the company, we've started a paradox map (as in Figure 3.4), not only on a chart in the front of the room, but using the room itself. We've marked two axes with "Flexibility" on one side of the room, "Control" on the other, upside "Values" represented at the front of the room, and downside "Concerns" to the back. I've asked the leaders to consider, for their part of the business, which of these forces needs more attention right now, and to stand up and move to that side of the room.

On their feet, the leaders make a mass migration to the side of Flexibility. In a room of 42 leaders, only 3 have chosen the side of Control. If these leaders were suddenly the only decision-makers in the company, it's easy to see how they might lead the organization into an overreaction toward flexibility. This is the first enemy of *And*: overreaction. This is exactly what's behind the "guardrail to guardrail" management style that bedevils many a company. We get so sick of the issues we've been dealing with recently—the reporting to headquarters, the endless forms to fill out, the obtuse decision-making paths—we would throw it all off in a declaration of independence before remembering all the upsides these controls have brought about.

Through the weight of their vote, these leaders have also diagnosed where the company currently is in this critical paradox: namely, experiencing the downsides of too much control. Earlier, in the classroom, they were laughing at me holding my inhale to extremes, but in a similar sense, the company could be said to be holding its breath of control too long. We turn to how they can create an oasis of greater flexibility for their people that still respects the value of control.

Working through the quadrants of the paradox map, I ask the mob of leaders on the side of Flexibility to move toward the "Value" front of the room and tell me what value they hope to achieve by making things more flexible. "Greater responsiveness to customer needs," "Taking advantage of new opportunities," "Better morale and engagement," come the first few answers. Asking them to now shuffle down to the "Concern" back of the room (which they are visibly reluctant to do), I query them on what they might see on the downside if they're too flexible for too long. "Missed commitments," "Too much started, too little finished," they offer. "Safety issues," one of the lonely three leaders on the Control side contributes. It's not surprising that this issue is voiced from someone favoring the other side of the paradox, for whichever side we favor, we see the other side first in terms of its concerns. Moreover, if we lock on to those concerns, we'll lock out any possible benefits.

One-sided voices are heard all the time: "If we go down that path, it's a slippery slope to letting the foxes guard the hen house." "The last time we did that, we had a drug rejected by the FDA." By imagining only the extreme downside of the opposite force, we stay locked on to the rightness of our one side. The leader who can see and show others that we're not dealing with a "slippery slope" so much as a "figure-8" of managing a healthy tension within bounds we can agree upon, moves the dialogue—and the company—to a higher level. The leader who can tease apart "what *exactly* did we do last time that caused problems?" and identify thresholds within which we can maneuver successfully raises the bar of performance.

Indeed, this raising of the bar is exactly why paradox is becoming the "new normal." Companies have gotten smarter and more competitive as they've learned to become "glocal"—managing the paradoxes of global scale with local familiarity, of standardized controls and flexible customization, and so on. As one executive of a company that globalized early and considered itself pretty good at it said, "We've come to think of globalization as a kind of quicksand we've learned to swim in. We almost want to lure our competitors into it with us, because we know how hard it is, and if they don't learn how to swim, they won't survive."

Back in the room, we turn to our three leaders on the Control side and ask them what value they hope to create with more control. "Delivering on commitments," "Consistent quality," "Protecting our reputation," they answer. Some of these items are opposites to the concerns of the other side, and others carve new territory. Even though we could simply flip around the concerns on one side to be the benefits on the other, it's surprisingly instructive to "stand" in each quadrant separately and sense its potential.

"And the downside of control?" I inquire. "We're living it!" pipes up one of the mob. "Too slow, lack of responsiveness, can't get anything decided, and we're losing some of our best and brightest stars." Again, not surprising that a member of the Flexibility tribe can instantly point out all that's wrong with Control. I finish out the map (Figure 3.7) and ask, What's the point of managing this paradox well? What is the overarching goal?

A few answers surface immediately around being "safely innovative," but this question of overarching goal is worth deeper reflection, for one begins to sense how the two forces not only benefit from, but *require* each other in order to function at their best. To create a business that is both agile and stable, flexibility *needs* control and control *needs* flexibility. What a breakthrough of understanding this is for leaders who previously defended only one side.

The next step, and the real art in managing paradox, is to identify measures on both sides that tell us when to shift. In the room, leaders cluster into small groups to fo-

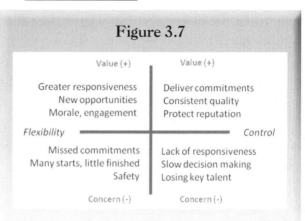

Figure 3.7

Value (+)	Value (+)
Greater responsiveness New opportunities Morale, engagement	Deliver commitments Consistent quality Protect reputation
Flexibility	*Control*
Missed commitments Many starts, little finished Safety	Lack of responsiveness Slow decision making Losing key talent
Concern (-)	Concern (-)

The map of flexibility and control.

cus on measures specific to their parts of the business. One group suggests we can get at employee engagement using a climate survey and set green flags (for example, a 4.2 on a 5-point scale is good enough) and red flags (3.8 out of 5 is a level we don't want to sink below) for when to shift. Another group proposes a way to measure the time spent in boards and reviews in a decision-making process; when it gets above a certain level, it's time to simplify some controls.

Near the end of the session, we gather into a conversation. Why, we ask, given that nearly every leader in the room sees the need for greater flexibility (and this is the case throughout the company), it's not happening. Some people offer answers that place blame higher up, and yes, the tone in the culture is set at the top. But how does this group play into it? "We like control too," someone observes, and, having seen the personality profile of the group, I know how right he is. "We've been successful as a company," another says, "if we've been holding our breath on control we're not dizzy enough yet." And herein lies the second enemy of *And*: under-reaction—when we keep ourselves comfortable, or things are going along well enough, and early warning signs of imbalance are ignored. If we wait for a crisis before shifting our focus to the other side, we create the conditions for later overreacting, and it's only a matter of time before we're rewarded with the crisis we've been waiting for.

We can do better. Knowing the dual enemies of *And*—the overreaction and under-reaction that lead to extremes—we can navigate a middle way.

The Zen Leader Flip 3: *Or* to *And*

The basic principles of this flip are simple indeed, and can be practiced again and again. Whereas a good deal of intellect is eventually involved in managing paradox, this flip begins in our physical senses. Just as in the frog and horse picture earlier, the flip from *Or* to *And* is triggered by a flip in perception that frees up the Zen leader in us.

See 2. Unlock from the certainty of a right answer to explore another possibility: this is what unlocks the flip from *Or* to *And*. It's fairly easy to practice on unemotional topics, such as seeing both frog and horse. We can flex our "See 2" muscles by noticing the competing forces in the organizations we're a part of, in the trade-offs we face as parents, or in the competing claims on our time. In a matrix organization, for example, we might notice how the customer service group gets pulled by the forces of efficiency on the one hand and customer satisfaction on the other. In our families, we might see the force of discipline in a tug of war with the force of leniency.

To See 2 becomes even more challenging and rewarding when you're deeply partial to one side, as in seeing the local view when you're at global headquarters, seeing a woman's perspective when you're a man, or seeing a liberal view when

The Zen Leader

Flip 3

Or to And

☯ See 2

☯ Map 4

☯ Manage the Figure-8

you're a conservative. Seeing at least two sides of any issue (often you'll see more than two sides), and identifying the forces at work on each side, creates an opening of mind.

"I don't care about an open mind," we may hear the little voice in our head protest. "I'm certain about this and I want to stay that way." When we meet such resistance, this is excellent progress, for we've come up against one of our "lock on, lock out" blind spots. Even if we can't get past it, seeing it is useful awareness.

Another way to increase our ability to See 2 is to examine something that seems like a garden-variety problem for the larger paradox it may be a part of. The example we used earlier was the decision to hire Jane, and how it could be part of a larger paradox of managing our talent pool for the short term and the long term. Similarly, you might consider an important problem you've "solved" recently, and whether your approach favored only one side of a larger paradox. That doesn't make it wrong by any means. Similar to breathing, our decisions in the moment almost always land us on one side or the other. It's being *aware* of the bigger picture and managing the dynamic of *And* through time that moves our thinking to a new level.

Map 4. Once we See 2 forces we want to manage a healthy tension between, we can Map 4: that is, draw a map of the upside and downside of each. We may see many more than two forces, but so as not to overshoot our cognitive (or artistic!) skills, we'll take two at a time.

To Map 4, we start with our first force and ask, "What is the value we hope to achieve by focusing here?" and identify two or three items. We then ask, "What might be the downside if we stay here too long?" and again identify a few items. To address these concerns, we would naturally want to bring in some of the opposite force. Moving to the upside quadrant of force #2, we ask, "What do we hope to achieve by attending here?" Finally, to complete our map we answer, "What might start to happen if we stay on this side too long?"

This sequential process—and it really helps to do it in this order—is depicted in Figure 3.8.

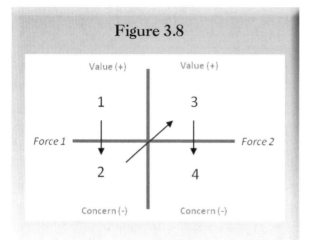

Figure 3.8

Map 4 by moving through each quadrant sequentially, and identifying a few items for each.

Some people find that physically changing their seat helps them shift their focus from force 1 to force 2. This is especially useful if we're partial to one force over the other. Just as tilting our head enabled us to see a horse, rather than a frog, changing our seat often makes it easier to see or imagine a different perspective.

When we Map 4, we don't have to keep it a solo exercise. Indeed, this exercise can make for excellent dialogue with another person or discussion with a team, especially if we involve players who can speak passionately for each side. Map 4 is just the beginning; it can open up a genuine dialogue where before there had been only attacks and counter-attacks. It also allows the next step.

Manage the Figure-8. Once we can acknowledge what's right and potentially concerning about both sides, we're ready for the art form of managing the figure-8 of *And*. Two questions will help us in this process:

1. What's the overarching goal served by managing this tension well?
   An overarching goal can be as simple as "keeping us alive" in the case of inhale and exhale or "sustainable growth" in the case of flexibility and control. Knowing this larger purpose can guide us in the 2nd question, which is:

2. When is it time to shift? What's good enough to serve our purpose? And when do we know we're entering dangerous territory?

Considering the two or three areas we identified in each quadrant when we Map 4, we look for those we can measure or signs we can watch for. Ideally, we can set some thresholds for "good enough" (green flags) and "we don't want to sink below this" (red flags).

For example, if we're a customer service group trying to manage the *And* of being efficient enough and responsive enough, we might measure our costs on the one hand and our customer satisfaction on the other. For customer satisfaction, we might set a green flag of 4.2 on a 5-point scale that says, "Good enough; turn back and focus now on costs." On the same scale, we might set a red flag of 3.8 that tells us, "Warning: Even if it costs a little more, improve your customer service." On either side we'll find the voices who would say, "Do better. If you can get 4.2, why not shoot for 4.5?" But we will generally find that improving one side worsens the other. Having measures on both sides lets us push the tension as far as we're willing to go, and still keep it healthy. On the other hand, if our costs are still in an acceptable range and our customer satisfaction rating is only 4.0, we know to keep pushing higher. In this way, we don't shift too early.

Above all, we want to avoid the mistake of measuring only one side. In examples like this, many leaders err by measuring only costs, and ignoring customer satisfaction. Even in managing our own work-life balance, many of us err by noticing only the signals that pertain to work, while ignoring early warning signs in our families or health. To manage the Figure-8, we need "time to shift" signals on both sides. If we "own" both sides of the paradox, some of these signals can be implicit or intuitive. But when we need agreements from others on when it's time to shift, objective measures are best. "If you can measure it, you can manage it," goes the folklore of the quality movement, which could just as easily apply to navigating the Figure-8.

*And*s Well Worth Managing

- Short term–Long term
- Flexibility–Control
- Creativity–Discipline
- Global–Local
- Doing–Being
- Individual–Group
- Cost–Quality
- Cost–Performance
- Speed–Quality
- Efficiency–Responsiveness
- Centralized–Decentralized
- Growth–Expense Control
- People–Task
- Work–Family
- Family–Personal
- Compete–Collaborate
- Liberal–Conservative
- Outcome (what)–Process (how)
- Shareholders–Customers
- Customers–Employees
- Action–Reflection
- Profits–Purpose

Putting It to Work: A Paradox You Need to Manage Well

No mystery in how to apply this flip, for paradoxes abound in leading today's complex organizations—not to mention our complex lives. Pick one. Pick a paradox that is particularly relevant to you right now. It could be a trade-off in how you spend your time, what you focus on, or a bias in how you make decisions that could benefit from counterbalance. If you work in a matrix organization and report more than one way, you might consider the tension in what each of your reporting lines expect of you. If you're achievement driven, almost certainly work-life balance is a tension for you.

Some *And*s worth managing well are given in the sidebar to stimulate your thinking.

See 2. Start your diagram. Identify your two forces as endpoints of the "x" (horizontal) axis.

Map 4. Starting with the upper left-hand quadrant, identify a few things you hope to achieve by focusing on force #1. Then, moving to the lower left-hand quadrant, answer what concerns would arise if you over-focus on force #1. Continue through each quadrant sequentially (as in Figure 3.8)—really feeling into that reality or potentiality—until you've identified key elements for the upside and downside of each force. You may find it useful to physically change your position as you consider the opposite-side force.

Manage the Figure-8. The first part of managing this *And* artfully is to understand what it's good for. Step back from the diagram and ask an overarching question, such as: "What are these two forces trying to achieve together?" Or, "What might be possible if I could get the best out of both?" Write down an overarching goal to managing this tension well.

Consider the elements you've written in each box for what could be some measures on both sides, or early warning signs of trouble. Based on your overarching goal, see if you can identify some thresholds for what's good enough, and what levels you don't want to sink below. Playing with several measures and thresholds, identify some maneuvering room: "altitudes" between which you can "fly" this paradox. Remember the importance of having measures on both sides, because the key question in managing *And* is not which side is right, or even better than the other. It's knowing when to shift.

The flip from *Or* to *And* starts simply enough—breathe in, breathe out—but it opens us to a most valuable way of looking, of thinking, of keeping our minds in motion, rather than stuck on a single right answer. With this flip, we transcend the dualism of *this OR that*—a skill we can now apply to far weightier matters, and our next flip.

The Zen Leader

Flip 3 Takeaways

Or to *And*

Understanding paradox is a leap in development in which we let go of single right answers and play in the pull of multiple forces.

To apply this flip:

- **See 2.** Identify an ongoing challenge and two opposing forces that keep it in play.

- **Map 4.** "Stand" in each quadrant in the order shown in Figure 3.8, and feel into the upside and downside of each force.

- **Manage the Figure-8.** Write an overarching goal that unites the two forces: What's the best of both? Then identify measures and flags on both sides that indicate it's time to shift.

4

From "Out There" to "In Here"

I'M AT A week-long Zen training session, intense for its long periods of meditation that both clear the mind and exhaust the body. I'm a few days into it, and a good 45 minutes into this particular "sit" when my body starts to shake. A quake first starts at my base, and then radiates through my spine, legs, arms, and my hands, as I both experience and watch with curiosity, hoping I'm not distracting my fellow meditators, or vibrating right off this cushion. An image comes to mind of being buffeted by the atmosphere, and suddenly I'm in a capsule, experiencing the dream of my childhood: being an astronaut. The buffeting gets more intense, and now I'm shaking all over and it's all I can do to hang on. And then, suddenly—flush—nothing. Complete smoothness, as if I've cleared the atmosphere and am drifting into outer space. Tears flow from my eyes as

I recognize in a flash that this—*this* experience—was why I wanted to be an astronaut: to break all bonds and be free. And now I see that the outer journey—all that we seek and do and struggle with—is a perfect mirror of the inner journey. Likewise, the inner journey *is* the outer journey; there is no real in or out.

In thousands of ways, I have watched this truth play out through the leaders with whom I work. For example, the leader who

- thinks large and creates a grand, overleveraged life.
- thinks small and creates a tiny, safe life.
- seeks outer greatness in answer to inner doubt.
- is outwardly impatient, because it's hard to control inner impulses.
- is relentlessly drawn to what's new to stave off inner boredom.

Who we are shows up in how we live, what we seek, and what world we create around us. Conversely, the issues we attribute to the people and situations around us are mirrored in our own internal tensions, where—good news—we always have the power to attend to them. "Drive all issues into one," Zen teacher Charlotte Joko Beck learned from her teacher, meaning to drive them into oneself, see where one is playing into them, and get to their inevitably singular root.

This chapter guides one into the flip of seeing where an outer drive has an inner source, where a difficult relationship has an inner cause, and where the things we don't like "out there" are mirrored in what we fear "in here." With this flip, one is freed from fear, and the Zen leader in us emerges to create a new world.

Slippery Ground

"Shit happens." Great bumper sticker; great phrase. It's the unlikely mantra of a former nun, Joyce. She's a wonderful teacher I'm getting to know, who has a rare circulatory disease that cropped up 10 years ago. She'll be dead in five years. She's in her early 40s, and I attribute her remarkable presence to this basic acceptance that, sometimes, shit happens.

There is no fairness in her disease. She didn't do anything to bring it on. And apparently there is nothing that can be done medically to stop its progression. It is what it is.

But Joyce has the disease; the disease does not get all of Joyce. In this week that I'm with her, she never plays victim. Indeed, her energy is beacon bright. She has so impressed me with her skillful guidance of this group of NASA managers (myself included) that I will eventually change careers to follow her example. She is also living the wisdom that we cannot always control what happens to us, but we can always control our response to it. A protégé of the great psychologist Will Schutz, she has opened my eyes to the mind-body connectedness of illness[1]: how her circulatory illness, for example, relates to (which is not to say was *caused* by, but simply *relates* to) matters of the heart and issues around openness. She opens up the possibilities of "choice" with such odd questions as, "Why did you choose your parents?" And by way of softening our startled gazes, adds, "Or if you had chosen your parents, what would you have gotten out of making that choice?"

Great question, I realize, as I can instantly think of a dozen reasons I would have chosen my particular set of parents, and realize how the very mind that is conceiving these answers was shaped by that "choice." (Try it!) The ground is getting slippery under my feet, as my ordinary way of looking at a world "out there" is getting turned on its head. Did I choose my parents, or did they choose me? Did Joyce choose her illness, or only her response to it?

Now that you've been tuned to paradox, you know the answers are neither simple nor static, and deeper truths can be found in all possibilities.

A World of Our Making

The idea of a world of our making does not mean we can consciously control everything. Whether it's winning the lottery or shit happening, events in this moment have been preconditioned by the past. Winning the lottery, for example, is only possible if some group has already organized a lottery, sold tickets, and we acquired one. Joyce's circulatory disease was apparently genetic. The idea that the past conditions the present is old and familiar, variously expressed as karma, action creating reaction, energy being neither created nor destroyed, or even "what goes around, comes around." Our choices in the moment are shaped by the past, and even the us that's choosing is preconditioned by all manner of nature, nurture, and previous experience. So constrained can our choices seem at times, that they can feel like no choice at all, and philosophers for ages have taken up this matter in weighty discourses on free will and determinism. Which one is right?

Surely you're onto it by now: it's another paradox. Yes, we are creative forces capable of imaginative leaps, awakened consciousness, and changing the course of history. And yes, we are corporeal beings living in a world where matter is governed by laws and causes have effects. In making the flip from a world "out there" happening to us to a world "in here" of our making, we come up a level in the game of life, dancing in a paradox of seemingly contradictory forces, in which we become not merely the one who has free will or is determined, but the Zen leader playing the game, free to use both.

The flip from "out there" to "in here" starts by accepting that reality contains much more possibility than, as a board player in the game of life, we can see. For example, most of us can think in two dimensions; really skilled spatial thinkers, such as architects, can think in three dimensions. Although theories to understand "out there"—so-called unified field theories in physics—vary in the number of dimensions they attribute to the universe, they agree it's somewhere around 10. Ten! We don't see all these dimensions. We can't think in all these dimensions. What we do see and think is "real" is more like a three-dimensional shadow (like a projection) of a 10-dimensional universe.

Consider for a moment the enormity of what this means. If you hold your hand up to a light so that it casts a shadow, you can get an idea of how much information is lost in going from your three-dimensional hand to its two-dimensional shadow. If you wiggle your fingers, you'll see that some form and movement information is preserved as you move from three to two dimensions, but color information is lost, as is depth. Imagine how much more information is lost in going from 10 dimensions to three! The flip to "in here" starts with the humble recognition that "out there" is vastly more complex and interesting than we can comprehend, and that we own the limited sensors with which we're sampling this vast pool, and the sense we're making of it. Because everything we experience is coming through our own filters, by the time it gets "in here" it has "me" written all over it. In the broadest sense, these filters can be as humanly common as eyes that register only certain frequencies that we call visible light. Because most people have similar eyes, billions of people around the world can roughly agree on what "blue" is, although their word for it may vary.

Somewhat more specific are filters that come from our society. For example, if we've grown up in America, we have a cultural filter (whether we personally agree with it or not) that asserts the rights of the individual ahead of the group (such as the state). If we've grown up in China, our filter would say the harmony of the group is more important than the rights of the individual. Within our respective societies, we might not even be aware of these filters, because "we all know" that's how it is. But bring our two societies into contact, and we can have grave misunderstandings about what it means, say, to protect human rights.

But potentially the most distorting filters are those specific to one's personality. For example, if I have an issue about being controlled, when someone tells me to do something, I may think they're trying to control me. They could just be trying to spare me from making a stupid mistake, but seeing the world through the lens of my own distorting issue, I will misinterpret others' actions, and this may trigger a chain of defensive reactions within me. This mistake, which happens all the time in relationships, is called false attribution: I falsely attribute aspects of my own personality or motives to others. As these distorting filters become more specific, and less widely shared, more room opens up for misunderstanding and false attribution. If I were at a pathological extreme of mental illness, virtually no one would understand or agree with my interpretation of "out there."

Even well short of the extremes, our layers of distorting filters based on our human limitations, culture, family, gender, age, strengths, weaknesses, experiences, fears, position in life, and on and on, create our perceptions and the meaning we make of "out there." Not only does this make for plenty of misunderstandings between people, but these filters also give rise to an even more insidious problem. Because we are never without them, even once we become aware of these filters, it's surprisingly easy to forget we have them. We forget that we're living in a world of our making. We actually convince ourselves that it's "out there." As the brilliant physicist David Bohm observes, "The mind creates 'reality' and then says, 'I didn't do it.'"[2]

In the flip from "out there" to "in here," we open up to the possibilities present in all that we don't know, and recognize that what we do know about "out there," and what we do with that knowledge, comes from "in here."

What World Are You Making?

Perhaps you've never thought of yourself as making a world. "I didn't make this world," our ordinary mind might say, "I stepped into it. And it'll all be here when I'm gone." In a paradoxical sense, that would be correct, and not complete. True, the entire world is a composite of the contributions from many people, many forces, and many causes and conditions all pouring into now. But we could just as easily flip that around and say the world is unalterably different because you are in it. Now how do you want to use that power? Depending on your self-image—consciously and subconsciously held—you will cast a net across the vastness and define your world.

If you regard yourself as small and powerless, you will create a tiny world in which you are often victimized by large and powerful forces.

If you regard yourself as a persistent, creative genius, like Walt Disney, you'll create a world of fanciful characters, transforming the entertainment industry.

If you regard yourself as a highly responsible person with something to prove, you will create a world where people rely on you, and life endlessly presents you with mountains to climb and challenges to overcome.

If you regard yourself as a dramatic person, you will create a world with plenty of ups and downs, conflicted relationships, and bold moves.

If you regard yourself as a disruptively creative entrepreneur who cheated death well before he succumbed to it, like Steve Jobs, you'll fearlessly create a world where whole industries leap to a new paradigm, and make a "ding in the universe," as Jobs was known to say.

"Your story is your destiny," proclaims Jim Loehr in *The Power of Story*,[3] which abounds in examples of how our deeply held self image—our "story"—creates our world. Jim helps people re-create their world by rewriting their story. Similarly, Betty Edwards[4] helps people connect their story to their world by having them write an important episode of their life, first from the perspective of a victim, and then from the perspective of a hero. No surprise that they find the second version vastly more empowering.

These are but two of the voices and bodies of research pointing to a world of our making. We could add to them the work of Martin Seligman and the Positive Psychology movement, the Law of Attraction, the "if you build it they will come" promise of a positive vision, and the only thing optimists and pessimists agree upon: optimists have better lives. Yes, we live in a world of causes and conditions. And yes, we define the scale, slice, or sliver of that world we operate in.

So what world are you making? The following exercise gives you a chance to think through some key elements of your personality and how they show up in your world.

What World Do You Make?

We don't normally look for connections between how we are on the inside and our everyday world on the outside, but when we do, the connections can be surprisingly revealing. Try this:

Start with your strengths. List five things you know you're good at, which might be specific skills (for example, math or music) or traits that have supported you through your career (for example, being good with people).

Then list five core values or beliefs—things that you stand for; qualities that even others would recognize as your "Leadership Brand."

Part 1: Consider your typical week, including both work and personal time. How does the week reflect the items on your two lists? Consider positive, satisfying connections, as well as things that irritate. Find a connection to each item on your list and, where one is not obvious, force a connection (a technique known to stimulate lateral thinking). As you write, also notice any feelings that arise.

Part 2: Considering your 10 items as a whole, answer the following:

- How big or small is my world, and how do my items play into this?

- How fast or slow is my world, and how do my items play into this?

- What role do people play in my world, and how do my items play into this?

This kind of awareness is invaluable, for it helps us see how we're playing into situations, even if we're not *causing* them entirely. It also helps us know the distortions of our filters, what we might be missing, and how we might misinterpret things. Just as navigators of the sea learned how to correct for the distorting difference between true north and magnetic north in their compass readings, so we can apply conscious corrections to our filters: for example, knowing we have a hair trigger for thinking people are trying to control us and that they may have other intentions.

A World in Our Image

"What are the people like in this town?" the allegorical traveler asks a village elder.

"What were they like where you came from?" the elder asks.

"Oh, they were very good people," answers the traveler.

"You'll find the people here are the same."

Later on, a second traveler arrives, meets the same elder, and asks the same question.

"What were the people like where you came from?" the elder asks in answer.

"They were scoundrels and thieves!" says the traveler.

"You'll find the people here the same."

This old story speaks to the way we unconsciously play into situations, giving roles to others that we, in some way, expect them to play as part of our deeply held self-image—our story. And because a human being is like a multifaceted gem, the part that we expect to see is often the only part that we *do* see. Now and then we might catch a surprise, but expectations are another way of saying that "in here" we've pre-tuned our senses to notice only certain things and to place certain interpretations on them.

I've just told this story to Jan in our coaching session because she's thinking of leaving her job. I'm not so sure that changing jobs—the "geographical cure"—is going to fix what she wants fixed. She says the people where she currently works are aligned against her. There may be some truth in that, but I'm encouraging her to explore her own role in the situation, her expectations, and what she gets out of feeling "aligned against." "I can't imagine what I'm getting out of it," she says, "I feel so alone!" I point to the report in front of us—a profile of her personality and leadership style that highlights her hard-charging ways. "This type of leader prefers working fast and alone," I tell her. "Maybe you're getting just what you want."

We review written feedback from others that she has also received this week, and the comments from her direct reports are particularly severe. "She doesn't make time for us," one says. "She's puts her own ambitions over the team," says another. On the positive side, everyone agrees that Jan is a real go-getter, "an achievement-driven machine." "I love to get stuff done," Jan agrees in part. "It's not that I don't care about my people, but they're old-fashioned and don't have the attitude to learn—especially from me! I used to be their peer, and they resent that I got promoted above them."

Becoming a boss of former peers *is* a challenging role. But as we talk, Jan sees how she went into the role *expecting* problems, and when she sensed something "off" in her early interactions, she was quick to read her expectations into it, as in: "They resent me; they're lining up against me," not "They're feeling their way through a new relationship with me and right now they're not feeling very good about themselves because I was the one promoted," which could have been another completely legitimate interpretation. Whether it was true for them or not, Jan was choosing to read resentment and retaliation into their actions.

Jan is also seeing the effect of her rapid-fire achievement drive on others, "No one else thinks they can keep up, so they give up, and I'm stuck doing the work."

"Perfect!" I say. "Here you are, a person who needs to achieve a lot, and you've created a world where you need to achieve a lot." She's still not convinced that this is her doing, but her puzzled expression tells me that she's beginning to doubt that all of this is simply happening to her from "out there." A possibility is dawning that she may be able to change something "in here" that would change her unpleasant world of work. By the end of the week, she will have built a plan of action in which she still explores other jobs, but also commits to a brave experiment to transform the role she's currently in, and leave her direct reports better off for having worked with her.

What's the Real Battle?

Mark is speeding along in the left lane of the expressway, doing the expected 10 mph over the speed limit, catching up with a driver who clearly didn't get the memo, and is creeping along. "Who said it was Slow Driver in the Left Lane Day?!" he bellows, pounding his fist on the steering wheel, flashing his lights. "Get the hell out of my way!" He does it to blow off steam, he says, and doesn't mean a thing by it. But he's visibly upset, as is now the driver in front of us. And I, sitting in the passenger seat, am getting that old familiar walking-on-eggshells-around-conflict feeling that I absolutely hate.

Let's freeze the frame and ask, What's going on here? Not in the usual blame-placing perspective—what's happening "out there" is not the story that interests us. Let's look instead at how each of us in this little scene is creating our world from "in here."

First there's Mark, driving along with an expectation that "we all know" driving in the left lane calls for going faster than the speed limit, and irritation flashes when that expectation is not met. Mark has a funny, boisterous, dramatic temperament, and his irritation triggers all of those traits. He has no doubt learned (he's a psychologist, after all) that big reactions like this make him the center of the drama, put other people on guard, and may lessen the chance that his expectations will be disappointed in the future. Let other people react as they will; he's staked out his territory.

Meanwhile, I'm riding along, I see the scene unfolding in the left lane, and suddenly the car is filled with sound and fury. Instantly, responsible me thinks I have to *do* something; calm this situation down, talk sense into this person. Why? What's my real battle? It's with conflict itself, and all the fear it unleashes within me. As a child, it would literally make my skin crawl and take my breath away (I have a long history of eczema and asthma to show for it). I'm sure one of the reasons I spent 30 years in martial arts is that I had to get a handle on my reactions to conflict. Good thing I did. Sitting in the car, I can still feel these vestigial pressures inside—*do* something!—but now in my world, they get very little of me. An earlier version of me in the car with Mark would have created a much more argumentative world.

And what of the person in the car in front of us? He was just driving along, minding his own business, perhaps more tuned in to his inner life than to outer conditions. Along comes some speeding Jeep on his tail, lights flashing, with the driver gesticulating wildly. What world will he create in this moment? If he's an easy-going fellow who knows he tends to daydream while driving, he might offer up a shrug, as if to say, "Sorry, spaced out," move out of the lane, and return to his dreamy world. If he's an angry driver, prone to road rage, he might just have to show Mark a thing or two, slow down even further, roll down his window, and jam a one-finger salute into the air. As it turns out, he's somewhere in between—a cautious fellow who has looked over his shoulder now three times to see if it's safe to move into the middle lane. But he doesn't like what Mark's done, or how Mark has made him feel about himself. He's grim-faced and determined, eyes straight ahead, as we sail by.

A late report, an infuriating e-mail, a warm exchange with an old colleague, a serious meeting, a jam-packed schedule, a slow car in the left lane of the expressway...our day is filled with scenes that trigger emotional reactions within us. The scene is just the scene. Where the real story and, in many cases, the real battle unfolds is "in here." How does it make us feel? What do we fear may happen? What do we fear may be true about us? By reacting a certain way, what fear do we reinforce? We may not normally reflect on everyday scenes with this depth, but it's surprisingly instructive when we do. For what we learn is that any outer conflict traces its roots to an inner fear. And once we can stand in that fear, get to know it, and make friends with it, our world becomes a vastly bigger, freer, happier place.

The Zen Leader Flip 4: "Out There" to "In Here"

This flip is best made in the spirit of open curiosity. We do well to suspend judgment, set aside any expectations of what we'll find when we start digging around "in here," and be guided by a sincere wanting to know—and a good sense of humor! Bring along your laughter. As you see into the mirror or find the root of difficulties "out there," you may think you're the only person carrying such baggage. The great joke is we're all born baggage carriers, and we also have the potential to be free of our baggage. Even baggage itself is neither good nor bad; the term may sound negative, but if you've ever taken a trip and had the airline lose your baggage, you know how comforting baggage can be. On the other hand, carry too much of it, and you don't go very far.

See into the mirror. We enter this flip by shifting our perspective from something happening "out there" to inquiring: *What is it related to "in here"? How am I playing into this? If, at some level, I chose this, what might I be getting out of it?* Any time we catch ourselves entering coping mode is a great time to practice this flip. For whatever has triggered our coping reaction is the very situation we want to explore, not in terms of how it appears in the world, but how it appears in the mirror of our self. We can support our inquiry physically by practicing the flips we've learned so far. In time,

The Zen Leader

Flip 4

"Out There" to "In Here"

☯ See into the mirror

☯ Find the root

☯ Claim your power

we can vastly accelerate our "inside" insight through meditation and other practices (see Sitting Meditation at the end of this chapter, as well as the Chapter 4 exercises online). In the moment, we can simply relax, center our self, release tension in the front of the body, and allow a sense of extension through the back, through our legs, arms, and fingers. We're ready to see into the mirror.

The mirror, of course, is a metaphor. And seeing into it calls for a bit of abstract thinking, in which we come up a level to make connections that may not seem obvious. As a player on the board, Jan, for example, couldn't imagine at first what she was getting out of thinking people were aligned against her. But as she came up a level to look at herself playing the game, she could see that her preferred style was to work fast and alone, that she valued achievement more than she valued relationships, and that she never felt that she had enough time. She could see how believing that people were aligned against her justified the way she wanted to work anyway.

Earlier you had a chance to write down several strengths and elements of your "leadership brand" and connect those to your world. Seeing into the mirror is being able to make these connections from self to world, as well as from world back to self. When we notice, for example, that we're irritated by a talkative visitor who has popped into our office, we can ask our self: *what is it related to "in here"*? We might not register these trifle irritations as full-blown fear, but we will almost always see they represent a violation of something we value. Ah, we may see our visitor violates our sense of order, our expectation that we control our schedule. Our knee-jerk reaction might be to dismiss this person, which would return us to our orderly world. This talkative person could be an irritating distraction, or could be bringing us a game-changing business idea; only by seeing into the mirror, and correcting for "order distortion," do we have a chance of telling the difference.

Seeing into the mirror is not meant to ignore that there are other players and other forces shaping the present moment. But it is meant to discover how we're playing into the contours of our world, and the choices we're now making. By sincerely inquiring into how we're playing into the situations we face, and what they relate to in us, we see more clearly how "out there" is mirrored "in here," where we have all the power in the world.

Find the root. Seeing is always the starting point, but before our actions can come from a deeper, fuller, freer sense of self, we have to find the root of what's holding our current story in place. We don't have to free up our whole story in one fell swoop, though there are systemic ways we can advance our freedom in leaps and bounds, especially through the core practice of meditation. But one can regard the sort of coping situation for which this flip is particularly useful as a little weed—something that crops up that we don't like. And similar to pulling a weed, if we don't find the root, our efforts are superficial, and the problem will crop right back up. But also, we don't have to unearth every root in our yard to deal with *this* weed.

Roots are our underlying fears. These fears might be that we're not good enough, lovable enough, strong enough to be present with difficult emotions, or name-your-own enough. These fears underlie what Hubert Benoit nailed as "The Great Lawsuit";[5] that is, the unwinnable case to justify or secure our ego's existence, to make this little, fragile self feel safe. Truly, as long as we regard our self as separate, we can never, once and for all feel safe enough. Hence, our little ego-token on the game board of life is bound to have fears. Lots of them.

To find the root is to inquire deeply into this question: *What do I fear in this situation?* Positive, go-getting people may at first think they don't fear anything, which was Jan's first reaction. But coping mode is itself evidence of fear. People who have truly mastered their fears don't spend much time in coping mode. I nudged Jan to go deeper with the question, "What does this situation make you fear that you may not be *enough?*" "Likeable enough," she answered instantly. "What kind of leader can I be if people don't like me?" This is finding the root.

Michael O'Brien, coauthor of *Quicksilver*,[6] helps his clients find the root all the time. He's categorized four of the most common fears as being:

- ☯ Stupid / Foolish / Idiotic (not smart enough)
- ☯ A Pretender / A Fraud (not good enough or authentic enough)
- ☯ An Outcast / Rejected / Unlovable (not likeable enough)
- ☯ Powerless / Weak / Ineffective (not strong enough)

This is a good list to start with anytime we want to find the root that is informing our story in a coping situation. These fears are crucial to recognize and name, because they are operating whether we recognize them or not. These fears are the tools the ego uses to keep its game going—for better or worse. The fear of death is perhaps the most obvious way the ego keeps its game going. But in subtle ways, all of these fears can trigger our ego's fear of death.

For example, you can imagine in the wandering tribes of our human ancestors, not being likeable and being banished from the tribe was a virtual death sentence, given all the predators ready to pounce on solo prey. Our nervous system developed through hundreds of thousands of years of this sort of learning, passed from one survivor to the next. Little wonder that the fear that we're not likeable is so primal. Likewise with not being strong enough, smart enough, and so on. At the same time, if our ego values achievement over being liked, we might subtly sabotage relationships to keep our achievement game going. Sometimes our poor, confused ego— our little token on the game board of life—doesn't know which fear it fears most, or which way to turn.

To find the root is to dig down and name the underlying fears in our coping situations. Once we can see our fears, they can no longer get all of us. For here's the good news: the awareness that sees the fear is not itself afraid. This awareness is the Zen leader in us, coming up to the level of playing the game, and claiming our power.

Claim your power. The truth about fear is that it can only do its dirty work underground and from a distance. From Franklin Roosevelt ("We have nothing to fear but fear itself") to Henry David Thoreau ("Nothing is so much to be feared as fear") to Francis Bacon ("Nothing is terrible except fear itself"), it seems we've known for some time that fear attacks in the dark. In the light of awareness, which is not itself afraid, fear loses its force. That's not to say it disappears altogether, but when we stand in our fear— move into the very thick of it—and act anyway, it loses its leverage over us.

Leverage. The word has become equated with financial meltdowns, but if you think back to a playground seesaw from your childhood, you know the principle of leverage: the farther away you are from the pivot point (the fulcrum), the more counter-balancing weight is needed on the other side, and a short drop on that end then puts you *way* up in the air. That's also how our fears feel and function from a distance: like a huge weight that we try to keep away from, and that somehow has us stuck up in the air (as in Figure 4.1a). Imagine the fulcrum represents our fear, and the weight represents how strong that fear is for us, which counterbalances how far we are from it. The closer we move to our fear, finding the root, getting it out in the open, the lighter it gets (Figure 4.1b). Claiming our power, we move right into it, stand right on top of our fear-fulcrum, and now our fear hardly weighs anything at all (Figure 4.1c). We're free to act. From inside out, we can extend our energy into the situation, and a problem "out there" is transformed by the Zen leader emanating from "in here."

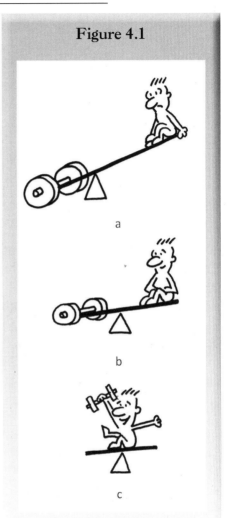

Figure 4.1

Moving toward the fulcrum of our fears, their weight lessens. Standing right in the fear, we are free to move.

How does this work in practice? In Jan's case, she was able to claim her power by accepting (there's that word again—always the hinge point between coping and transforming) that, okay, maybe her people don't like her, or they don't like how they feel about themselves around her. After all, she hasn't been giving them much attention. But now she wants to help them feel more capable—she cares about these people. Jan knows she can't control whether she's liked, but she can control whether she invests in her people, and let the liking fall where it may. She's determined to make the investment, not for the sake of being liked, but because she knows it's right for the people, right for the company, and right for her. It's as if a weight she's been avoiding suddenly lightens.

Here's another example. I'm in a conversation with a prospective client who wants a leadership program for 100 high-potential directors—and I want to sell it to her. We're talking about possible designs and I keep bringing up our unique approach to whole leadership and mind-body oneness, which is the reason I think someone would come to me for a leadership program. She keeps dismissing what I'm saying. I reword, try again, and get the same dismissal. I'm feeling like I'm pushing upstream, and I'm growing more uncomfortable in the conversation. I can see how I'm playing into this: the more I push, the more she pushes back. I believe in the value of my work and I want her to see it too. What is my fear? That she won't see it; my work won't be valuable to her; *I* won't be valuable—and I'll lose the deal. Claiming my power, I stand in the middle of these fears and say to her, "Maybe I'm not fully understanding what you want, and I'm just telling you what we're good at. Tell me what you're really going after here, and if I can't deliver it, I know I can connect you with someone who can." Completely different conversation.

For the leader who thinks small and creates a tiny, safe life, claiming your power might be to stand in your fear of things getting out of control, or your fear of not being 100-percent dependable, and making a larger decision anyway.

For the leader who seeks outer greatness in answer to inner doubt, claiming your power might be to stand in the middle of your fear of being insignificant and still making the most valuable, seemingly insignificant contribution you can offer in the moment.

For the leader who gets impatient listening to others, claiming your power might be to own your desire to blow up or run away, and still choose to be present. "I'm afraid if you make this too long, I'll tune out," you might say, "So please make sure I hear your most important point."

Claiming your power is moving into the space your fear would otherwise occupy. It is bringing your fear so close it can no longer operate on you. It is regarding yourself with the deepest curiosity and compassion—your ego-token on the game board of life—seeing your fears, and bringing the ego and fear together, revealing *there's nothing there*, except greater space for freer action. This is leading fearlessly, which doesn't mean fears never happen, but that by merging with them, you become bigger than the ego that had been avoiding them. Through this merge, your Zen leader emerges to change the world from "in here."

Putting It to Work: Turning a Difficult Relationship

A great place to apply the flip from "out there" to "in here" is where something seems to be happening "out there" that we don't like. Difficult relationships are perhaps most interesting, because they involve another person onto whom we can project our fears, assign a role, and engage in staggering misunderstandings—all subconsciously! So start by thinking of a relationship that you find difficult, or that is important to you to make even stronger than it is, and jot down answers to the following questions.

1. Describe the current reality of the relationship. What's a typical exchange? Where do things go wrong? What pattern recurs that troubles you? How do you feel about this person? How does he or she feel about you?

2. **See into the mirror.** Looking over the current reality, answer the following:

    ❧ How am I playing into the way things go wrong?

    ❧ What pattern keeps cropping up in me? Where in my life have I seen this pattern before?

    ❧ How does this person make me feel about myself?

    ❧ If I had chosen to put this person in my life to learn an important lesson, what would I be learning?

3. **Find the root.** What are some of the fears this relationship triggers in you? Either things you may be afraid are true about yourself, or fears about the consequences or the future. Answer:

  ❧ What am I afraid will happen? What will that lead to? And
  that lead to?

  ❧ What do I fear may be true about me? What am I not *enough*?
  (For example, not strong enough, smart enough, likeable
  enough...)

4. **Claim your power.** Look over your list of fears, recognizing that
these are discoveries about yourself; it's impossible to say whether they have truth beyond that, but their power over you comes
from the fact that they're *your* fears. Remember that fears are the
way the ego keeps its game going. With that in mind, go through
each of your fears, stand in the middle of each one, completely
accepting that it's a fear operating in you, and write a statement
of intent for how you will act in the relationship regardless of the
fear. How might you change the game your ego has been playing?
For example, if this difficult relationship makes me fear that I'm
not likeable, a standing-on-my-fear statement of intent might
be, "I will help this person be successful, whether she ends up
liking me or not." Or if one of my fears is of being weak in conflict situations, my statement might be, "I will be real and present in the relationship and let tempers fall where they may."
Completely move into the fear, and declare what freedom you
find there. Remember, you are more than the ego who has these
fears. The awareness in you that could uncover these fears is not,
itself, afraid. Using that awareness, stand on the fear and declare
your larger intent.

Because you're reading a book at the moment and probably not engaged in that relationship, you may have to wait a bit to put these intents
into practice. But perhaps you can already feel the empowering possibility they represent. You can do these things and no one can stop you!
Such is the power of acting from "in here." And because you've freed up
a fear that had been operating "in here," you will see that the contours of

your world "out there" can now change. That's not to say everything you want to happen will automatically happen; things take time, causes have effects that have to play out, and every person around you will be in his or her own state of readiness to accept something new from you. But in time, you'll notice that things that have become non-issues for you also cease to be issues in your relationships with others.

We could run through this same process (including most of the questions, slightly reworded) to explore transforming a difficult situation. For example, say we're worried about money, or irritated by the many demands on our time. How are we playing into it? What are we afraid will happen? What do we fear about ourselves in this situation? And how can we move into that fear and claim our power anyway?

In applying this flip, we need not limit ourselves to difficulties. My opening story about my experience while meditating shows what insight we can gain from seeing how our outward goals relate to inward yearnings. What do you seek "out there?" What does it relate to "in here?" In the case of a goal, we might ask, "If I attain this goal, what will that do for me? What fears about myself do I hope to lay to rest?" Achievement-driven goals, for example, often find their root in proving we're good enough, smart enough, or powerful enough. There's nothing wrong with this, but only by finding the root of even worthwhile goals in our life can we use them productively, rather than them using us.

We can also apply this flip to consider great opportunities "out there" for what needs to change "in here" to take advantage of them. Seeing into the mirror, we might ask what strengths or values "in here" would be served by moving in this direction. What would it call out from us? How satisfying would it be? Finding the root, we could probe what fears might hold us back or sabotage our success. How are we likely to get in our own way? Claiming our power, we can move into those fears and decide whether to move forward on the opportunity. If we do move forward, we know what fears we have to master to move fearlessly.

The flip from "out there" to "in here" is widely applicable and endlessly empowering. In making this flip, it becomes increasingly clear that there is no real "out there" separate from "in here," but only one thing going on, in which we're a creative player. In making this flip, the Zen leader in us is able to use both what's free and what's determined in any moment. It's as if we're able to shift out of being merely a token on the game board of life to being the one playing the game, using broader awareness to illuminate and dissipate the fears that are part of the game as we know it, and then send in a better game plan to our token-selves on the board. In the flip from blaming "out there" to claiming our power "in here," we cultivate fearlessness. We also develop the extraordinary awareness that allows us not only to play to our currently understood strengths, but also to vastly strengthen our play, which we turn to next.

The Zen Leader
Flip 4 Takeaways
"Out There" to "In Here"

What we seek or avoid "out there" relates to yearnings and fears "in here," where we have the power to master them.

To cultivate fearlessness:

- ☯ **See into the mirror.** Ask, *How am I playing into this? What is this related to "in here"?*

- ☯ **Find the root.** Ask, *What am I afraid of? What may be true of me? What am I not "enough?"*

- ☯ **Claim your power.** Merge with the fear, accepting it, not as a judgment, but as a discovery about yourself. Find your freedom to act and declare your intent.

The Zen Leader

Core Practice: Sitting Meditation

Our ability to see into the mirror and find our root fears can be accelerated by practices that build awareness and relaxation in the body. Sitting meditation is a core practice for doing that. In meditation, sitting still with all our senses open, we can cultivate a condition of complete relaxation and complete awareness, inside and out, all at the same time. After about 20 minutes of "sitting" (that is, "sitting meditation,"), people commonly experience an abrupt drop in tension. The best way to learn meditation is with the guidance of a skilled teacher. But to get started on your own, or refresh what you already know, the following will guide you.

1. Loosen up your neck and shoulders, shaking out any superficial tension. Sit on a cushion or chair, with your spine as naturally straight as it would be if you were standing. Your hip joints should be slightly higher than your knees (see Figure 4.2a and b) Eyes take in 180-degree vision, with your gaze splashing off the floor a few feet in front of you.

2. Arc your arms into letter Cs, with your shoulders relaxed and the blades of your hands on your center (*hara*), palms up, one hand on top of the other, slightly below your navel. Here, your hands can feel the breath move to and from your *hara*. Fold in the thumb of your lower hand and close your upper hand around it.

3. Breathe quietly in and out through your nose. As you start to exhale imagine two things: first, a slight current of energy extending through the balls of your feet (or through your knees, if on a cushion) down into the earth. With this slight extension, you'll notice a "thereness" or set feeling in your *hara*, and a sense of extension through your spine and out the top of your head (Figure 4.2c). Second, in your

mind's voice, link your exhale with a deep vowel sound, starting with "ahh," and working through "ay," "ee," "oh," and "uu" on successive breaths. Let the imagined sound penetrate all the way through your exhale, making it as long and slow as you comfortably can. After you finish "uu" (or if you lose your place at any point), go back to "ahh."

4. At the end of your exhale, relax completely (quit extending energy) and allow the inhale to happen on its own, from the bottom up (Figure 4.2d). Continue in this way, alternating slight extension as you exhale and relaxation as you inhale. As thoughts or impulses arise, simply watch them without getting lost in them, and blend them with your breath and voiceless vowel sound. Sit for 20 minutes.

Figure 4.2

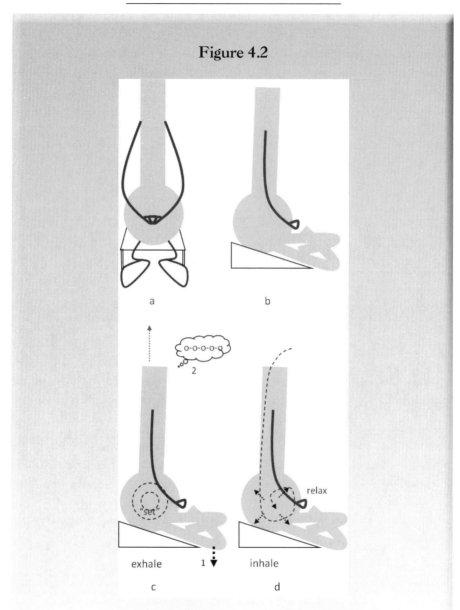

Posture for sitting meditation.

5

From Playing to Your Strengths to Strengthening Your Play

"THE PURPOSE OF Hojo training is to drop every habit from the day you were born." Say again? Welcome to my confusion when I first heard this line from Tanouye Roshi, a brilliant Zen master who headed up Chozen-ji, where I did much of my Zen training. Confusion notwithstanding, I knew everything he said mattered, so it lodged in my brain as a riddle to be solved later. Hojo is an obscure branch of Kendo, with four sword kata (forms), each named for a season and manifesting a specific kind of energy. Why was he so enamored with it? What did this have to do with habits, and why did habits have to be dropped anyway?

Train as I might in Hojo, it would be years later and 4,600 miles away, in a dance studio with choreographer Betsy Wetzig, when the light would go on. Betsy's lifelong work with movement had led her to learn about four movement patterns based in the nervous system and known since the 1930s, but hardly known in the everyday world. We all have access to all four patterns, from nature, nurture, and years of conditioning, and we also have a preferred pattern order. Betsy recognized these movement patterns related to personality—or "habits," to use Tanuoye's word—and she catalogued many of their psychophysical connections. I saw they were the essence of every "personality test" I'd ever taught or taken. They were a powerful framework for connecting "being" and "doing"—that is, how we are on the inside with how we show up in the world. They were the perfect tool for helping leaders grow authentically and embody learning, or "be the change." They were the underpinning of every business and organizational need I'd been addressing, from strategy to communication, to team climate, culture, and handling conflict, and, yes, they were the energy patterns of the Hojo. If you could be facile in any of them, you would flip from being a prisoner of personality to being able to *use* your personality fully. To paraphrase Tanouye Roshi, you would be as flexible as the day you were born!

Throughout the years, the field of leadership development has gone back and forth on whether leaders should find and fix their faults, or play to their strengths. Which is right? As usual, a greater truth is more paradoxical. Between these forces, a higher-level goal is possible: Play to your strengths, but don't become a victim of them; get to know *all* facets of the Zen leader in you, and field the right player for the situation.

In this chapter, you'll meet four aspects of yourself; four energy patterns that represent ways your nervous system can function. You'll find that some of them you know quite well, whereas one or two might feel less familiar:

1. The intensity of the **Driver**
2. The stability of the **Organizer**
3. The engaging fun of the **Collaborator**
4. The flow of the **Visionary**

You'll first have a chance to discover what strengths you normally play to, and then learn how to make the flip that vastly strengthens your play.

Putting the Whole *Person* Back Into *Personality*

Maybe it was Descartes and his famous dictum, "I think therefore I am," that propelled us down the path of regarding personality as only a "head thing." Or maybe it was the idea that thought is what sets us apart from animals that made it the focus of our inquiry into human personality. However we got here, it's clear that most models of personality focus on the neck up. Through the stages of development, which we grow through individually and societies grow through collectively, we've gone back and forth between emphasizing the body (basic survival, "might is right") and emphasizing the mind (becoming logical, rational: "I think therefore I am"). Now that you know the power of paradox, you can appreciate that we reach an even greater truth when we embrace the *And* of both. But that means integrating the whole person—body and mind—in our view of personality. Fortunately we live in a time when all the ingredients for doing that are in place.

We can stand on the shoulders of ancient wise ones, such as Hippocrates, who characterized four "humors" related to types of people and their physical health. We learn from archetypes embodied in myth and story ("the warrior," "the magician"), which endure through time because they speak to aspects of all of us. We have the wisdom of Carl Jung, who turned archetypes to temperaments, and Karen Horney, who noticed that some people push against the world, others withdraw, and a third group goes along.[1] We can build on the work of those who characterized personality types and gave us ways to measure them, such as Isabel Myers and Katherine Briggs, and the popular MBTI (Myers-Briggs Type Indicator).[2]

As computers became commonplace, researchers could discern which personality traits group together into fundamental factors—"primary colors"—of personality. The so-called five-factor personality models emerged, which might better be described as "four factors plus a basket of things that could go wrong." Instruments to measure these factors likewise emerged, such as the NEO PI (Neuroticism-Extroversion-Openness Personality Inventory),[3] the Hogan Suite,[4] and the HBDI (Herrmann Brain Dominance Instrument).[5] Even though we've mentioned the body once or twice here (it would be hard, after all, to push without a body), this is all pretty mainstream psychological stuff, focused on the mind.

Rewind the tape to the 1930s, and we can trace the body side of this story. We find Josephine Rathbone at Columbia University,[6] using some pretty rudimentary techniques—moving people's arms—yet noticing something very interesting. Her subjects are all relaxed and in the same position, but as she rotates their arms, she detects four different unconscious, residual tension patterns in their muscles. Knowing that movement happens through the coordination of opposing muscle groups—what we might think of as engine ("agonist") and brakes ("antagonist")—she discerns four distinct patterns of neuromuscular regulation. Paraphrased, one would be: "Apply engine and brakes at exactly the same time." Another would be: "Just go with your engine and get to the brake if you need it." You can imagine if these were real drivers on the road, their driving patterns would look very different, from the cautious to the cavalier. And so they do in movement as well.

Fast-forward 30 years, and Rathbone's research resurfaces in the laboratory of Valerie Hunt, where electrode recordings are now possible.[7] Hunt and her colleagues are able to measure four patterns of neuromuscular firing corresponding to Rathbone's patterns. Hunt speculates on the connection to personality, as did Rathbone before her, but her research goes off in different directions. A graduate student in Hunt's lab, Sally Fitt, is invited to speak on this movement research at a national dance conference in 1977. The audience is filled with choreographers and people who live in their bodies and move for a living. One of them is Betsy Wetzig, and her world will never be same.

Our world is better for it. For Betsy finds in these patterns the answers to questions she's puzzled about for years working with her dancers. For example why this one practices with such discipline, and is so good at the precision of ballet, but can't get the flow, while that one gets the flow effortlessly, but can't get to rehearsals on time. Betsy recognized these were patterns of body *and* mind, patterns of personality all the way through, and she started mapping the links between them.

Then, 20 years later, I'm meeting Betsy in a dance studio outside Atlanta. I've come from a dojo where I teach Aikido and Zen when I'm not on the road doing leadership programs, and I've brought some students with me. The light bulbs start going on as Betsy leads us into each of the "Coordination Patterns,"[8] as she calls them. I'm watching my students and seeing what Betsy must have seen in her dancers—how the patterns they move in most easily match their personalities. I know from my leadership work how important it is to know and build on one's strengths. And then I remember the Hojo, and Tanouye's description of its purpose: to make one agile in any energy. By the end of the day, I'm nearly bursting with the possibilities these patterns present. "These patterns can really help people!" I blurt out to Betsy, as if she doesn't already know that. "Where is the book on this?"

"Why don't we write it?" she answers, which led to *Move to Greatness*,[9] and began a new phase in my work when I started writing, living, breathing, teaching, and seeing patterns—patterns everywhere in leadership, teams, organizations, business models, market trends, cultural differences...you name it. In the world of management, where measurement matters, developing a tool for measuring these patterns became especially important. Working with Mark Kiefaber, my psychologist husband whom you met behind the wheel in the last chapter, we developed the FEBI[10] ("fee-bee," which stands for Focus Energy Balance Indicator). In researching and validating this instrument,[11] we put the FEBI through all the standard psychometric paces and found, indeed, that it measured four distinct factors of personality, and predictably correlated with the "mind" aspects of other psychological instruments.

What Do You Know About Your Strongest Game?

In the last chapter, you had a chance to build a list of your strengths. You can refer to that or develop it fresh.

1. List 5 things you know you're good at, which might be specific skills (such as math or music) and also traits that have supported you through your career (for example, being good with people).

2. Describe a time when you felt completely "in your game"—that is, completely engaged and able to bring out your best.

   ☙ What skills and attributes were you able to bring to that situation?

   ☙ How did you feel?

3. List one thing you've often wished you were better at.

So now all the pieces are in place for these two streams to come together—the psychological and the physiological, mind *and* body—in a way of understanding personality that integrates the whole person. As we'll see, this integrated view has many advantages over a mind-only view when it comes to moving from awareness to action, from talk to walk, and from playing only to our strengths to strengthening how we play our best game.

What Strengths Do You Play To?

Before we delve further into the energy patterns, it's useful to pause and recall what you already know about your strengths. You may have started building a list of your strengths in the last chapter; the sidebar exercise gives you a chance to take that further, and also consider something you've always wanted to be better at. We'll use these answers later when we look at the flip to strengthening your play.

Maybe you have strengths that you're not conscious of. One reason instruments like the FEBI are so useful is that they make connections you may not be aware of. If you'd like to take the FEBI, visit *www.focusleadership.com*; if you've already taken it, great! Pull out your report. Otherwise, you can get a sense of your strongest patterns by completing the mini-FEBI that follows.

This is all good fuel for the journey on which we're now embarking: a journey into your own nervous system where you'll find you can play any of these four energy patterns, just as a radio plays multiple stations.

Mini-FEBI

On a scale of 1 (never) to 10 (always), indicate how true each statement is for you. Use as much of the 10-point scale as applicable. A "5" means average; in other words, this statement is about as true for you as you think it is for people in general. (Scoring is given on page 114.)

When facing a big task, I break it down, and take it one step at a time.	1.
I am direct and to the point.	2.
My moods go up and down.	3.
I love to win.	4.
I'm conscientious about commitments.	5.
I enjoy the energy of networking.	6.
I have many stacks of papers, articles, and so on around my office and home.	7.
When faced with obstacles, I push harder.	8.

I have a hard time finding where I put things.	9.
I make work fun.	10.
I know how to work the system and get cooperation.	11.
When people are upset, I remain calm and rational.	12.
I do things in a hurry.	13.
I used to daydream in school.	14.
I think life is flux; nothing is fixed.	15.
I can get stuck and not know which way to move under pressure.	16.
I like to let go and see where events will lead.	17.
In conflict, I fire back.	18.
I'm an optimistic person.	19.
I'm steady and dependable.	20.
I often go back and forth on tough decisions.	21.
I come up with highly unusual ideas.	22.
It's important to me to do what's expected of me.	23.
If something isn't getting done fast enough, I'll just do it myself.	24.

© Focus Leadership. Used with permission.

Experience the Patterns

Heavy metal, country and western, New Age—just as different radio stations specialize in different kinds of music, so each of the energy patterns has its own specialties. Just as we have preferences for what music we listen to, so we have preferences among the four energy patterns. The pattern we most prefer (our favorite radio station) is called the Home pattern. Not only do we play it the most often, but even when we're playing the other patterns, it's still humming along in the background. The pattern we least prefer, or patterns that are particularly weak for us, are potential risk areas, as we might not use those patterns when they're called for, and instead stumble around misapplying our strengths.

Misapplied strengths are not strengths at all. When we bring the wrong energy to a situation, it's like playing Christmas carols on the 4th of July—something doesn't match and doesn't work. So it's good to know what each of these energy patterns is essential for, and the best way to build that understanding is from inside out. Let's go.

Push into the Driver. Sit forward in your chair and push your feet into the ground. Stare into this page as though your eyes were lasers trying to burn a hole in it. You'll notice a furrow comes into your brow, as your concentration intensifies. You can take this further—but you'll have to set down the book—by straightening your arms out in front of you, pressing your palms together, pointing your index fingers straight ahead like a gun, and interlocking the rest of your fingers. If you now feel like Dirty Harry ready to tell someone to "Make my day," you've got the right attitude. And you might notice how your attitude itself has shifted from just a moment ago when you were casually reading a book. Words like *aggressive*, *angry*, and *determined* come up when people describe how they feel in this pattern.

How does this pattern move? If you take a few steps in your Dirty Harry posture, you'll find your movements are clear, fast, straight, and direct. This could just as easily describe the thought process of this pattern: no nonsense, get to the point, let's move on. This is the Driver pattern, based in pushing or thrusting. Physiologically, our nervous system has put on the brakes and then gunned our engines into overpowering strength (sort of the way a drag race starts). Being all about pushing, this pattern pushes against goals, pushes other people, and pushes against the clock. It's a pattern in a hurry, making it the accelerator pedal of business. It can also be impatient, poor at listening, racing ahead or running over people. In various stages of life, it is the pattern of early defiance (as in the "terrible 2s"), teenage rebellion, the warrior, the fierce competitor, and, in its most mature phase, the great protector.

If you're racing to get to the next paragraph, this pattern probably feels familiar.

Step into the Organizer. Sit up straight in your chair and place your knees together, feet flat on the floor. Hold your head high, as if it could balance a book, and hold this book high as you read it, as if you were in a choir. Hold this posture for a bit and you can feel the upright character and properness that is the Organizer. Notice how different this is from the Driver: much quieter, more composed, and yet all we've done is changed postures.

The Organizer pattern is based in holding form and giving shape to a messy world. Physiologically, the nervous system is giving instructions to the engine and brake muscles to proceed together, step-by-step, and get this thing right, which makes for precise, disciplined movement. Picture a regal procession, or better yet, stand up and take a few measured, regal steps yourself, drawing up your back foot before stepping again. This may not be the fastest way you ever walked, and, in its need to be correct, this pattern sometimes struggles to keep up in an ever-quickening world. But because it's also disciplined about deadlines and correct about commitments, it will try and try to keep its word.

This is the pattern of conscientiousness. It is a pattern of planning the work, working the plan, making the list, checking things off, taking big thorny problems and breaking them down into—what do you think?—*steps*, that can be acted upon, managed, and measured. Organizer energy is the voice of operational excellence, safety, quality, and ethics in an organization. Business couldn't even function without the Organizer keeping things running on time. On the other hand, this energy can get stuck in its ways as the world changes, or worry so much about getting little things right that it gets big things wrong. In various stages of life, it is the pattern of early ritual ("the Teddy bear goes here, not there!"), the boy scout or girl scout, the good soldier, the dutiful wife or husband, the upright citizen, and, in its most mature forms, the matriarch, the patriarch, the responsible ruler.

Now that you've checked off this pattern, you're ready to go to the next.

Swing into the Collaborator, baby. Forget all that still stuff and loosen up a little. Start rocking in your seat, left and right, going a little farther each time, and letting your head and shoulders get into the motion (hint: relax your neck). You might start noticing a rubbery feeling in the body. You can feel this through your whole body if you stand up, and keep shifting your weight from foot to foot, relaxing into every shift. You might recognize this rhythm is the basis of agility in many sports, and the ability to move easily with others, as in Aikido or dance. The back-and-forth ease of Collaborator energy naturally engages others. And if you're like the thousands of leaders I've watched move in this pattern, the smile on your face is no accident either. This is a happy pattern.

The essential movement of the Collaborator pattern is back-and-forth, to-and-fro, or swinging. From handshake greetings to rocking a baby, this pattern conveys the warmth of human connection. Physically, the nervous system has let up on the brakes (relative to the Organizer pattern), going into oscillation and triggering engine then brake, engine then brake. In finding this rhythm, it's easy for this pattern to play in the give-and-take of relationships, to spin a marvelous story, to deliver a punchline with just the right timing, to see my way, and also your way, to find irony and humor in the most ridiculous situations, and hence to roll with the punches, find its way around obstacles, and talk on and on in run-on sentences.

In the workplace, Collaborator energy strengthens the bonds between people, making teams work better, influence work at all, and work a lot more fun. Like the Driver, it's an extroverted energy, but oriented to people (whereas Driver is focused on goals). Long under-appreciated in the world of business, it's now a pattern on the rise as companies try to get closer to customers and keep their employees engaged. It's no coincidence that some of the best salespeople have strengths in this pattern, enabling them to easily connect with others. Too much of this pattern, and one's life resembles a cornucopia overflowing with relationships, distractions, and commitments that cannot all be met. The Collaborator might have a hard time being taken seriously, or have a hard time *being* serious. And did I mention this pattern likes to talk? In various stages of development, Collaborator energy emerges as learning to play with others in the sandbox, the social butterfly or networker, the clown, the lover, the entertainer, the magician, and, ultimately, the charismatic savior.

With the Collaborator, we've moved over to the so-called right-brain patterns of thinking (Driver and Organizer being solidly in the left-brain category). You might notice that as we've progressed through these three patterns, we've let up on the brakes, which reduces the "front" side tension we dropped earlier in our flip from tension to extension. So what do you think happens when we take the brake off altogether and go where it goes? Who knows?

Drift into the Visionary. The experience of this pattern is all the more striking in contrast to the Driver. For a moment, re-assume the Dirty Harry position. Sight down your gun-barrel index fingers as if your life depended on it, hands pressed together, feet pressed into the floor, focus, focus, focus, and then—poof!—let that go. Let your hands drift to the sides of your head in (as in Figure 5.1), seeing both at the same time in your peripheral view. Already you may notice a felt difference in your head as the blood flow shifts to the brain's lateral lobes; imagine you could see through your ears. Sit back in your chair, relax, and let your eyes drift wherever, as your ears register every sound and you see the entire dome around you. Let your hands drift down, supported by air, to rest, palms up, wherever they light. Open your mouth slightly, and let air trickle in on its own and out when it's ready—so very slowly and silently...the air itself is not disturbed.

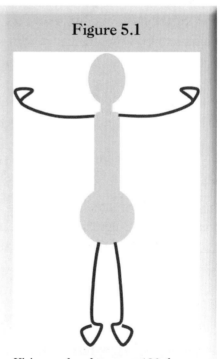

Figure 5.1

Open, boundless, and *free* are words people frequently use to describe this energy flowing through them. Visionary is the pattern-of-no-pattern; its essence is spontaneous, non-repeating movements that extend through the body...drifting, hanging in the eternal Now. This energy gives rise to leaps in imagination, connecting ideas, and truly seeing the big picture (which most leaders think they do, but face it: in Driver energy, you're looking through a periscope). It senses the larger forces at work, and naturally moves to harmonize with them in setting a vision and leading on purpose.

Visionary hands open to 180 degrees, as do eyes and all the senses.

In businesses and organizations, the Visionary is great at dreaming things up, finding the future, and leaping to the next game-changing paradigm. Like the Collaborator, this energy pattern is also on the rise, evident in broader, "greener" thinking, and increased emphasis on purpose and innovation. An insatiable learner, the Visionary doesn't attempt to keep up by moving faster, but instead by scanning, connecting ideas, and sensing the essential. But hang out in this pattern too much, and you may have a million ideas that go nowhere. Throughout development, the Visionary energy emerges as the inquisitive learner ("where do stars come from?"), the explorer, the philosopher, the sensitive artist, poet or naturalist, the counselor, and, in its Obi-wan maturity, the sage.

You've now experienced all four energy patterns, so you know that the "radio" that is your nervous system can play any of them. You probably also have a sense about your favorites; can you guess which pattern(s) underlie your strengths? Or which one could help you most in the area you've always wanted to be better at? Say your Home pattern is Driver and you need more strategic thinking and game-changing boundlessness. How do you get your nervous system to play Visionary? Could it be as easy as a flip from a Dirty Harry stance to open-palmed extension?

Yes. But not at first.

Flipping Patterns, Changing Style

Early research on these patterns showed that when one part of the body moves into a pattern, the rest of the mind and body follows. You may have experienced this moments ago when you consciously moved into each of the patterns and noticed simultaneous changes in emotions and thought processes. This connectedness through the layers of our whole self is exactly what makes the patterns so powerful in working with our life and leadership.

That said, we are more than a conscious mind. At an unconscious level, our Home pattern is still lurking around in the background, in the

If Your Nervous System *Were* a Radio...

Here's how the four energy patterns might show up on your radio dial:

Driver: Jam with WDRV as it blasts out heavy metal, the ROCK in rock and roll, or the thump-thump of hip-hop; music that makes you stomp or *thrust* on the beat.

Organizer: Tune into WORG, and enter the orderly world of Bach and Mozart. You might also hear folk ballads and songs of simple symmetry, for which you step or *place* on the beat.

Collaborator: Roll on down to WFUN for good times, good dance tunes (*swing* on the beat!), rhythmic jazz, or swing-your-partner country and western.

Visionary: Catch the drift on WFLO for some New Age bigness, or jazz that goes all over the place; if you can even detect a beat, just *flow* with it.

Similar to people, most music draws from multiple patterns in a particular order. The strongest pattern, what we might call the music's Home pattern, is carried in the beat (and if you can't pick out the beat, it's probably Visionary). The music's style comes from the combination of Home plus the second strongest pattern (for example, rock and roll reflects Driver-Collaborator).

The energy of music is more than an interesting metaphor for the patterns. Indeed, music is a particularly good way to sense or access the energy patterns, because sound frequencies create matching resonance in the human body.

Using Your Strengths as a Springboard

Here are some ways you might use the strengths of your Home pattern to approach practice.

Driver: Use your speed and competitive edge to practice in short bursts; set a target and keep score; make a bet with a friend, or make a friendly competition out of reaching your goals.

Organizer: Draw on your disciplined, orderly nature by setting a regular time for practice, practicing in bite-sized steps, keeping a log of your practice and progress, and checking off activities successfully done.

Collaborator: Engage your playfulness, sociability, and sense of rhythm to play with your practice—turn it into a game. Make it fun; involve friends. Alternate between a couple of activities to find the right rhythm.

Visionary: Use your imagination, curiosity, and risk-taking to practice as an explorer, pushing the envelope of your comfort zone to see what happens; try different things and explore what practice works best.

same way that our muscles carry residual tension, even when we try to relax them. As we move into different patterns, the parts we can consciously access change their functioning, and the parts we don't have access to stay in whatever pattern they were in—generally the Home pattern. The result is what we call "style," which is a blend of our Home pattern with another pattern. Music is a good example of how energy patterns blend together in a style (see the sidebar "If Your Nervous System *Were* a Radio").

Agility in the patterns comes when we're able to use not just our favorite couple of patterns (our primary style), but any pattern when it's called for (backup styles). For example, if our usual Driver-Organizer style isn't appropriate for the brainstorming session we've just entered, we could call on our Visionary pattern, and engage in a more Driver-Visionary style. Our ability to fully and deeply access weaker patterns improves with two things: *awareness*, which is how we make the unconscious conscious, and *practice*.

Awareness in our body gives us conscious access to more of its moving parts. That's why mindfulness in the body is the foundation of training in any martial art or sport, as well as dance, yoga, music, physical therapy, body therapy, meditation, relaxation techniques, and on and on. Awareness is the key to unlocking more of ourselves. The more awareness we develop in the body, the more we resemble the "soft and pliable" baby (think of a practiced yogi) and the more fully we can express any pattern. We further increase our agility by becoming aware of how each pattern functions in us, and flipping between patterns as the situation demands.

The second requirement, practice, is needed to lay down new paths in the nervous system as alternatives to the old, well-traveled path we have been using. If we don't practice, we can still consciously access a weak pattern, but as soon as our conscious mind moves onto the next shiny thing, our nervous system reverts to its same old style. For a period of time—generally three to six weeks—we have to practice through a phase of "conscious competence" in order to build a new unconscious competence in a weak pattern.

What we practice should match the energy pattern we'd like to cultivate. For example, we might do fast, clear, score-keeping activities to bring out the Driver, whereas, if we want easier access to Collaborator, we'd do things that are fun, social, or rhythmic. Table 5.1 gives a number of ways of using work behaviors, our senses, or physical movement to stimulate any of the patterns we'd like easier access to.[12]

How we practice should build on our strengths. Knowing that our Home pattern will still be playing in the background, we're more likely to stick with our foray into a different pattern if it has some vestige of the familiar. If your Home pattern is Organizer, for example, the whole idea of disciplined practice speaks to you: set up a schedule for it, put it on your list—it'll get done. But if Home is the Visionary pattern, you might want to make a more open-ended exploration of practice: when is the best time? Which of three or four different activities works best? The sidebar "Using Your Strengths as a Springboard" gives some ideas for how you can use your Home pattern to adapt your practice.

Table 5.1

Ways to Develop Any Pattern

	Driver	Organizer	Collaborator	Visionary
Work Behaviors	Know your top three priorities. Measure something you're doing—and cut it in half. Get to the point. Set stretch goals. Reduce distractions. Enforce clarity and action.	Make a list. Organize your day. Make sacred time for planning. Break big jobs down into steps. Always know your next step. Under-promise and over-deliver.	Put fun into your day; celebrate. Build your network. Build a bond on a team you're working with. See both sides. Find your way around obstacles; work indirectly. Work through people.	Add spontaneity to your day. Make time for reflection. Brainstorm, ideate. Widen your perspective (surf the net, solicit many points of view). Create some chaos; stir things up.
Physical Activities	Movement: thrust, push	Movement: shape, hold form	Movement: swing, rock	Movement: hang, extend
	Running Karate Weightlifting Cardio machine (hard and fast) Kendo, sword work Bicycling (hard and fast) Aggressive sports Skiing (hard and fast) Tennis Racquetball	Ballet Yoga Meditation Walking Dressage Ceramics Housecleaning Organizing a space Woodworking Needlepoint Anything done step by step	Ballroom dance Ice dancing Aikido Golf (the swing) Skating, rollerblading Swimming Bicycling (slow and easy) Skiing (slow and easy) Weaving Bowling (the set up, social aspect)	Tai Chi, Chi Kung Meditation (*Samadhi*) Sailing Hang-gliding Scuba diving Snorkeling Archery Photography (in the moment) Being out in nature

With awareness, we *see* the patterns functioning in us—rather than just unconsciously *being* in this or that pattern. With practice, we make it easier to play any pattern we need. If we think of these patterns as making up our own inner team, with practice, we build our bench strength. With a fully capable inner team, we can fully show up as we need to in any situation.

"Makes the Numbers, Rough on People"

That's the buzz on John, which is why he's asked me to be his coach. For the past several years, he's been targeted for promotion to the executive team of this $10 billion company. But the promotion isn't going to happen, the head of HR tells me, until John learns how to build bridges with his peers and develop the people who work for him.

John is great guy: sharp as a tack, energetic, and witty. People who have worked for him for a long time are deeply loyal to him. "But he pushes too much," they tell me in interviews. "He tries to do too much himself." Meanwhile, his peers are saying, "He doesn't listen." "He's always in a hurry, and you get a sense that he doesn't have time for you." And then there's the temper. "Bureaucracy drives me crazy," John admits. "We need 20 people in the room to make a damn decision!" You've only just

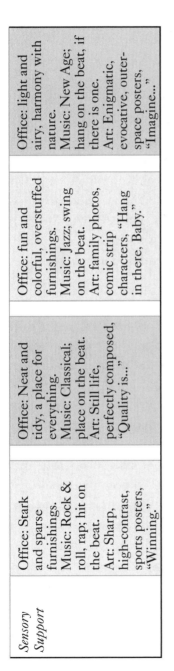

Sensory Support

Office: Stark and sparse furnishings. Music: Rock & roll, rap; hit on the beat. Art: Sharp, high-contrast, sports posters, "Winning."

Office: Neat and tidy; a place for everything. Music: Classical; place on the beat. Art: Still life, perfectly composed, "Quality is..."

Office: fun and colorful, overstuffed furnishings. Music: Jazz; swing on the beat. Art: family photos, comic strip characters, "Hang in there, Baby."

Office: light and airy, harmony with nature. Music: New Age; hang on the beat, if there is one. Art: Enigmatic, evocative, outer-space posters, "Imagine..."

met John and just learned about the patterns, but perhaps it's already clear to you that he's quite the Driver, and the key to his future success is more Collaborator.

As I get to know John, it's clear that more than a promotion is at stake. He has high blood pressure and a history of heart trouble—all that Driver pushing takes its toll. Even without the promotion, he's already too busy. The relentless pace makes him more impatient and ill-tempered. "I feel like a one-armed paper hanger," he tells me during one of our early coaching sessions. "I can't keep doing this. I've got to change."

John is ripe to flip from playing to his strengths to strengthening his play. As we review his FEBI report in which Collaborator shows up as the weakest energy, we explore ways he could build this bench player. John quickly rules out dance ("No way!"), but notices "golf," which he has enjoyed in the past, though he's made it a highly competitive, smash-the-ball game. He'd have to work with a golf pro for awhile to get out of his old Driver habits and into an easy, Collaborator swing, but he likes that idea. I also encourage him to really slow down when he plays, and use his Driver strength to protect his golf time as sacred.

The ideal practice combines physical activities—such as golf—with daily work behaviors that also reinforce the desired energy. John agrees to try a practice borrowed from improvisational comedy, which we call "Yes, and." His usual way with people had been closer to "No, but," as in "*No*, we considered that, *but* we don't have the resources." Little wonder peers never felt heard by John. In this new practice, which he good-naturedly tells several peers about, John promises to start every response with "Yes," and figure out how to build on it. Sometimes it will come out a little odd, as in, "Yes, and I have no idea how you came to that view. Will you explain it to me?" But this way of speaking always creates an opening. John's challenge is that he normally doesn't feel he has time to open up dialogue with his colleagues. What he's starting to see is that his whole relationship to time has been conditioned by the Driver pattern: hurry, hurry, hurry. It's a legitimate way of being, but it's not the future he wants for himself.

A few weeks later, John is on a layover in the Charlotte airport. He notices the rocking chairs in the terminal and people rocking in the chairs where you'd normally find only Mad Hatters running this way and that. It gives him an idea, and a few days later, a couple of rocking chairs arrive in his office. "They remind me to slow down," he tells me. They've also become the setting for real conversations between John and his colleagues. It seems people actually want to come into John's office now, and rather than treating those conversations as a waste of time, John is learning to build on each one as a tool of leadership. He's getting more done now through others than he ever used to get done through speed. And, unlike speeding up, this method scales up. Can you feel the relief?

The Zen Leader Flip 5: Playing to Your Strengths to Strengthening Your Play

This flip starts by popping up a level to *seeing* your personality, rather than just unconsciously *being* your personality. To borrow an image from football or soccer, in this flip we move from being just a solo player on the field to also being a player-coach who is seeing the whole field and fielding the right player. First, we have to know our normal player strengths and when we are likely to get into trouble. The energy patterns provide the perfect framework for seeing this. Plus they help us take the next step, which is shoring up our bench strength of other players who can take the field as the situation calls for it. This is not being other than we are, so much as reclaiming *more* of who we are. Ultimately, we can read the situation unfolding on

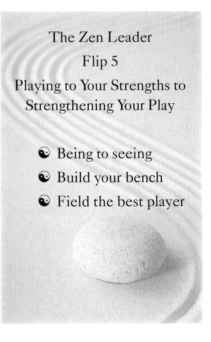

The Zen Leader

Flip 5

Playing to Your Strengths to Strengthening Your Play

- ☯ Being to seeing
- ☯ Build your bench
- ☯ Field the best player

the field and authentically show up as our best player by flipping into the appropriate energy. Try it.

Being to seeing. You may have started this flip earlier when you reflected on your strengths and the area you've often wanted to improve. Using the FEBI, as well as your own experience of the patterns, perhaps you can already identify your strong and weak patterns. If not, you might build this pattern awareness by asking people who know you well which patterns they see you functioning in most and least. Or reflect on the voice of each of these patterns in you; which ones "speak" all the time in your mind chatter, and which ones get little voice?

Building this awareness is the seeing. Awareness transcends our ordinary pattern mindset to see what is going on. The energy patterns give us a simple framework for understanding the energy we're expressing, and awareness lets us see where we are in that framework. Although there are no good or bad patterns, all pattern profiles have implications. Pattern strengths can become weaknesses if used at the wrong time. And all weak patterns can become strengths if we cultivate them, which leads to the next step.

Build your bench. Once you can see the patterns functioning in you, it's easier to identify the pattern you'd like easier access to. It might be the pattern that best supports that thing you've often wanted to be better at. Or it could be a pattern you simply want more of at this stage in your life. Building this bench player is not meant to detract from your strengths; rather, it's only by building your whole inner team that your strongest patterns can fully flourish. We focus on strengthening a weak player simply because this is how we create new capability in the nervous system. It's not enough to remind ourselves not to overdo or misapply our strongest patterns if we've given ourselves no alternative.

Pick a pattern you'd like more of and flip into it right now. You might re-read the relevant paragraph that introduced the patterns earlier and repeat the core movement of your desired pattern: push, hold, swing, or flow. As you think about it, you can make this flip instantly—at least part of you can. You may notice, for example, if you flip into Collaborator, only part of you gets into the back-and-forth rhythm; your neck is still stiff, your ribs aren't moving, and your mind is saying *This is just plain silly*. Building your bench is systematically letting go of whatever's stuck or resisting until Collaborator is just Collaborator, and you can completely go there. Flipping into the composure of the Organizer, jumpy you may notice it's hard to sit still; you're a person of action, and maybe you resent all that rule-following forced upon you as a child. Building your bench is entering this resistance, until Organizer is just Organizer and calm composure can pervade your nervous system.

If you'd like fuller access to a weak pattern, even when you're not thinking about it, you'll want to build a practice. You can build a practice from among your hobbies, work habits, or the practice suggestions in Table 5.1 (pages 122-123): pick one or two activities in the right pattern and make a practice of them. The more we build our bench, the more comfortable we become moving into any pattern at a moment's notice. Only when every pattern is ready to play do we have the option to field the best player for the situation.

Field the best player. If all we have is a hammer—as the saying goes—everything looks like a nail. Put it into pattern terms: If all we normally do is push, every situation looks as though it can be handled by pushing. But once we have a well-rounded inner team of pattern players, we are more ready and able to read life situations for the best way to approach them.

How do we know the best approach? In time, this intuition grows as we learn to read the energy of situations. But we don't have to get hung up on finding the perfect energy for every moment. All we have to notice is when our usual approach *isn't* working; when our usual player on the field doing its usual player thing is getting into trouble. Then we want to ask, *What's another way to play this?* If pushing isn't working, maybe try engaging, and field our Collaborator. If that's not working, maybe the timing is wrong and we have to hang loose for a bit; put in the Visionary. Fielding our various players, we'll eventually hit on the best player for the situation.

My sister tells a great story of how noticing when something isn't working and fielding a new player saved a meeting and a good deal of business. The president of an advertising agency, she and her head of business development, Tim, were calling on a marketing director who was one of their regular clients. As she tells it, "Both of us were Drivers and had worked together in the past at these pitches with reasonable success. But this time, it wasn't going so well. The marketing director was shutting down the more Tim pushed. He was starting to back-pedal on initiatives we thought were already concrete. He even started showing physical signs of irritation, which prompted me to take the lead on this meeting and switch into Collaborator mode. 'I hear what you're saying...let's talk about this more.'"

Fielding her best Collaborator energy, she shifted the energy of the meeting to positive, we're-all-on-the-same-page collaboration. The more she listened, the more the marketing director talked his way back into the initiatives they'd been discussing. On the way back to the office, even Tim remarked on the dramatic turn the meeting took, and, as she says, "It was an extraordinary lesson for both of us."

Another way to build our intuition about fielding the best player is to learn from the success of others, and notice how they blend the patterns. We might notice, for example, how a skilled CEO turns around lackluster performance by pushing a culture of accountability (Driver, Organizer), even as he creates community (Collaborator) and instills a sense of purpose (Visionary). Or we might study the phenomenally successful launch of Apple's iPad, and notice a mix of visioning the future (Visionary), ripening the market (Driver, Collaborator), building successful partnerships (Collaborator), and managing timely execution (Organizer, Driver).

The more sensitive we become to the energy patterns around us, the better we read situations, and field our best player. Each time we experience a bit of success, a bit of learning comes with it, and we progressively build a catalog of what works best when. Indeed, we're operating with such a catalogue right now; it's just that our unconscious catalogue developed by habit and happenstance, and may not draw upon our full inner team. But once we've built our bench, fielding the best player for the situation becomes as natural as choosing the right golf club, or dancing to the beat of a song.

Once we can field...

- ☯ the Driver to protect, focus, or push.

- ☯ the Organizer to plan, order and get stuff done.

- ☯ the Collaborator to engage, influence, and play well with others.

- ☯ the Visionary to let go, sense the essence, and make connections.

what could possibly stop us? Flipping it around, which of these could we possibly ignore and still play our best game? From being a solo player on the field of life with habitual pattern strengths, we can flip to being the one playing a much stronger game.

Putting It to Work: Build Your Bench

Which pattern could help you most right now? It may be the one you like least. Or perhaps it's one you enjoy, but don't feel you have time for. Our likes and dislikes, and our sense of time, all relate to the patterns themselves, so they are not reliable indicators of which pattern would help us most. But look at your life, or that area you identified earlier that you've often wanted to be better at, and pick one of your bench-player patterns that you'd like to strengthen.

To build a practice for this pattern, *what* you do should be something that lets you access this energy. Table 5.1 gives you a good start in recognizing what sorts of activities let you access each of the patterns. *How* you practice best builds upon your Home pattern strengths. The ideal practice combines a regular, physical/sensory activity (for example, John's golf, or the rocking chairs) with a work behavior (for example, his "Yes, and" practice) that you can do again and again.

"Do something that makes you uncomfortable," Tanouye Roshi used to say. Or, as Arnold Schwarzenegger (from his bodybuilding days) advised in his distinct Austrian-English: "You muhhst confuuuuse da body." The irony of practice is that if it's too comfortable, we're not learning, and if we're learning, it's not too comfortable. Yet, if practice is too uncomfortable, we won't stick with it long enough for it to take effect. If you can find that place in the paradox where you will consciously accept the discomfort of functioning in a weak pattern for three to six weeks, it will be weak no longer.

Expect the discomfort of practice to arrive in sneaky forms. For the Organizer, doing anything remotely unproductive will bring anxiety, whereas for the Visionary, anything routine may bring discomfort. Slowing down can feel excruciating to the Driver, and shutting up can be pure hell for a Collaborator. Far from being signs to give up in our practice, such inner resistance is a good sign that something new is happening with our inner team. A bench player who didn't used to see much action is being called upon; a strong player who used to dominate is relinquishing the reins. In this way, we build our bench, and our entire team is stronger for it.

Using your strengths as a springboard, you can adopt and adapt these three points for designing a practice as they work best for you:

1. **A work behavior.** Identify a specific work (or non-work) behavior you can do daily in the desired pattern. Consult Table 5.1 (pages 122-123) for ideas—including the ideas that pop into your mind as you read these ideas. Don't be timid about trying a few behaviors on for size before you find one that fits.

2. **A physical way.** Identify one to three specific sensory or physical ways to access your pattern that you could do several times a week, or add to your environment. It might be practicing a suitable martial art, sport, or yoga. You might change your office space to include more clarity, order, fun, or nature. Calling this a "Way" (as in "Tao" or "Do") is no accident, for the deeper the training, the greater possibility you open up in yourself. Ideally, work with a teacher or coach in your physical practice, so you can move beyond your usual habits in how you approach it. This underlying support to your desired pattern will not only help you stick to your behavioral practice, but will also help make it authentically successful, rather than a perfunctory surface act.

3. **A symbol.** Create or select a token or symbol that reminds you of your intent—something you can keep in front of you that continually refreshes your commitment. On my desk sits a small Play-Doh sculpture that reminds me to play, along with a tiny Post-It note that asks, "Who?" to remind me to always engage others, and not do too much by myself. These are a couple of the symbols that have supported my Collaborator practice throughout the years. Sit back, relax, and imagine a symbol that would support your practice.

Build your practice; build your bench. You'll find a natural balance, a sense of ease, with time, and things that you couldn't do well in the past become ever easier in the present. "Doing excellent things the easiest way" is how Betsy describes the functioning of the patterns. But don't take her word for it; run your own experiment.

Even more important than the specific activities we choose for practice is the awareness we bring to doing them. Awareness grows as we bring mind and body together in the present moment, feeling our entire body all at once. Making these inner shifts between the patterns, being the one who shifts what player we field, rather than being the clueless player on the field, allows us to play a much stronger game. It also loosens up our self concept. In playing with these parts of ourselves, we discover we are more than we thought we were. Yes, we are the ones endowed with some natural strengths, but we are also the ones who see those strengths and know how to use them. We are not only our thoughts, but the one who sees our thoughts. We are not only our emotions, but the one who sees those emotions. Strengthening our play, we can move effortlessly among these four aspects of our self. This is great freedom indeed, yet flipping between these patterns is but a limbering up for even greater flips to follow.

The Zen Leader

Flip 5 Takeaways

Playing to Your Strengths to Strengthening Your Play

Awareness and *practice* are key.

Being to seeing—See the patterns you're using, rather than blindly being in a pattern.

Build your bench—Design a practice.

☯ **Work behavior.** For the pattern you want to develop, identify a work (or non-work) behavior you could do every day to access that pattern.

☯ **A physical way.** Augment the above with a physical activity you could do in that same pattern several times a week and/or sensory cues in your environment.

☯ **Symbol.** Select or create a symbol of your intent to keep in front of you, refreshing your commitment.

Field your best player—Read the energy of the situation and enter with the right pattern. Notice when you're getting into trouble and flip into a different pattern.

6

From Controlling to Connecting

LYNN IS A perfectionist, which she thinks is a good thing, but everyone who works for her sees it differently. "She gets stuck in the details," says one of her people in a feedback report that I'm reviewing with Lynn. "It's almost like she's looking for the fault in everything you do," says another. "She over-controls everything."

"I don't want to be that person!" Lynn protests. "But every time I let up, I get burned. They say they want me out of the details, but when I back out, no one else steps in." Another example, I tell her, of how the world we create around us mirrors our own issues. From her own need to control she has created a world she needs to control. Perfect!

Now that you can work with the framework of the energy patterns, it's not hard to see that high control needs and the need to get it right—two components of perfectionism—emerge from the Driver and Organizer patterns. Nor would you be surprised to learn that those two patterns dominate in Lynn's FEBI results. In the body, these are the two patterns that create the most physical tension and make us feel most separate: apart from, not a part of. With that separation comes a largely subconscious fear that one has to protect or secure that separate, little being against whatever forces "out there" could threaten it. Let the "take charge" game begin!

Rather than misapply her Driver-Organizer strengths, Lynn sees that she could play a much stronger game by engaging her Collaborator and Visionary. In so doing, she'd be making a flip from controlling to connecting, as these patterns impart a sense of connectedness, be it in a relationship or group, (Collaborator), or the web of life or universe (Visionary). Lynn wants this connection, and starts using her fierce determination to haul herself to Aikido class several times a week, even though she's afraid it could be a waste of time. In time, she learns how to connect with and lead others' energy. She learns that over-controlling an Aikido technique destroys it. Perhaps what surprises her most is she's having fun. Lynn is still Lynn, and her controlling ways are still a deep part of her personality. But now she knows how to flip into connecting mode. And her own experience tells her that she feels stronger, happier, and more capable when she does it.

Similarly, this chapter invites you into the flip from controlling to connecting, first as a physical sensation, and then as empathy and joy, which arise from the connected state and the play of the Zen leader in you. Although control may feel like a surer bet when it comes to getting things done, what becomes clear is that our controlling self drives results from too small a place, while keeping us locked into too small a sense of self.

Control as Camouflage

Self-control. Quality control. Span of control. In so many ways, we regard control as desirable: that which makes us feel in charge, secure, or confident. To explore the flip from controlling to connecting is not to do away with control forever, any more than we could do without the Driver and Organizer aspects of our self. But for those of us who strive for control, and attempt to control our world, the flip to connecting is freedom, indeed. It opens up vast new territory for having a broader, more sustainable impact in the world.

Why? Because as we peel back what's really behind our need to control we find a frightened ego. It may not appear frightened at first—so full of itself, seemingly confident and striving—but control is its camouflage to keep its game going. If I control my income, I can pay my bills and not have anxiety about going broke. If I control my temper, I can get through this meeting without angering people and jeopardizing my career. If I control the quality of my work, I can receive praise for it, or people will reward me. Control implies an "I" controlling, and that "I" is fundamentally about preserving itself. Not that self-preservation is wrong; it's our most basic instinct. But the smaller our sense of self, the more vulnerable we feel, and the more our efforts to control come from too small a place.

Now, as we'll see, our sense of "I" is always changing. As young children, our sense of self is no bigger than our self-in-our-skin. The center of the universe, we make everything about us; we see our shadow, for example, and think the sun is following us. This stage of development, what psychologists call narcissism, is natural for children, but vestiges remain well into adulthood. The ego hates giving up its starring role.

As we get a bit older, somewhere in the range of 6 to 9 years old, our minds develop the capacity for thinking more abstractly, and we start to sense how other people see and feel about things. This is the beginning of empathy, and, like the second child in a family, it has to find its place alongside its older sibling, narcissism, in our now larger sense of self. "I feel like I have a little elf on each shoulder," as a friend once described this uneasy alliance, "One voice is saying, 'share the cookie,' and the other voice is saying, 'eat it yourself.'" Both voices we identify as "I," but one speaks from empathy, the other from narcissism.

This is but one example of how our sense of self naturally expands as we develop. In the flip from controlling to connecting, we invite this expansion on an ever-grander scale until it embraces the universe.

The Illusion of Control

Write your name. Really. Find a pen and a piece of paper, and write your name two different ways. On the first side, take control of the pen, grip it good and tight, and, making sure you don't slip in any stray marks or slightly misshapen letters, write your name. Now, turn the paper over. Rock gently in your chair, and, holding the pen so lightly that it barely stays in your hand, write your name like a cloud.

Did you notice how small and tight you felt in your highly controlled name writing? And how a sense of bigness and openness came in when you turned the paper over and wrote "like a cloud?" If you were a hand-writing expert analyzing the personality of the side-1 writer, what words would come to mind? As you look at the name on side 2, how would you describe that character? If you got into the spirit of this simple exercise, you found yourself flipping from Driver-Organizer to Collaborator-Visionary. Depending on your Home pattern, in making this flip, you were either leaving home or entering it, so you may find one of the sides closer to your natural handwriting. Regardless of which side you like better, it's pretty clear that the name on side 1 is more reproducible and easier to read, and would net you a higher mark on penmanship from your 2nd-grade teacher. You've already proven to yourself how quickly and instantly you can flip from the controlling patterns (Driver, Organizer) to the patterns of connection (Collaborator, Visionary). In the radio analogy, it's as simple as changing stations. What makes this flip difficult is relinquishing a way of being that has historically netted us lower risk, higher quality, and greater rewards.

So why bother with this flip at all? Maybe we don't care about expanding our sense of self; we're already having enough trouble navigating the speed, complexity, and sheer busy-ness of our day. But that pressure is exactly what's pointing to the shortcomings of control. Because it shows us that we can't keep playing the game the way we have been, and that we don't control all that we think we do. Even when we can control a situation, we can't control its consequences as they chain react into the future.

Consider for a moment the speed, complexity, and busy-ness of your day, as compared with, say, the days of your ancestors living around the year 1800. In 1800, it would take six weeks for a letter written in England to reach Massachusetts. Most people concerned themselves with growing, gathering, and preparing food. And in those simpler, slower days, people could prosper wherever the climate supported a fairly reliable link between planting and harvesting. Our forbearers might have felt a sense of control planting seed in the spring, with every reason to expect a harvest in the fall. Of course, not all plantings led to harvests, and nature has a way of reminding us how little we truly control. But the illusion of control lingers longer when less is going on. When things change slowly, our predictions are more reliable, and we get the sense that we can control outcomes (the harvest) by controlling what we do (planting). We might liken these early days to a slow, lazy river, with a smooth, predictable current; I can float a reed in the river at one point, and predict where it will be in a few moments. Perfect control.

But now look at today. In the time it's taken you to read this sentence, more than 6 million messages have flowed from England to Massachusetts. More than 6 million people have picked up fast food at McDonald's. If today were a river, it would be whitewater everywhere, tumbling and boiling among pebbles and rocks, constantly changing. I might be able to control how I place a reed in the water, but how can I say where it will be in even a few moments? Replace the reed with something you truly want to control—your children's behavior, making your numbers in the third quarter, having enough money for retirement, whatever—and you can appreciate how many tumbling forces stand between anything you do and any of these outcomes. Let's say you've done everything possible to make your third-quarter numbers: you've planned, you've segmented the market, you've shown your people how to focus on the best customers, you've done it all. And then a competitor's product gets a favorable buzz on Twitter. Then a virus infects the manufacturing plant of your Chinese supplier; they're forced to delay shipments, creating stock-outs in the Midwest, and half of your salespeople have nothing to sell.

Yikes! Are you going to give up? Not if you're the Driver-Organizer achievement machine that today's fast companies reward you to be. You're not going to take setback sitting down. Why, you're going to make *war* on those third-quarter numbers! Controlling-you takes charge, and forces your own buzz onto Twitter (*Follow me!*), puts a contingency plan in place with three new suppliers (two of which you'll drop in a month), relentlessly pushes on decision-makers in your company to redistribute stock from Canada, and works your people 12 to 14 hours a day. And, after all that, you can proudly announce at the next quarterly review that you've taken all these extraordinary steps to close the gap to your third-quarter numbers. Your ego is so vindicated. But if we were also to follow any of the chain reactions kicked off by your war, we'd find an endless stream of unintended consequences, from bad publicity to broken relationships to burnt-out people. If you can feel a tightening in yourself even as you read this way of working, that's no coincidence either. Forced control makes us tense and tight. Although it may seem as though we're winning the battle, in fact, we've created the war. We may think it's coming from "out there" and all those market conditions and competing warriors. But the moment we're in it, it's our war, fed by "in here"—whatever our ego is afraid of.

Does that mean when the going gets tough the tough give up? If we're not going to make our third-quarter numbers, or whatever it is we're trying to control, do we just say, "too bad?" Do nothing? Giving up is no more an option in business today than not planting in response to a bad harvest would have been for our ancestors. As always, a greater truth is found in paradox. We have to recognize that our usual way of controlling is not, and cannot be as complete in our world today as it was in simpler, slower times. We have to find a different way to function, something bigger than narcissistic control. And that comes through connecting.

The Connection of Empathy

Anything we're trying to make happen as a leader involves other people, and the fact is, most people don't have to follow us. They don't have to believe in our great ideas, buy our great products, or do what we want them to do. Even when we have authority—as parents of teenagers will tell you—our power doesn't go very far without others believing that what we want them to do is in their best interests. The pull of connecting to others and their interests is far more powerful than the push of control, especially when we find the intersection between their interests and our goals. How do we know what's truly in someone else's interests?

"Become the other person and go from there." It's the best piece of coaching advice I ever received, coming from Tanouye Roshi, and it applies equally to influence, negotiation, conflict, sales, teaching, and communication of all kinds. To become the other person is to listen so deeply that your own mind chatter stops; to listen with every pore in your body until you can sense how the other's mind works. To become the other person is to feel into her emotional state, see through her eyes, think like she thinks, and see how she views you, your proposition, and the situation at hand. To write it out or read it in serial fashion makes it sound like a lengthy, time-consuming process, but in fact, deep empathy conveys its insights in a flash, and our ability to empathize deepens with practice, as we learn to quiet our own inner state.

Once we become the other, we can sense what's in her interests, and influence becomes a matter of showing how our idea connects with those interests. That doesn't mean she will always agree with us or do what we want, but it does mean that our thoughts and actions are now coming from a larger place: one that accords both our interests and hers. Extending this empathetic approach, person by person, group by group, through your world, you can see where your actions start to be informed by an ever larger context. Consequently, your ideas, actions, and direction will start to resonate within that larger context. You can start making big things happen, not by controlling, but by connecting; not by making war on them, but by becoming the people whose interests are served by those big things.

In a pattern sense, we can make this flip by starting in a quiet, listening, Organizer place, and then relax completely. We invite a kind of permeability into the boundary of our self-in-our-skin and sense another's rhythm. We can listen for their breathing, their pulse, sense their entire being all at once, and we enter the Collaborator's empathetic engagement. If the talkative Collaborator is Home for you, your challenge might be to access the quiet listening of the Organizer as a starting place. If you normally live at the Driver's speed, you may find it hard to slow down enough to sense depth, rather than racing over the surface. If you normally live with the Visionary's expansiveness, you may need enough centeredness to connect without losing yourself. Whatever your challenge, you now know how to access the energy pattern that can support you in building a practice of connecting with empathy.

Become the other, and it opens up a world of understanding, in which communication becomes naturally influential, and influence becomes just another authentic dialogue. We'll return to this matter of influence when we look at applying the flip from controlling to connecting. But first, let's look at how big connecting can get.

Become One With Everything

The flip into connecting can embrace not only people, but all kinds of things and ideas as well. Become one with the keyboard you're typing on and your fingers naturally find the right keys. Become one with a vision to bring books and literacy to the world, as John Wood did in *Leaving Microsoft to Change the World*,[1] and you find a world of donors and supporters. Becoming "one with" is such a common expression of a Zen-like state, it's become trite, even a punchline (as in, What did the Zen master say to the hotdog vendor? "Make me one with everything."). Because it's so common, we may think that we know what it means and miss it altogether. Indeed, if we think we know what it means we *are* missing it altogether. For this oneness is not a state of knowing at all, but a condition of not-knowing, non-thought, and non-self-action that we attempt to describe as the boundless expression of the Zen leader.

This sense of connectedness with everything is a flip into the Visionary's bigness, which may start with the intention of "I" making the flip, but evolves into simply being the whole picture, where no "I" stands apart. In becoming one with Now, we might sense the causes and conditions that have poured into Now from the past. We might sense the context and consequences that will create the future. We might sense how two seemingly unconnected ideas connect. This insight will come, not with effort, not with order, but in a flash, before thought has time to think. Just as our left hand doesn't have to seek our right in order to clap with it—they are, after all, part of one system—as we merge with the moment we don't have to seek anything for wisdom to arise. What we sense and what sense we make of it will depend on our condition and how completely we make this flip. But it surely increases with practice. And the only time to start is Now.

The Zen Leader Flip 6: Controlling to Connecting

This flip calls on us to relinquish a sense of self-in-our-skin control, and trust that a larger sense of self and greater capability will emerge by connecting. It is difficult because it feels like a little death for the ego, and our ego will always put up resistance to changes in the game as it knows it. Yet you'll find, if you haven't already, that the ego is remarkably adaptive to a larger sense of self, like a snail shedding one shell to grow another. You can trust that eventually, the ego will take pride in this growth—even take credit for it. Sneaky ego.

The energy patterns provide a convenient framework for making this flip, because they help us flip into different modes in which we can play our nervous system. As we've seen, this flip takes us from the Driver and Organizer patterns that concern themselves with I-centered control (being in charge, self-control) to the Collaborator and Visionary patterns that connect with people and possibilities.

This is a more difficult and real flip for those of you who normally live in the Driver and Organizer patterns, and this chapter is particularly dedicated to you. But even if you claim the Collaborator or Visionary as Home, that doesn't mean you've been spared the need to control. We all pass through stages of development where we attempt to control our world. But if Collaborator and Visionary are your strongest patterns, you might find this is less of a flip and more of an application of existing strengths. For you, the challenge may be having enough grounding to be fully present when connecting, and you may want to focus on centering and meditation practices (such as the ones at the end of Chapters 2 and 4).

In making this flip, I've paired the patterns in a particular way—Organizer flipping to Collaborator, Driver flipping to Visionary—because these pairings represent physiological opposites, and more easily "undo" one another. But the flip into more Collaborator or Visionary energy can start in any pattern, including your Home.

Less Organizer, More Collaborator. We enter this flip from the Organizer's consummate self-control. For a moment, sit up straight, place your knees together, feet flat on the floor, and hold this book at eye level, as if you were singing in a choir. Feel the held stillness of this posture, and just listen to the sounds around you. You may notice that it's easier to listen when you're holding a sense of quietude on the inside. This ability to listen is an essential starting condition for making this flip.

The Zen Leader

Flip 6

Controlling to Connecting

- ☯ Less Organizer, More Collaborator
- ☯ Less Driver, More Visionary
- ☯ Less is More

Continuing to listen—pausing as you read words on this page—gradually lessen the Organizer as you relax your body, and let go of "holding" stillness in place. Particularly relax your shoulders, soften your ribcage, relax your heart, let out a sigh of relief. From the very bones you're sitting on, feel a gentle, rocking rhythm start to come into your body. Don't try to force it; simply invite it, and let Collaborator energy engage more of your body, until your torso is rocking, and your relaxed neck is letting the rocking come right up through the top of your head. This flip into the Collaborator's easy rhythm, without losing the Organizer's keen listening, is perfect physiological support for connecting with other people.

That doesn't mean we literally rock our way through every conversation with others, so much as apply this sense of "listening rhythm" to sense the rhythm of others. If we listen for it, we'll easily sense the rhythm of their speaking and gestures, which relates to their rhythm of thought. We'll sense if this is the right time for a difficult conversation, or if their emotional state is too volatile. We'll sense the patterns they're functioning in and whether this is a conversation that needs to get to the point quickly (Driver) or explore possibilities (Visionary). If we try too hard or think about it, we'll be falling back into controlling ways, and our efforts will be unsuccessful and exhausting. But if we play with it, make a game of it, and get insatiably curious about sensing the rhythm and minds of the people we're with, we'll find we can build this sense as surely as we can build an eye for good art or a taste for good food.

What we're building is empathy. You may not be able to practice with anyone in this moment, but you might pick a few people in your life with whom empathy is particularly important and practice with them as occasions arise. Playing with this practice, you might notice a quiet joy arises when you're party to this human connection. That's no coincidence, for joy accompanies the shedding of separateness, and any time we feel more connected, we move closer to the truth.

Less Driver, More Visionary. The second stage of this flip comes as we shed our need to control outcomes, and connect with a broader sense of possibility. To get a feel for this stage, start with something (or someone) you've been trying to control that's not going so well. It could be the work of a direct report (or family member) you've been trying unsuccessfully to turn around, or a thorny issue that you can't quite put to rest. Think of some person or situation you've been pushing on, trying to get him, her, or it to go your way. For a moment, set your jaw, bore your eyes into this page with the Driver's determination and get to the point: What do you want to make happen here? As rapidly as possible, jot down a few words that capture the outcome you're driving toward.

Now, sit back, relax, let out a sigh of relief, and let go, opening your hands, palms to the ceiling. Take in the two questions that follow, and then let your eyes drift up to the ceiling, as these questions drift through your open mind for a few moments.

☯ What are the larger forces at work that you could work with?

☯ What wants to happen here?

Regardless of what insight or answers come to mind, notice how the condition of your body and mind has changed: more relaxed and bigger, less tight and separate. As you regard some of the larger forces at work with your person or situation, which of these could you merge with? Not as separate from yourself, but as a natural extension, in the same way as great sailors become the wind to get where they're trying to go. As you regard what wants to happen, how would it change you—and how might you change to accord it?

Less is more. When becoming other people, merging with larger forces, our actions naturally become informed by a larger sense of self, in which "I" embraces a bigger picture. Less self-in-the-skin effort is more enduring in the world "outside" our skin. Less I-centered trying is more supported by natural law. Less is more.

We can experience this flip when we do less ourselves and reach out to others more. When leaders have delegated away many of their everyday tasks in order to attend the programs I teach, I always caution them about how much they take back when they return on Monday morning. Who can help? Who can learn from this? Where else in the organization could we get support? The more we can connect with people and ideas around us, the more we scale beyond the capacity of being merely a "one-man-band." Not only does connection help leadership scale to greater levels, but it's even essential for the uptake of our individual efforts.

"I have so many great ideas and tools, but nobody at this company wants to hear about them," laments a consulting firm manager in one of our coaching sessions. I ask him why he doesn't develop those ideas and tools *with* the people who could use them. Why not get them involved early on, let them test early versions? He admits that he prefers working alone because he gets to control the entire project "without interference." The flipside of "without interference," I tell him, is "without buy-in." Who needs to give input to this? Who can help? Asking ourselves questions like these can flip us out of control mode into connect mode where we remember that beauty is in the eye of the beholder and usefulness is in the experience of the user.

We can experience this flip when we *do* less, period. Slow down from 40 furious activities per day to a few big things done well. Slow down from speaking five words per second to three words per second. Slow down from breathing 10 times per minute to three times per minute. All of these are frequencies in our body, mind, and life, and when we do less, we drop into a lower frequency that can be more settled, impactful, and enduring. We could even go all out and stop for 20 minutes in meditation. Slowing down our life by this much is like slowing down the blades of a fan until we can see, not just a whir, but through the blades of the fan itself. Doing less, we sense more.

We can experience this flip when we *own* less. Owning is another form of control, and many people seek to control their lives by owning a great deal. This shows up in organizational life as managers wanting to "own" people (and not, heaven forbid, have to work through pure influence). This shows up in everyday life as wanting to own stuff (as in, "the person who dies with most toys wins"). But the truth is: That which we own also owns us. If we own three houses, three cars, or have three direct reports, every one of these defines something about how we then live our life. Owning less opens the opportunity to connect more. For example, instead of "own-ing" a small group of people in the organization, I might connect across the organization and lead projects through far broader influence.

I recall as a young child being asked—no, *told*—by my parents to clean the basement. It was a mess, and they had every right to insist that I clean it up. But I didn't feel like doing it. I was angry, resistant, and just hated all this stuff I had to clean up. So I put all my toys in a couple of large cardboard boxes and dragged them up the stairs, through the living room, past the watchful warnings of my parents ("You'll regret this"; "If you throw those out, we're not replacing them"), straight out to the curb to be collected as garbage. I came back to the basement and felt positively free! Space all over. And even though I couldn't articulate it then, somehow I felt more space to grow into—not like a kid with a bunch of toys I'd outgrown. Less past, more possibility.

We can experience this flip when we *know* less. "I know" is possibly the most self-limiting phrase in any language, for it stops our mind on an "I" that is certain of a conventional delusion. Seriously, that's all we can be sure of. Not because we're stupid, but because we're working with limited sensors, vaguely grasping a three-dimensional projection of an at-least-10-dimensional universe, through the biases of personality, culture, and so on, selecting what we notice and how we make meaning. In conventional matters, such as knowing the rules of the road or where we keep our toothbrush, conventional knowing works just fine, and we'd exhaust ourselves if we constantly questioned it. But in assumptions we make about the world, our customers, the future, the people closest to us, or the possibilities for innovation, we can get huge mileage out of knowing less and learning more. Suspend knowing. Hang out in not-knowing, and dissolve into boundless possibility: connected, as if in solution, before "I" has a chance to distill out and make a claim to "know."

To know less is to be more. To have less is to be more. To do less is to be more. When we cease to control from the self-we-think-we-are, we flip to connecting more to the self-we-truly-are. How can we sense when we've made this flip? Joy invariably arises.

Putting It to Work: Connecting for Influence

As big and boundless as this flip can be, it is also the most practical flip a leader could make. For it is the flip that gets people moving with us, not because they have to, but because our connectedness brings them along. Moreover, how we move with connectedness is naturally modified to accord a larger picture. Influence is a two-way street, a give and take, a mutual learning. If I think influence is about getting another person to accept or act upon my idea, and that I will come away unchanged, I've mistaken it for control. The less "I" in influence, the more likely influence will occur. Influence has nothing to do with the strength of my argument, my data, eloquence, how loud or long I talk, how right I am, or how many big and powerful people I have behind me. Influence is not about me-in-my-skin at all. It is about the person I want to influence perceiving that my idea is in his or her interests.[2] That's it. And as we've said, the surest way to do that is to become the other person and go from there, a practice you now have a chance to apply.

To get started, think of a person you want to influence on an important matter. It could be a person involved in the situation you started thinking about earlier that's not going so well. It could be a manager or coworker whose support you need on a project. It could be a family member whose life may go off the rails if she doesn't change her ways. Pick a particular person and write down his or her name (for simplicity, I'll use a universal "she" in what follows). These steps won't guarantee you'll get exactly the results you desire, but almost certainly you'll get at least one new angle on how to approach this person.[3]

1. **Deeply understand your own needs and interests.** What do you want from this person and why? Be clear about your own needs and interests in this situation. Try to dig beneath your surface position, to why you really want this, and what it will really do for you. In digging beneath your surface position, you may start to see some needs that are not so important, or alternative ways to get some needs met. Whether any insights come to you at this point or not, write down as much as you can unearth about what you want from the other person and why. When you're done, set this aside.

2. **Become the other person.** Sit back; relax. From the very bones you're sitting on, invite a subtle rocking rhythm. Imagine yourself becoming the person you would influence: see through her eyes, hear with her ears, think with her mind, and look back at yourself and the whole situation as that person regards it. How does she feel about you and your proposition? How do you make her feel about herself? What else does she care about? Feeling into what it's like to step into her shoes, write down as much as you can about how her world looks at this time, and how your

proposition fits into her world.

3. Finally, consider each energy pattern as you become the other person, and sense the extent to which she operates with:

- ☯ The Driver's sense of urgency, love of numbers, and need to win.

- ☯ The Organizer's sense of order, rationality, and the need to do the right thing.

- ☯ The Collaborator's concern for people, love of stories, and the need to play with ideas.

- ☯ The Visionary's big thinking, sense of possibility, and need for purpose.

Identify which one or two of these matches her best.

4. **Go from there.** Starting with what you now know about your person's interests, look back at what you want from her and ask, How is this truly in her interests? You may see several possible connections. Additionally, you may surface other ways to get your needs met, other ways this person could help you, or other things you might do for her in exchange for her help. Even the relationship with you may be something she truly values. The stronger your connection with her, the more likely she is to help you for the sake of the relationship alone. Conversely, the stronger your connection, the more likely anything you're trying to get her to do really *is* in her interests.

Once you can see how your idea—or something you can trade— is in the other person's interests, the only remaining piece for influence to work is to *show* it in a way that is compelling and overcomes her resistance. The energy patterns are again a source of insight into how to show effectively:

- ☯ For a Driver, don't waste her time; get to your point with numbers, and show how your idea is a win for her.

- ☯ For an Organizer, give her time to think, perhaps relevant information to read; show how your idea is the right thing to do.

☯ For a Collaborator, let her play with your idea and make it her own. Let her talk it through, and be ready for some give and take. Show how this will strengthen your relationship or be good for people.

☯ For a Visionary, expect to wander around a bit and let her connect your idea to grand ideas of her own. Go where it goes; help her imagine the future with your idea in it, or how it is an elegant or essential solution.

So what's the best way to show that your idea is in her interests? Write down a couple of ideas for how, having become the other person, you can go from there.

Sitting here reading a book, you can't be certain of the outcome. But almost certainly, you will have reached the goal of having at least one new angle on how to approach your person. It might also change your whole attitude of approach, and the confidence and caring you express.

This is exactly my experience with Jim Loehr. It's 2007, and I've just finished writing *Move to Greatness* with Betsy Wetzig. My publisher has asked me to contact the most famous people I know to ask them to write an endorsement, which I look forward to about as much as I do a root canal. But Jim is someone whose work I've long admired. He's authored and co-authored many books, including *The Power of Full Engagement*, which became wildly popular, and put forward the importance of managing energy. Yes, Jim's endorsement would mean a great deal to me. Although I sort of connect to Jim though my network, he and I have never actually met. As I pick up the phone, I'm thinking, *Here I am, calling a person who's never met me, and asking him to endorse a book he's never read. This is about as cold as a call gets!* I put the phone down.

And I do this exercise. I think through what I really want and why. Yes, the endorsement, but it also becomes clear to me that our work really does connect around the theme of energy, and there are ways our combined work could help people. And then I become Jim. Not having met him, I'm working only from his writing, but I can tell he's a Driver (his tagline, "Accomplish the mission!" was a hint). *Don't beat around the bush with Jim*, I decide; *put it out there and show how this can be a win for him.*

Which gets me thinking, *How* could *this be a win for Jim?* Well, because his last book was so popular, I imagine his business is really taking off, and perhaps things are bit discombobulated around the office; I could offer to do a teambuilding session with his people. I could also show how my work helps his work, and how the patterns help people manage their energy. After only few minutes in Jim-mode, I'm actually looking forward to this call.

A different me picks up the phone—not so weak or empty-handed. And the Jim who answers the phone is sharp, vibrant, and wonderful. He appreciates the potential connection of our work and my offer to do a session with his team. "Perhaps sometime in the future," he says. "Of course, send the manuscript. I'll read it over." On reading it over, of course he sees where it adds to his work and he writes a wonderful endorsement. I haven't done the session for his team yet (the offer still stands, Jim), but in so many ways, I find myself promoting his work, recommending his book to clients, and singing his praises (I think I just did it again). So his endorsement truly did turn out to be in his interests as well.

This is what I continually find with connecting and influence: things never turn out exactly as I expect, but they always turn out. The outcomes of connection—grounded in context, reality, and the real needs of others—are bound to be more connected and enduring than the solo efforts of a separate "I."

That said, let's also remember that the flip to connecting doesn't mean we can, for ever after, do without the Driver and Organizer's sense of control. Driver and Organizer still have their place, and no leader, team, or business could function well without them. The beauty of truly understanding connecting mode is that we can—at last!—give control its rightful place, and not misapply it. Want to find an innovative solution to an intractable problem? Don't start in Driver mode; you'll race right past a solution without recognizing it. Flip into Visionary mode, become the whole picture, the whole problem, and sense what's possible. Once you sense a solution, now is the time to apply your Driver's sense of urgency to make it happen. Maybe then you want to flip back into the Collaborator's connecting mode, engage others in this solution, and let them make it their own. Now bring in enough of the Organizer's process and planning to keep everyone's efforts aligned. And so on, endlessly, like inhale and exhale, now after now, naturally operating with a sustainable rhythm.

The more completely we make the flip from controlling to connecting, the deeper we "breathe" in this rhythm. Moreover, flipping from control to connect extends the sense of self toward its true boundlessness. When we first approach this flip, connecting is but another act of the ego. "I" flip from less Organizer to more Collaborator. "I" flip from less Driver to more Visionary. That's completely natural, but eventually, we lose the sense of "I connect" to simply *connect*. This is where "I understand you" shifts to true empathy; where "I am dealing with this change" becomes simply according the myriad changes. This is where "I" disappears—not permanently; it will be back—but for this moment, dissolving us into a state of complete connectedness called *Samadhi*.

Despite the foreign-sounding word, this is not a foreign concept—only an old one—available to you here and now and every time you flip into complete connectedness. If you'd like to invite or deepen your access to this Samadhi condition, the breathing series at the end of this chapter is an especially useful practice.[4] The everyday practice of becoming one with people we would influence or problems we would solve also invites and deepens this Samadhi connectedness. Good thing, too, for we need this connectedness for every flip that follows. Starting with attracting the future.

The Zen Leader
Flip 6 Takeaways
Controlling to Connecting

Connecting happens through more Collaborator (less Organizer), more Visionary (less Driver).

Less is more. If you *do*, *know*, or *have* a great deal: *do* less, *know* less, and *have* less, to connect more.

Influence works through connection:

☯ **Deeply understand** your own needs and interests: Go beneath the surface to unearth what you *really* want and why.

☯ **Become the other.** See through her eyes, think with her mind; sense its patterns. Consider what is truly in her interests.

☯ **Go from there.** Show how your idea is in her interests, either directly or through an exchange you offer.

The Zen Leader
Core Practice: Invitation to Samadhi

Samadhi is a state of complete connectedness, in which thought is suspended, as no "I" stands apart to think. This connectedness is not an exotic condition, but a natural state that arises when we're absorbed into our setting. For example, in a thrilling baseball game when the pitch is thrown, the bat is swung, a moment of collective Samadhi arises in the absorbed tracking of the ball. Or at the end of a momentous symphony, in a brilliant performance that has captured the audience, the quiet of Samadhi rides on the end of the closing note before thunderous applause erupts.

As these examples illustrate, Samadhi arises on its own. It cannot be willfully entered, because that which would "will" it is none other than the stand-apart "I." That said, the body and breath can be developed in ways that become conducive to this condition arising. And the exercises themselves are relaxing and rejuvenating. Without trying to make anything happen, invite your body and breath into the exercises that follow. Let the quiet of Samadhi come to you.

First, Establish the Center

1. Stand with feet hip-width apart, arms at sides (Figure 6.1a). Beginning a long, slow **inhale through your nose**, let your arms drift straight up in front of you (Figure 6.1b). When they're parallel to the floor, moving ever so slowly, open the arms 180 degrees, letting your vision expand at the same time (Figure 6.1c). Continue to inhale, and lift your arms overhead, palms to the sky. Stretch slightly towards the sky at the end of your inhale, slightly lifting your heels, shifting your weight toward the balls of the feet (Figure 6.1d).

2. Set (meaning set down your heels), maintaining a slight pressure from the balls of your feet into the earth, and feel a connection to the base of your *hara*. **Exhaling slowly through your mouth,** make the sound of **"aaay"** (long ā) as if from the *hara* itself. Through the base of both palms, extend outward, turning the wrists back 90 degrees, and slowly arc your arms back to center (Figure 6.1e). At the end of your exhale, relax completely and begin again. Repeat for five to 10 breath cycles.

Figure 6.1

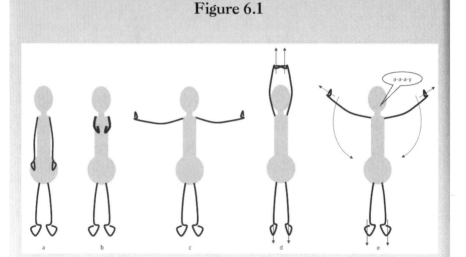

Second, Release What's Holding

1. Stand with feet in a wide, but comfortable horse stance. **Inhaling through your nose,** and hunkering down slightly, gather your forearms together in the middle of your chest, as if to metaphorically gather any worry, concern, or thought of any kind (Figure 6.2a).

2. **Exhaling through your mouth,** make the sound of
    "ahhh" as you straighten your legs, open your arms, and
    release any and all holding. Let the sound of "ahhh"
    resonate through your entire being, with nothing held back
    or bound. As your arms open, let your eyes also drift to
    180 degrees, and "see" with your ears. At the end of your
    exhale, pause for a moment to hang in this open-ended
    Now. (Figure 6.2b). Draw in your arms and inhale for the
    next cycle; repeat for five to 10 breath cycles.

Figure 6.2

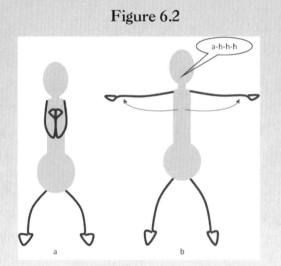

Third, Hear/Feel Your Entire Body All at Once

1. Stand with feet in a wide, but comfortable horse stance,
    shoulders relaxed, eyes taking in 180 degrees of your
    surroundings. Lightly press your palms together at your *hara*,
    fingers pointing downward (Figure 6.3a). **Breathe in and
    out quietly through your nose.** As you begin **each exhale,
    slightly extend the balls of your feet** into the earth, and
    maintain this extension through a long, slow exhale. Relax on
    the inhale, and let it happen on its own. Repeat several breath
    cycles.

2. Continue breathing the same way as above. Leaving your left hand where it is, rotate your right elbow so that your right hand points upward, thumb side touching your chest. As you feel the contact of your hand, **release any tension in your chest**, so that the touch can be "felt" all the way to your spine (Figure 6.3b). Repeat several breath cycles in this posture.

3. Continue breathing the same way as above. Leaving your left hand where it is, extend your right hand just over your head, pointing upward, near the back of your skull, where your spine would extend if you had a few more vertebrae (Figure 6.3c). As you exhale, feel both the **groundedness of *hara*** under your left hand and the **extension of your spinal energy** through your right hand. Repeat several breath cycles in this posture, opening your senses and feeling/hearing everything within you and around you.

4. Continue breathing the same way as above. Leaving your left hand on the *hara*, rotate it so that the palm faces up. Draw your right hand back down to chest level, fingers pointing upward, as in the second posture (Figure 6.3d). Again, as you make contact with the chest, empty any tension that has accumulated, feeling the contact all the way to your spine. Repeat several breath cycles in this posture, **feeling/hearing your entire body all at once**.

5. Continue breathing the same way as above. Leaving your left hand on the *hara*, palm up, rotate your right elbow so that your right hand, also palm up, comes to rest on your left. Fold in the thumb of your left hand and gently cup it in the right; this is the same hand position as for sitting meditation (Figure 6.3e). Repeat several breath cycles in this posture, feeling/hearing your entire body, your entire world, all at once.

Figure 6.3

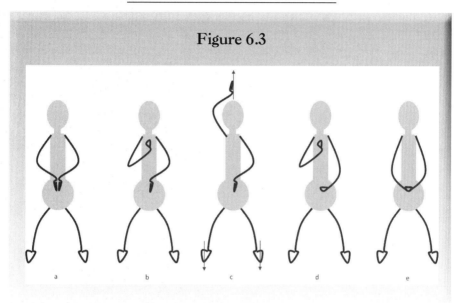

7

From Driving Results
to Attracting the Future

"DRIVES FOR RESULTS." "Results-oriented." "Makes war on his numbers." I'm reading the comments on a 360-degree feedback report for a leader I'm working with this week, and these are his strengths. I reflect on the assumption that making war on numbers is unquestionably a good thing. Business rides on this assumption, yet it's not without consequence. I can almost predict what I'll read next describing this leader's weaknesses: "Doesn't listen." "Doesn't have time for us." Nearly half of the reports I review for this week strike a similar theme. I know there will be a good many Drivers in the program: people who have been rewarded their entire careers for driving results—otherwise they wouldn't be here. But just as the shell of a snail is perfect for one stage and too small for the next, these leaders will learn that the energy of the Driver, although indispensable for driving results, lacks the larger view of what kind of future is worth driving toward.

Contrast the drive for results with the so-called Law of Attraction, which didn't pass my physics-trained litmus test of being a real "law" when I first heard of it (more like New Age mumbo jumbo): Who could believe that by simply visioning a future, a leader could *attract* the people and conditions that would bring about that future? Imagine a CEO declaring at a meeting with analysts, "These are the numbers we're visioning for next quarter and we'll attract the future to them." In our everyday way of looking at things, this is nonsense.

But it is our everyday way of looking at things that is the problem. Rooted in dualism, even our concept of a "Law of Attraction" is of *this* attracting *that*, where *this* and *that* are separate. Do the left and right hand attract one another in order to clap? We could think of it that way, or we could just say they're part of one system, operating from the same program. As we saw in the last chapter, in flipping from control to connect, we open up the possibility of sensing a much bigger picture, whether it's the subtle signals of the colleagues we would influence, or the unmet needs of customers we would serve—not apart from any of these, but a part of the same vibrant ocean of energy. If, in a state of complete connectedness, the thought arises to form a business, one could say I'm attracting that future as I start the business, or one could say the future is using me to bring the business about. "I" and "the future" are not two separate things.

Building on connectedness, in this chapter we explore the further flip by which the future becomes the present, not by driving the present toward the future, but by attracting the future into Now. This is a flip from I-pushing to manifesting a connected pull, from driving *my* agenda to sensing the larger picture and letting it activate my doing. We can apply this flip to our own vision and purpose—revisiting the one we developed in Chapter 2—and ask: *What future do I attract? How do I know this is right?* Although attracting the future cannot be faked, the potential for self-delusion and the ego re-asserting itself is ever-present. You'll learn a reliable litmus test for telling the difference between necessary endurance toward a worthy goal and worthless driving toward an unrealistic vision.

The connection between leaders and the future is not a small or incidental matter. Some would say finding the future is the very essence of leadership. As Richard Strozzi Heckler puts it in his book, *The Leadership Dojo,* "A leader declares the future." Put another way, if a leader doesn't match a slice of the future, is he or she leading at all? In the flip from driving results to attracting the future, the Zen leader in us brings that future into Now.

Driving Results Drives Business...Sort Of

It's a classic business analysis: What's our target? What's our current reality? What do we have to do to close the gap? Whether we're closing a gap in our budget, in our number of customers, or in the skills of our people, this way of thinking—a so-called gap analysis—is so common it would be hard to imagine work life without it. We might depict it as in Figure 7.1a, where our target exists as a desired future state, and current reality is where we are today.

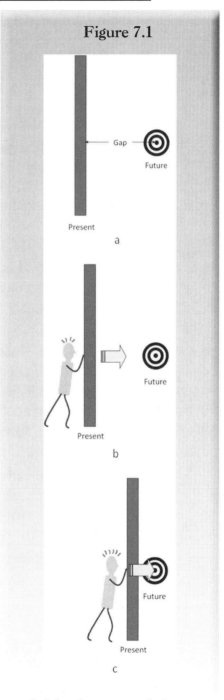

Figure 7.1

Driving the present to the future.

Figure 7.2

Attracting the future through personal transformation.

To close the gap, we push that reality toward our target (Figure 7.1b), and, if we're successful, we'd say we "hit our target" (as in Figure 7.1c). The reason I tease apart this common example in such detail is that every aspect of this way of looking at things—no matter how common it is and how much it drives business thinking—is backwards, starting from an "I" that's doing the analysis and ends up doing the pushing. It is, at best, a one-sided story.

We could flip the entire analysis around, take the controlling "I" out of it, enter a state of complete connectedness, and sense the future, the present, and our entire existence all at once (as in Figure 7.2a).

Insight arises, translates into thought, and differentiates into a vision of the future on the one hand, and clarity about the present on the other (Figure 7.2b). In the same flash of insight arises the internal understanding of the personal

transformation required—the knowledge, attitudes, and actions—to work with the present and manifest the future state. Through this personal transformation, the self becomes "larger" and the future becomes Now (Figure 7.2c).

In the conventional way of looking at a gap analysis, a relatively fixed player—"I"—pushes reality toward a desired target. In the connected way of looking at it, the transformation of self, which is the working of the Zen leader in us, is exactly what brings the future into the present. When self changes, a new world is possible. In truth, self is always changing, which should give us a hint as to which of these views is closer to reality. But it is the nature of our development as human beings that we always start out conceiving of a relatively fixed "I" at the center of things—it's our narcissistic heritage. So it's not surprising that a good deal of conventional business thinking would function at this level. And if it works well enough, why mess with it? Why bend our minds with this flip, when we can go on doing conventional gap analyses and driving results? Because driving results—pushing the present to the future—is but another form of control, which, as we've seen, doesn't hold up as well as well as it used to. Too many forces converge ever more quickly between the present moment and any future I might target. In the roiling whitewater of today, assumptions about the future get dashed on the rocks faster than you can say "There's no reason for any individual to have a computer in his home" (which, in fact, Ken Olsen, the CEO of Digital Equipment Corporation, did say in 1977).

Moreover, driving results is inadequate for finding the future because, think about it: Driving comes from behind. If a cowboy is driving a herd, he's behind the herd, pushing it forward. If we're driving a car, we're behind the wheel, pushing on the gas pedal. In driving mode, all we focus on is the goal in front of us and getting there.

Of course, in the world of work, *there* keeps changing. Hitting a business goal is not a one-time event. Rather, one goal morphs into the next: My third-quarter target becomes a fourth-quarter target, gets reset by currency fluctuations or the lagging performance of a sister division, and morphs into a stretch target for next year; no sooner have we reached *this* target than *that* target is what we need to be driving toward.

In other words, we never arrive once and for all. We rarely catch up, much less leap ahead to see what future might lie beyond our present-minded assumptions. How often have you heard a busy colleague lament that he or she is so behind and racing to catch up—or felt this way yourself? This endless footrace against time becomes habitual and exhausting, and may even lead us to question whether it's worth it. Just as the targets we pursue in this way are generally set by others, we also come to expect our rewards for hitting them to come from "out there." Those rewards often do come for a while: from good grades in school to a good job, a raise, a bonus, and a promotion or two. But we will always encounter places where our efforts outpace the rewards. Then it's easy for dissatisfaction to set in, as in, "After all I've done for this company, all I got was...," fill in the blank: a lousy bonus, a crappy rating, more work, whatever. This can lead to a downward spiral, all traceable to our own backward thinking. We mistook ourselves as (relatively) fixed and time as moving—all too fast—and thought the trick was to catch up with our goals. Flip that around, and you come to a much deeper truth: Time is Now—period—and we're changing; our goals are realized as we manage that change in our self.

In addition to the exhaustion and disillusionment that can come from driving the present toward the future, even more problematic is the fact that this is no way to *find* the future. If we've accepted a target that represents a desired future state, such as to graduate from school, increase our market share by 3 percent, or develop a razor with six blades, then Driver energy might work just fine. It will help us push past our fatigue or discouragement, push our people, or push technological limits. But it will never tell us whether this future is worth driving toward: whether our schooling is in line with our passion, whether this market is worth growing in, or whether the world really needs a razor with six blades. For finding a future worth creating, we need a different kind of thinking, one that does not come from behind; one that is not based on an "I" pushing.

Being Now

This different kind of thinking arises from a connected state. At its best, it's not something "I" think at all, but rather a Samadhi-arising insight that we translate into thought, much as a visual artist might translate a vision into a marvelous painting. Thought happens so quickly (compared to, say, painting) that we commonly equate insight with thought, but insight-derived thought is day-and-night different from ordinary I-based thinking. To flip from driving results to attracting the future, we have to flip into this connected state, which also flips our relationship to time. What does our relationship with time have to do with attracting the future? If you immerse yourself in this next experiment, you'll see: everything!

Oftentimes, leadership programs start with an exercise of building a timeline of one's life and career, noting significant milestones, events, and people along the way. I invite you to build such a timeline now, but in a particular way:

1. Take a blank piece of paper and put a dot dead-center that represents Now (Figure 7.3a).

2. Draw a horizontal line through that dot, representing the past to the left and the future to the right (Figure 7.3b).

3. Now, using just a few inches of the line to the left of your dot, locate a second dot where you were born. Between that dot and the present, create a compressed timeline of your life and career, noting a few of the most pivotal people, events, or milestones that have made you who you are today (Figure 7.3c).

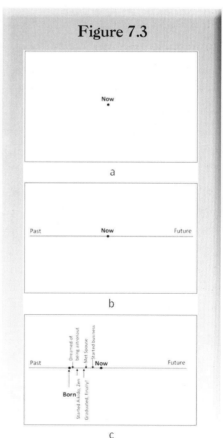

Figure 7.3

4. Using a few inches to the right of Now, locate a third dot representing your death. Between now and then, fill in several future milestones you'd like to attract. These could be goals, achievements, or items on your "bucket list" (things you want to do before you die, or "kick the bucket"; Figure 7.3d).

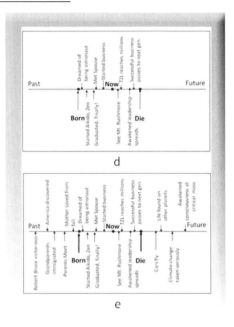

5. Now, stepping back from your individual life, put your life into a broader context. Using the whole rest of the timeline and paper however you like, fill in some events from your family's past and from history that shaped the conditions of your birth. Fill in some events that may follow in your family, in your business, or in the world after you die—even long after. Speculate freely! (Figure 7.3e).

Let's pause for a moment. This is how we're used to thinking about time: something that flows along a line from the past to the future, like a road we're driving along, with the past behind us and the future ahead.

But now I invite you into a different perspective: Break into your timeline. Imagine yourself standing at the dot of Now, merged right into your timeline page, looking at the past and future "end on." Looking down the past, all the historic and family events, all the pivotal people and meaningful milestones are superimposed, one on the other, all spiraling into Now. Sighting along the future, all possibilities you wish for—those that could arise next month and those that might happen a century from now—are all visible, connected to where you stand, spiraling out of Now. Stand here for a moment, being Now. What you see is that everything from the past feeds into where you stand, and everything that is to happen flows out of it; endless chains of cause and effect interconnect through Now. Through you. Perhaps you've left out some important historical causes, or are off in your speculation on future effects, but the details are not important. What's important is the flip in perspective. Being Now, you see all possible things and all things possible arise in you.

Instantly, your head may start to throb with the mind-boggling possibilities that being Now presents. *Hey, wait a minute!* your rational mind may protest, and start in with such questions as, *If I'm Now, who are you? And who is Jane over there? How can we all be Now?* Mind-bending as it is (sort of like physics near the speed of light), we might think of Now as an inexhaustible flame that could light countless number of candles. You're lit by Now and, no less than you, I'm lit by Now too. Or we could think of Now as an infinite, inexhaustible Internet in which you can do your searches and feel as though you're at the center of, just as I can: Your use of the Internet Now doesn't preclude mine. Indeed, the fact that we're both here is perfect proof that we can coexist in Now, both being Now. It's so in-your-face obvious, we miss it (I missed it for years!). But the more we stand at the dot of Now, the more the kaleidoscope of past and future possibilities becomes as our own arms and legs.

So on the one hand we have a view of ourselves in the ordinary, everyday world, what we might call a spatial world: a nominal three-dimensional world (which has many more dimensions that we don't sense). We see ourselves as an "I" moving through space; time flows by, "I" gets older, but it's still "I," and we can depict this process by drawing a timeline, as we did a moment ago.

On the other hand, we can experience our existence as being time, or simply being Now. If you can imagine yourself being Now, you will notice that all things arise in you, all things intertwine through you, and nothing exists without you. Applying a bit of memory to your Nowness, you will also notice that everything changes from one Now to the next in accordance with its nature (in other words, people change more quickly than do rocks), including the body with which you're conducting this thought experiment right now (hey, there's another thought, another change!). Yet Now itself does not change, while supporting all things changing within it. It is never then; it is always Now.

This is the essential flip by which we become any future we would attract: from being a relatively fixed "I" moving through time to being Now in which a constantly changing picture—including "I"—unfolds. Being Now, I am connected to the whole picture. Connected to the whole picture, insight arises that is not yet realized—it is either a fantasy or the future. If I bring it through me, because I am Now, I attract it into the present. In the ordinary, spatial world, it feels like I'm moving toward it. In reality, I'm manifesting it through my existence in Now.

In addition to our boundless connectedness, we also live in the ordinary world. And in that ordinary world, not all visions of the future can be manifest. The bigger my vision, idea, or dream—the broader its horizon, the more people it involves—the more broadly it has to resonate within a common, shared reality in order to come about. If my vision involves 10 other people—such as the direction of a small business or a special Thanksgiving dinner—it needs to be in accord with the reality of those 10 people; it has to become part of their world too. If my vision involves 10 million people—such as introducing a new product or building a new city center—it has to "click" and find support within a broadly shared reality. Leaders who can attract great visions into the present create a new shared reality among a great many people. In organizational life, this shows up as a change in culture.

Attracting the Future to XL Capital

For years, XL Capital has been a great place to work, committed to developing its leaders, which is how I've gotten to know this relatively small, specialty insurance company. But here it is, 2008, and the company has gotten hammered by three years of grave misfortune, from three major hurricanes in one season to a partly owned subsidiary completely melting down in the financial crisis. A resilient company of great people,

XL Capital shouldered these difficulties, but is not thriving. In one of our leadership programs, participants are distracted by ever-worsening news on their BlackBerrys, as they watch their company's stock price tumble from $15 to $10 to less than $5 in one week. People are scared.

In comes a new CEO—Mike McGavick—with an impressive resume of business and political leadership. A consummate communicator, from day one he is both reaching out and listening to the people in and around XL. He speaks to the leaders in our program, and tells it like it is—which isn't pretty—even as he charges them to act with accountability and ownership for this great company. He brings a buzz into the room, which remains even after he leaves (the hallmark of leadership that endures). Later, over dinner, I'm talking with several participants who tell me how, in the space of a few months, Mike has signaled a sea change in accountability. "I never thought I had a budget to manage," one manager tells me. "Now I'm scrutinizing every line."

This may sound like just another "great leader" story, but what strikes me while watching Mike is that more than being a great leader, he is the *right* leader for XL. Why? Because he sincerely wants the job, and has taken it with a crystal-clear vision of the brighter future that could become XL's present. "I see this as a place where the best underwriters in the industry come to practice their craft," he tells people. Only a few months earlier, competitors were raiding XL's best talent, and now the CEO is declaring the culture that would attract the best and brightest.

Culture is like the collective personality of an organization, and Mike knows that the personality of the company needs to personify success in order to bring that success into the present. So, for example, he redefines the model XL leader in terms of the behaviors and attitudes that will be emphasized and rewarded going forward. This is, to paraphrase Ghandi, being the change you want to see in the world—which Mike embodies, not only as an individual leader, but also by transforming the collective personality of the company.

Would the company be acquired? Could it make it on its own? From a distance it seems that Mike faces some mighty struggles in his first year, and some of the directions he tries turn out to be blind alleys, but they never become sticking points; only temporary experiments. This ability to learn and move on is the signature of leaders who attract the future, whereas leaders who only drive results tend to keep pushing, even down blind alleys, far too long. The beauty of attracting the future is that one never stops listening for the future and learning from the present.

Part of Mike's tremendous effectiveness is that it's not about Mike. I send him a note after one of our programs, thanking him for his participation amidst all the fires he was attending to. His note back to me says it all: "I will work tirelessly for the people of this company, and being with them last week reminds me why it's all worthwhile."

In 2009, XL Capital was one of the biggest stock market success stories of the year, up by more than 500 percent. Just saying.

Pumping the Swing

Not all futures we attract will necessarily be lucrative. After all, the "I" that may be attracted to lucre is the very part of us that lets go in making this flip. Attracting the future comes from the inherent connectedness of who we are, but that doesn't mean that insight alone is enough. Insight alone would not have given XL Capital a brighter present. Quality in execution is also needed—the Driver and Organizer getting stuff done. But this quality of execution differs from the blind drive for results in two important ways: First, it arises from and hence serves our boundless connectedness, not merely our local ego trying to make good for itself. Second, it is not blind. Rather, it's constantly listening, sensing, becoming one with the larger forces at work and using them to great effect. With this openness of mind and intentionality of vision, synchronicity can operate. This is the quality of action that Lao Tzu calls non-action because there is no actor standing apart: "In non-action we do everything."

In addition to connectedness, this quality of action manifests what Tanouye Roshi called "driving rhythm," which is perhaps easiest to understand in the context of music. My colleague, Roger Nirenberg, is a symphony conductor who applies his art to leadership, and vividly demonstrates the role of driving rhythm. He gives an orchestra a piece of music to play—a Mozart symphony—and leaves the podium. He's gone. They play along without leadership. Their performance is technically correct, but there is a felt flatness to the music and it grows perceptibly slower. He then returns, and with tempo-driving baton and gestures, the music springs to life, fills with energy, and turns on a dime. Roger's driving rhythm makes the difference between an uninteresting performance and an outstanding one.

You know about driving rhythm from the playground of your childhood. Remember sitting on a swing? If you start out by just rapidly pumping your legs, nothing much happens, even though you're working very hard. But if you straighten your legs, push your body back, and start even the smallest oscillation, you can grow it by timing your pumping to its leading edge.

In physics we call this sympathetic vibration, and it's a way to bring about big effects through the timing of small ones. To create sympathetic vibration, we have to *sympathize*—catch the rhythm of, become one with—the larger forces at work. It takes only a bit of training to learn a driving rhythm for pumping a swing. It took Roger years of training to sympathize with the composers, orchestras, and audiences whose training, tempo, and temperament he factors into his conducting. Mike McGavick's leadership has matured through years of sensing the timing and larger forces at work in the complex world of business and politics. He understands that to create a driving rhythm in an organization is to work with its culture.

The trick with setting a driving rhythm—as with using any aspect of Driver energy—is to do so in a way that keeps listening (Organizer), connects with others (Collaborator), and is in accord with the whole picture (Visionary). In other words, it is to engage our Driver's edge, even as we remain our connected selves. If we can dance in this paradox, we will find inexhaustible support for our vision, because our vision itself will naturally transform as conditions change. Moreover, as we apply our driving rhythm to the current conditions, our impact will grow in a way that doesn't exhaust us, any more than does pumping a swing.

The more facile and self-aware we become with the energy patterns, the more easily we can live this paradox. The exercise at the end of this chapter and additional Chapter 7 exercises available at *www.thezenleader.com* give you a chance to simultaneously experience (or quickly flip between) all four patterns, and play with creating a driving rhythm from a connected state. You might want to flip to the end of this chapter and try the exercises now to prime the pump—or pump the swing—into making this flip.

The Zen Leader Flip 7: Driving Results to Attracting the Future

To drive results is to push the present toward the future. As we've said, it always comes from behind, and a relentless habit of it makes us feel like *we're* always behind.

To attract the future is to create the pull of working with larger forces. In one sense, creating pull is nothing new to leaders. Basic marketing, for example, teaches the importance of creating pull from customers, not merely pushing one's products and services onto them. But what many leaders do find new in this flip, especially Driver leaders in fast companies, is slowing down enough to actually sense the market—not only what's happening, but what's missing. That's why we start by slowing down, and stopping, if only for a moment, to give the mind a chance to change gears, and sense opportunities. We then want to listen for the future, which requires relinquishing the safety of *knowing*, and hanging out in not-knowing, if only for a while. Finally, if we are rewarded with insight that resonates with us as a worthy vision, goal, or even direction for the day, we come to the final step, which is transforming our selves to realize that intention.

Attracting the future is not a heroic act, so much as unifying our intention with what's ready to happen, and bringing it about through our actions. In effect, we're creating sympathetic vibration—pumping the swing—as we listen for and work with the needs of people, the surrounding context, the timing of situations, and even nature itself. Because we're working with larger forces, we can enable bigger effects that are non-exhausting, non-depleting, and more sustainable. Far from propagating a preconceived agenda, we attract the future by simultaneously listening for it, and transforming our self in the present. Luck is sometimes defined as opportunity meeting the prepared mind. In this flip, we prepare the mind to sense opportunity and create its luck.

Slow down...stop. The flip to attracting the future is simply connectedness applied to sense what future is possible and how to bring it into the present. I say "simply" because it's not complicated, but it *is* subtle. If we're driving results full steam ahead, and not getting where we want to go—or not wanting what we're getting—we have to slow down to even approach this state of connectedness in which acute sensitivity gives rise to insight. Better yet, stop. Already our listening improves as we give our nervous system a chance to come out of Driver mode.

> The Zen Leader
>
> Flip 7
>
> Driving Results to Attracting the Future
>
> ☯ Slow down...stop
> ☯ Listen for the future
> ☯ Transform [in] the present

We can slow ourselves down into this flip as a thought experiment, as we did in becoming the dot of Now in our timeline. Stepping into this dot, looking at the past and future "end on," we see all possibilities intersecting through us. The future is but another leg of our boundless expanse.

The more we can fully immerse ourselves in this dot of Now, the more a Samadhi state of connectedness arises. We cannot will this state, for the "I" that chases this condition is the very "I" dissolved by it. But we can, with practice, create the conditions in our body and mind whereby this connectedness arises on its own. It is exactly the condition cultivated in meditation, and people have been cultivating it for thousands of years. It is exactly the cultivation of the Zen leader in you.

We can slow ourselves down into this flip by slowing down our breath. Breath functions both consciously (we can control it) and unconsciously (it's still functioning when we're not thinking about it). Hence it plays a special role in our mind-body system because it can reach into parts of our self that we cannot consciously access. Slowing down our breath reduces the rate of mind chatter. When we breathe just a few times a minute (as opposed to the average 12 times per minute), in a physics sense, we lower our overall frequency into a more stable and sensitive range. Try it.

Slowing down our thoughts helps us see more clearly. If you imagine each thought as a ripple in the pool of mind, high-frequency thought is like a jumble of ripples, all colliding with one another and distorting any image they reflect. As thoughts slow down, there is less collision and the waves form a more even pattern. Although I'm speaking metaphorically, these smoother waveforms are exactly what neuroscientists find in the EEGs of seasoned meditators[1]: more coherence, less noise—which pretty much matches one's psychological experience. In this more coherent state, we can sense more subtle things, just as we can see more detail reflected in a calm pond than in a turbulent one.

Slowing down also helps us find the natural frequencies for getting other people and situations working with us. Having only one speed is like rapidly pumping our legs as we sit on a swing; we can work very hard to very little effect.

In an energy pattern sense, when we slow down...stop, we move out of Driver mode and into the quieter patterns of Organizer and Visionary. The Organizer is a good listener, and its quiet centeredness will serve us well, but we cannot sense the future by stopping within the walls and assumptions that the Organizer knows. We have to leave the realm of knowing, and open into the Visionary. Even "I" entering Visionary is not the same as Samadhi connectedness, but it moves us in the right direction. In the Visionary's boundlessness, dissolve into essence; be Now.

Listen for the future. Listen with your eyes, with every pore, curious and open. What you're listening for is not your usual mind chatter; it's a different-quality signal that seemingly pops up out of nowhere.

"Call Aunt Jean" popped up as I was listening this morning, and I know today to call my wonderful aunt. "The future" is not confined to grandiose visions, though the other thing that popped up for me this morning was how to tell the story that will help people understand this book. I could have labored for hours writing promotional pabulum, but it never would have been as clear as what popped out on its own.

I use myself as an example because I can't tell you how much I've complicated things throughout the years, with all my effort and striving for achievement. This make-it-happen mindset is also common among the leaders I work with. But in listening for the future, we suspend trying to make anything happen, and *trust*. This morning, I didn't need to make anything happen, so it was easy to trust, easy to listen. I had a question concerning the day and this book, but I didn't grasp it as some kind of problem to solve. More like...*What wants to happen here? Surprise me!*

In listening for the future, we open ourselves to surprise—and luck. We may get a brilliant idea for a mobile phone with no buttons. We may get a marketing insight. We may get "call Aunt Jean." Who knows? This pop-up experience is not foreign to us. "Where are you when you get your best ideas?" I've asked leaders on four continents. And the winning answer? You guessed it: in the shower. Most people don't take a shower in order to make something happen or get a good idea. Yet, when the warm water hits our skin, our body relaxes, we open up, and—voila! It's what happens when we *quit* trying to make something happen. What I've noticed is that if I'm quiet enough to truly listen for what wants to happen, it's always there, always playing. But in my everyday mind, my usual mind chatter plays over this signal—like one radio station playing over another—and I can miss it. If I try to force it, it's "I" forcing and I miss it even more. We all can miss it. Slow down...stop, dissolve the "I," and listen: we can all hear it.

In listening for the future, we are also listening to ourselves, because we and the future are not two different things. We are listening for our interests, passions, perhaps a sense of calling, or the joy that comes with expressing our gifts. We are listening for what holds us back from the future we aspire to, what is too stuck, too small, or too afraid to move forward. As our self-awareness grows, the future we wish to attract naturally becomes a more realistic match to who we are. How could it be otherwise?

In listening for the future, questions that help us listen from a connected state are best: *What are the larger forces at work? What wants to happen here?* Or my question this morning: *What wants to happen today?* Our question may even be subconscious. I'm sure this morning a deeper question was lurking regarding how to spread understanding of this book. It wasn't conscious, but it didn't have to be. Pouring myself into this book day after day, I can trust that this question is operating.

The same is true for you. Listen for the future with questions like, *What's next? What's ready to happen?* Listen to your self with questions like, *What holds me back? What's the next thing that needs to open up in me?* Listen and be surprised.

Transform [in] the present. Of course, not all surprises are pleasant. And even pleasant surprises—brilliant insights—are not always convenient, and may call on us to exert a great deal of energy to bring them about. But that is attracting the future to the present: the transformation begins in here. The difference between a great idea that becomes a breakthrough innovation and one that dies on the vine is the ability of the leader who has it to transform the present, which is to say, transform him- or herself.

Not all ideas can or should be realized. Ideas that come from a disturbed mind may not resonate with enough people to ever come about. Even ideas from a great mind are a dime a dozen, and most of them are fantasy. But who decides? The first decider is the idea-haver. If we are only lukewarm about an idea and it will require red-hot levels of effort, it dies a natural death in our own mind.

But say we're completely excited about an idea and want to pursue it. Then we go to the next level of transforming the present: *Can we generate interest? Can we pump the swing on this?* In this way we start to test whether this idea can or should be realized. In a driving rhythm, we transform a bit of our activity to test whether our idea resonates within a larger context, be it family, friends, customers, colleagues, communities, or whatever slice of the world our idea applies to. Perhaps our transforming activity creates changes in the climate of a group we lead or in the culture of an organization, in which case it will start to spread to others. Or perhaps we will pursue our idea as something of a skunkworks because the larger context is not yet primed for it. Perhaps our next set of transforming activities plants the seeds that get people ready for our idea. This is exactly what Apple did with the iPhone to move people beyond keyboard-based computers and ready them for the iPad. Pretty smart, huh?

Again, not all ideas are brilliant future products and not all futures we attract have to be game-changing. Some "futures" may be as short-term as what we're going to do today. But when ideas are large, long-term, and involve many others, the key to attracting them is to maintain a driving rhythm informed by listening and learning. This is how we will tell whether our idea is fantasy, or that our idea may be sound but we've gone down a blind alley, or that—wonder of wonders!—our idea is starting to sprout.

Our transforming in the present is supported by a perfectly reliable indicator of whether we're on the right track: joy arises. Joy doesn't come from any old thing that we do. Rather, when our doing arises from connectedness, joy arises with it. This joy may be more subtle than the "jump for joy" variety. It may feel like full engagement in what we do, and a quiet satisfaction arising. It may feel like energy that keeps renewing itself, much as pumping a swing seemingly gives us more energy than it takes.

This joy is mighty contagious, attractive, and impossible to fake. If our idea involves others, joy will draw them, and enthusiasm will build. The word *enthusiasm*, which comes from the Greek word for *God*, speaks to the embodiment and expression of universality through our being. As Eckhart Tolle observes, "With enthusiasm you find you don't have to do it all yourself. In fact, there is nothing of significance you *can* do by yourself. Sustained enthusiasm brings into existence a wave of creative energy and all you have to do then is 'ride the wave.'"[2]

Riding a wave is not a passive act, but a consummate example of driving rhythm. To ride a wave is to stay on its leading crest and use its enormous force with agility. This driving rhythm is a state of complete sensitivity and perfect timing that uses larger forces, often pulling others along. It's what allows a leader to change the direction of a group when circumstances change. It's what allows Roger to get an orchestra turning Mozart on a dime and delivering a most enthusiastic performance. It's what allows Mike to push a culture of greater accountability that meets with enthusiasm from people at XL because it matches who they want to be.

Transforming in the present with an intention about the future, we will encounter obstacles. A big obstacle will be when we get in our own way, which we'll talk about more in the next chapter. Just as we get turned off by leaders if we sense they're in it for themselves, so we also stink up our own ideas when we contort them to serve our needs. Being aware of this possibility, watching for it, we can remind ourselves (or re-experience!) that in connectedness, no self arises to take or need credit.

Other obstacles we'll encounter come from other people and situations. They may not be ripe for our idea. They may have competing interests. A few steps into execution, new information may tell us that things are not proceeding quite as we expected. If we are still clear and convinced by our idea, we can negotiate every one of these obstacles with listening and further adjusting. Because even what we regard as an obstacle (this goes for our self as well) assumes a particular intent or direction. It may be that we have to adjust our direction, or pace, or make some change by which an obstacle becomes a springboard. The history of innovation is rife with stories of how the first time something is tried it doesn't work so well, and only in the learning, adjustment, and re-launch do things come together.

The obstacles may be so overwhelming that we find our enthusiasm waning. This may be a sign that we need to re-energize, that our idea is unrealistic, or that our approach needs adjustment. If, as a matter of course, our enthusiasm disappears and joy is replaced by strain and effort—not momentarily, but as a common occurrence—it's time to go back to the beginning: slow down...stop. Whatever future we're attracting (for example, a performance bubble with broken relationships and high blood pressure on the side) is not one we truly want, and our own lack of joy and energy are telling us with the utmost clarity.

Putting It to Work: Your Vision Revisited

We've covered some distance since Chapter 2, when, by way of aligning energy, you were invited to craft a statement of your vision or purpose, and how you might approach it. Hopefully you can find or recall what you wrote, because now is a good time to revisit that vision and apply this flip. We'll also use the timeline you had a chance to build earlier. Reflecting on your vision for the next few years, and opening to the connected state available to you now, you can get a sense of how pushing toward it contrasts with attracting it.

1. **Slow down...stop.** To start, write down a few things you know about your vision and how you are going about realizing it. You can use what you developed in Chapter 2, or start fresh.

   Now relax. Breathe deeply and ever more slowly into your *hara*. "See" through your ears. Open to this state for a few minutes. (Hint: Put the book down.) Bring your awareness to the vision and approach you just wrote, and identify a few concrete goals or milestones that you want to make true some time from now— six months, a year, or no more than three years out. Using (or re-creating a simplified version of) your timeline, state them as realities and locate them as entries in the future. Identify a few concrete things you've done so far to realize your vision, and locate them as entries in the past.

2. **Listen for the future.** Step into Now. In your imagination, enter your timeline, be Now, and consider past and future "end on." All that you have done toward your vision pours into Now. The future vision you would attract flows out of Now. Rest in this open state for a moment and listen. Listen. What wants to

happen? What's next? What's true about yourself? Don't try for any answer. Simply listen.

- ☯ You may hear nothing.
- ☯ You may sense that something you wrote earlier is off.
- ☯ You may sense a different goal, a different future possibility.
- ☯ You may remember something that seems completely disconnected. Don't lose it. It may later connect in surprising ways.
- ☯ You may sense a next step.
- ☯ You may sense resistance or fear regarding a next step.
- ☯ You may be flooded with thoughts; relax your breathing and let everything flow through you without obstruction.

If anything noteworthy arises, honor it with a note. But don't force it. Nothing necessarily has to happen in this moment. If you can remember and return to this general process, when something needs to arise, you'll be listening for it.

3. **Transform [in] the present.** As you continue being the dot of Now, ask:

- ☯ Regarding the past, what have you been doing to drive results toward this vision that is not working, that feels like strain and effort? What can you stop doing?
- ☯ Regarding the future, what could you do differently that might work? How can you "pump the swing" and work with larger forces? What's the next thing you need to learn, let go of, or open up to?

Recognize that what is transforming in the present is *you*. And when you exactly match the you of your vision, that future will be exactly Now. Between that moment and this, changes in what you value, how you spend your time, what you learn, and who you connect with and how effectively, will percolate into chain reactions of cause and effect. If your future vision is able to be realized, joy will accompany your progress, and a wave of enthusiasm will build. If your vision is unrealistic, you will hit stuck points where your driving rhythm has no more effect than a woodpecker attacking stainless steel; where there's no path forward, no learning is taking place, and no joy is present. Conversely, if you keep listening from a connected state, your vision will auto-adjust to the oneness that is you, and will inform your rational mind what to do next.

After writing your answers, take another look at your vision statement and current approach and see if you'd make any adjustments that match you better. In the back and forth between transforming "in here" and listening to "out there," we are both *being* and *creating* the change we want to see in the world. Allowing a bit of time for conscious reflection helps, not because it drives the process so much as aligns our conscious mind *with* the process.

Attracting the future doesn't mean we forever stop using the Driver's push or the Organizer's plan; both are indispensable to getting stuff done. But they are infinitely more useful when they serve the insight and vision arising from the connected state, rather than blundering along blindly on their own. Conversely, the insights of the connected state can be all idea and no action without the driving rhythm that sets a pace and gets people moving with us. Learning to function in this paradoxical tension, we appropriately flip between the connectedness of the Visionary and Collaborator and the get-it-done-ness of the Driver and Organizer. The more we engage each of these patterns, the more unconsciously competent we become at flipping between them, until moment by moment we manifest whatever energy is needed. The core practice at the end of this chapter ("All Patterns at Once") invites you into this state of spontaneous agility.

With every pattern available to us right Now, what can possibly stop us? We are the future we attract, able to sense its contours. We are Now, able to sense the hearts of people, the practicalities of cause and effect, and the natural timing of situations. We are the transforming agent. We are the driving rhythm. We are Lao Tzu's non-actor, and, "In non-action, we accomplish everything."

And yet. Even if we have caught glimpses of our boundless possibility, the reality for most of us is that something holds us back from manifesting this clarity in our daily lives. An ego-body, full of needs, asserts itself in the moment, asking, even *insisting*, that whatever is going on, *Make it all about me.* How do we flip that around and come to a greater peace in this paradox of human existence? How do we get out of our own way and let the Zen leader in us emerge in service of others? We turn to that next.

The Zen Leader

Flip 7 Takeaways

Driving Results to Attracting the Future

You are Now. You are the transforming agent. As you match the future, you bring it into Now. To realize this:

- ☯ **Slow down...stop.** Enter the connected state, being Now.

- ☯ **Listen for the future.** Throw in an open-ended question: *What wants to happen? What's next?* Or simply trust that deeply rooted questions are functioning. Listen with an open mind; invite surprise.

- ☯ **Transform [in] the present.** Test a possible a future idea first in the body of your own interest. Manifest a driving rhythm, listening and learning, to build momentum. Let joy and enthusiasm be your guides.

The Zen Leader
Core Practice: All Patterns at Once

Hopefully, you've already experienced all four energy patterns, and have a sense of how each of them plays differently through you. The more easily and instantly you can move between any of them, the more all of them are simultaneously available to you right Now. This exercise helps you experience all four patterns at once. It's simple, but subtle, and deepens with practice. Additional exercises using all patterns at once are available on *www.thezenleader.com*.

1. **Establish the center and extension.** Start with the centering breathing exercise that was the first step to the Invitation to Samadhi (end of Chapter 6; see Figure 6.1). This time, as you press the balls of your feet into the earth and extend your palms upward (Figure 6.1d on page 154), pay particular attention to the base of the abdomen. This is the Driver center (lowest "star" in Figure 7.4 on page 184), and you can feel it firing whenever you push. As you open your arms on the exhale (Figure 6.1e), notice energy moving out the top of your spine and through the top of your head. This is the Visionary "center," which is not fixed in the body, but extends upward and outward (the "star" above the top of the head in Figure 7.4). Notice both solid foundation (Driver) and extension (Visionary) at the same time. Repeat several times until you can feel both patterns at once.

2. **Add rhythm and stillness.** Breathing in and out through your nose, start shifting your weight from foot to foot, feeling a gentle rhythm come up from the earth through your entire body (Figure 7.4a). Let your head move as well, and your hands make figure-8s (Figure 7.4b). Pay particular attention to your belly as the center of this Collaborator swinging (the belly "star" in Figure 7.4c). Keep sensing

Figure 7.4

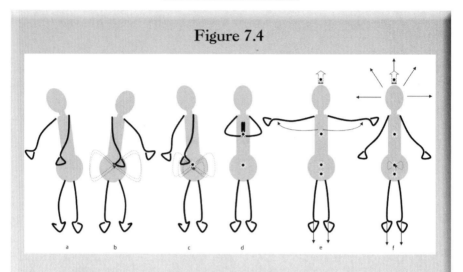

that belly center as you cut the motion by half, and half, and half again, like a string damping out, but still capable of vibration. In this dynamic stillness, touch your palms together just above your solar plexus (don't press), with your forearms making a straight line from elbow to elbow. Notice the uprightness and calm of this Organizer center coming to life (the heart "star" in Figure 7.4d). Feel the rhythmic potential of the Collaborator and the stillness of the Organizer at the same time.

3. **All at once.** Breathe out through your nose, extend through the balls of your feet into the earth, open your arms wide, and feel your eyes, ears, and all senses open (Figure 7.4e). Relax on the inhale and continue breathing in this rhythm: extend on the exhale, relax on the inhale (Figure 7.4f). Feel the Driver's power, the Collaborator's rhythm, the Organizer's calm, and the Visionary's extension all at once.

8

From "It's All About Me" to "I'm All About It"

"I'M NOT SURE what I want to get out of this program," says Glenn quite honestly. He's one of the people I'm coaching in this week's leadership program, and he's not sure he wants to be here. "I think the company was just throwing me a bone, putting me in this program because they didn't give me the promotion I'd been promised and they're afraid I'll leave."

"So it's all about the promotion?" I ask. And Glenn unleashes all the reasons he deserves the promotion, the political intrigue that kept him from getting it, and the undeserving people who got one instead. For the past six months he'd been working with a coach who had given him advice about how he should show up in meetings in order to impress the right people. Now it all feels wasted. "Don't you want to be free of all this baggage?" I ask. "Absolutely!"

he answers. I suggest that freedom should be his goal for the program. He agrees tentatively, not sure that such a thing is possible. "Forget the promotion," I tell him. "Focus on the value you want to create in the world, and let the rest fall into place."

Glenn looks at me as though I've just tricked him. Forget the promotion? "Forget it." I repeat. "As long as you're locked onto whether you're going to get this promotion, you're drawing everyone into the question with you. *Is he ready? Why hasn't it happened already?* Meanwhile, no one's paying attention to the value you're creating—not even you. Only after you let go of the question will others let go of it, and will your full value be apparent." Glenn's face visibly softens and his shoulders drop half an inch. "You mean I can just forget it?" he repeats, more to himself than to me. And for the rest of the week, he seems lighter, more engaged, coming to morning meditation sessions, exchanging easy banter with his colleagues, not with some kind of "hasn't been promoted yet" cloud hanging over him. Glenn is a joy to work with, and through the week he builds a vision, and commits himself to this newfound freedom and a practice to sustain it. Promotion or not, Glenn leaves the week a happier, more effective leader.

As Glenn learned, this flip from "it's all about me" and the need, in his case, to be recognized, appreciated, and promoted, to "I'm all about it" is a flip to freedom. The boundless personal transformation that attracts the future is stunted when we get trapped by the issues of our self in the moment. We lose our agility and fall into coping mode when we're stuck to the dot of self, reacting to something "out there" that doesn't serve us. Moreover, the "self" that we're stuck to is yesterday's news. It's habit and baggage from the past, but not necessarily what this moment calls for. How do we approach this moment with freshness? We can never do it by focusing on a self that becomes stale the moment we focus on it.

This flip from "it's all about me" and my needs to "I'm all about it" is a flip from narcissism to serving others. We might at first approach this sense of service in order to be seen as a good person, or because narcissism sounds bad and serving others sounds good. But ironically, this flip to "I'm all about it" isn't just for the sake of others. It is—as Glenn found—what frees us from our own smallness. "Where focus goes, energy flows," quips Anthony Robbins. When our focus is riveted on our little, local selves, our energy gets drained down that hole. Unaware of all that could replenish us, we grow smaller and weaker, completely blind to our true, universal nature.

This chapter serves up the flip from "life should serve me" to "I serve life." We'll explore how this flip frees up the value we can add and changes our way of leading from regal governing to empowering others and forming partnerships. We'll also look at what makes this flip difficult, which is the fear that our personal needs (for approval, safety, and so on) will not be met, and how we can cause this fear to lose its grip. It is through this flip from "it's all about me" to "I'm all about it" that the Zen leader in us emerges boundlessly, and without chains.

It's Like High School

It's completely natural that we start out in the place of "it's all about me." As we said earlier, it's the natural journey of development to form an ego (we'd be psychotic without one), and to start out by viewing everything from "I" at the center. Even for humanity as a whole, this was our first view of the universe, attributed (in the West) to Ptolemy. The earth was at the center and everything revolved around it; that is, around *us*. Young children similarly see the world as revolving around themselves, which is how a 3-year-old child can close her eyes and say with sincerity, "You can't see me." This is the stage of narcissism, named after the mythological Greek hunter, Narcissus, who gazed into a pond and fell in love with himself.

But just as Ptolemy gave way to Copernicus in the 16th century (not without upheaval from the threatened establishment, mind you), and the truth emerged that we revolve around something larger, so that same awareness begins to form in us (often with great upheaval from our own threatened establishment). First-born children are often jolted into the beginnings of this awareness when a younger sibling comes along, and suddenly they find themselves sharing the stage of their parents' attention. A rude awakening! Parents may try to help their children bond and minimize the rivalry. But rivalry is natural when "it's all about me" collides with "it's all about me too"! Little by little, we become aware of the thoughts and feelings of others, and the fact that our life revolves around a larger context. We learn, as we grow, that actions have consequences, that the world follows rules not of our making, and that other people feel pain.

This growing empathy, as we said earlier, is like a second child having to find its place alongside its older narcissistic sibling. And for some time, the voice of feeling for others has a hard time standing up to "it's all about me." Moreover, no matter how developed we are, we can always regress to this least common denominator in human experience. It's the basis of greed and fear. It's so common, in fact, that populist politicians invariably play this card in speeches: "It's about you! Your money should come back to you!" And countless ads remind you daily of products and services that are all about you.

So yes, it's natural that we enter this stage of "it's all about me", but just like high school, we do well to graduate. It's part of the journey, but we don't have to make it a stopping point. For nothing makes our life smaller than revolving around "I." Nothing makes leadership smaller than an "I" that serves itself first, and never quite makes it to what's second. As for Narcissus, it didn't end well for him either. Unable to tear himself away from his own image, he wasted away and finally died.

The Many Faces of "It's All About Me"

I don't hear many of the leaders I work with say it's all about them. Now granted, I'm fortunate to work with a fairly mature lot of leaders. They take an interest in the learning journey of leadership. They engage in development programs and coaching. They've generally had distinguished careers in challenging companies, and have been battle-tested through ups and downs, promotions and layoffs, and good bosses and bad. By the time I work with them, most leaders have cast a wider net of concern than purely themselves-in-their-skin. They may be about winning for the company, developing their people, creating jobs in their country, providing for their families, and so on. Hardly any of them would say, "I'm out to get my own needs met."

And yet. And yet, the need to meet our own needs is deeply human, and doesn't disappear the moment we start caring about others or connect ourselves to causes. We speak of survival as an *instinct*, not an option, because these needs are deeply pervasive and mostly subconscious. Tanouye Roshi jolted me into a disturbing awareness of just how deep and pervasive these needs run when he spoke once about the "death seat."

We don't use this term so much anymore, now that seatbelts are widely used. But when I was growing up in the 1960s, seat belts were not common and traffic fatalities were. It was common knowledge that the person most at risk in an auto accident was the passenger in the front seat; hence the term, "death seat." And why was this? The commonly accepted reason was that the steering wheel somehow protected the driver from flying headlong into the windshield. But Tanouye Roshi saw through this flawed reasoning. Sure, for slight bumps, the steering wheel might provide a stabilizing hold. But for the sort of impact that causes fatalities, the steering wheel is just another hard object to be blasted against. The reason the passenger ends up taking the brunt of the impact is because the last person to decide the direction of the car, the one who makes the final swerve, is the *driver*.

Wow, I thought. *Could we really be so selfish? Could I really be so selfish?* Of course I wanted to believe that I'd make a different decision in the moment of truth, but don't most of us want to believe that about ourselves? It's not polite to put ourselves first—most of us learned that as children. The first time I said, "Me and Diane are going out to play," I was promptly corrected that it's "Diane and I." The first time I had tea with my grandmother and served myself first, I was taught to serve others first. Our cultures and language are filled with ways to mitigate this instinctive me-first-ness. We might think we've so transcended that self-in-the-skin selfishness, but it only goes underground, and surfaces as so many disguised faces. Those faces don't literally speak the words,

It's all about me, but that's what they're saying in so many ways. Here's a smattering I hear all the time from high-flying, highly skilled leaders who indeed care about the people around them.

- ☯ Only I can do this (fast enough, correct enough, and so on).
- ☯ I'm right.
- ☯ I (or my team) want credit for this.
- ☯ I need to market myself better.
- ☯ I'm worried about money.
- ☯ If our groups get merged, I may be out of a job.
- ☯ I don't care what you think (or I'm just not listening).
- ☯ How does this affect my bonus?
- ☯ We're only rewarded for our numbers, so I'm not going to collaborate with that other department.
- ☯ I didn't get as much of a raise as that other group, so I don't want to cooperate with them.
- ☯ It bothers me that my peers don't like me.
- ☯ I'm burning out; I work too hard.
- ☯ I don't care what our lofty mission says, the only thing that matters is winning.
- ☯ I need to be heard (or respected, or promoted, and so on).
- ☯ I make a decision about people and those in my "in" group I'll help.

Is it wrong to think this way? No. It's completely natural, and in certain contexts, these lines of thought may be appropriate. But again, as with high school, these are not places where we want to hang out forever. Perhaps even reading through that list you could feel the tension forming in your body and the smallness of mind created when we're locked into these ways of thinking. Yet we don't move beyond these thoughts by denying or ignoring them. Rather, by knowing ourselves deeply and seeing how we tend to self-in-the-skin needs—or the fears that arise when we're not sure we *can* get our needs met—do we find peace with these needs, and know they don't have to define us any more than does our shoe size.

The great psychologist Abraham Maslow recognized well the depth of these human needs and gave us a simple way to understand how they build on one another. Maslow's hierarchy[1] (depicted in Figure 8.1) rests on the foundation of lower-level needs (for example, physical needs, and the need for security) that must be met at some level of sufficiency before we can mature to tending to higher-level needs (for example, personal power and self-actualization). As dynamic, biological systems living in a dynamic, unpredictable world, we don't scale this hierarchy only once, or in a simple, linear fashion. Rather, we're always going back and forth—down to the physical level when we're hungry, up to self-actualization when we're doing our best work, down to security when a terrorist attack threatens our city, up to personal power when we're passed over for promotion, and so on.

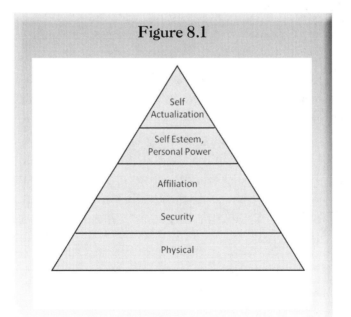

Maslow's Hierarchy.

Mapping the many faces of "it's all about me" into Maslow's hierarchy, we can see some of the human needs behind these sentiments. For example:

- ☯ Only I can do this (fast enough, correct enough, and so on). → self-actualization
- ☯ How does this affect my bonus? → personal power
- ☯ It bothers me that my peers don't like me. → affiliation
- ☯ I'm worried about money. → security
- ☯ I'm burning out; I work too hard. → physical

In doing this mapping for your own favorite needs, which the sidebar exercise guides you through, you may find a statement mapping to a more than one need.

For example, "I (or my team) want credit for this" may map to the need for personal power as well as to affiliation for a team you care about. "I'm burning out; I work too hard," can represent a tug of war between physical needs and self-actualization.

Really understanding how our needs function, not as a judgment against ourselves but with curious exploration, moves them from being faces in disguise to faces we recognize. In light of this awareness, we can start to see, "There I go again, meeting my own need for self-actualization." Or , "There I go again, trying to be something." Once we can see where our own needs color our response to a situation, we can start to ask, "What really serves here? What's really being called for?" In light of this awareness, we are ready for the great flip into using our needs, rather than them using us.

Be All You Can Be

The tiny pinnacle of self-actualization at the top of Maslow's hierarchy represents a creative, recursive process in which self transforms and transcends its earlier self. Whereas we are always changing, the fully actualized self is forever growing in a way that, say, a self stuck tending to its security needs is not. In this sense, being "selfish" can be a growing act if it comes from a place of actualizing a growing self. Hence the Dalai Lama's sage advice: "If you're going to be selfish, be smart selfish, not dumb selfish." Being selfish for our self-in-our-skin, we can get stuck in "high school," feeding our insecurities and taking things personally, which makes them "all about us." Being selfish on the largest possible scale, we become "all about it," whatever *it* we embrace as our world.

This expansive possibility is not foreign to us; it is our very nature, and can be brought out under the right intention and conditions. "Be all you can be," goes the U.S. Army recruiting slogan, with the implied promise that military experience pushes one beyond purely self-in-the-skin concerns. A young military recruit enters boot camp, and immediately his head is shaved, his clothes are the same as everyone else's, his private space and time are gone, and he begins a rigorous battle of training with cohorts he will come to rely on. This de-individualizing process creates a cadre that cares for one another, often more than for personal security or physical needs. To

Which Face of "It's All About Me" Do You Recognize?

Read through the list of I-centered statements and make a note of those that you catch yourself saying or thinking most often.

Add to this list any other I-centered concern that is one of your personal favorites—that comes up for you again and again.

Map these statements to the need (or combination of needs) in Maslow's hierarchy that is trying to get met or is afraid it won't get met.

Get to know these faces of "it's all about me" so that when they surface you can make a choice about them. And get to know this spot in Maslow's hierarchy where you have a tendency to get stuck. Awareness doesn't make these needs disappear, but it does make them progressively less consuming.

the point where a soldier like Private First Class Ross McGinnis literally lays down his life on a live grenade to save his crew.[2]

Or a young Albanian nun hears a "call within the call" to leave her convent and live among the poor. She forgoes personal comforts, promotions, and annual bonuses and starts a school for the destitute and starving. Others are drawn by her example. She opens an orphanage, a hospice for the poor, and a home for those with leprosy, and her work expands to other countries. A documentary covers her journey, and the world takes notice. The support she receives, including the proceeds of her Nobel Peace Prize, are plowed back into her mission. Through her prominence, she brokers a temporary cease fire in the Siege of Beruit, and rescues 37 children trapped in a hospital.[3] By the end of her life, Mother Teresa's Missionaries of Charity are operating more than 600 missions, schools, and shelters in 120 countries.

"Saints" and "heroes," we call people such as these. The words not only praise them, but also elevate them beyond our seemingly more meager selves. But we are not more meager. The people we would praise, like us, operate from a hierarchy of human needs. What their example shows us is how completely the top of that pyramid can supersede the bottom: how actualizing a boundless self puts one's physical existence to its fullest use.

And what is that fullest use? It's different for every one of us, based on our nature, development, core competencies, and conditions of our life. But actualizing our authentic self for the benefit of others is not merely the realm of saints and heroes, but the functioning of the Zen leader in us. Rather than life being about securing our physical existence—which cannot ultimately be secured (I hope I'm not the first one to break that news)—we flip into using our physical existence to serve life. If we're a soldier, we might say we're serving our country. If we're Mother Teresa, we might say we're serving God. Because "God" and "country" can hold different meanings for each of us, we'll speak of this flip as simply connected with Being and serving life. In making this flip, we convert an endless battle toward a losing proposition into truly being all we can be. What could possibly make more sense than that?

It's All About My Dream

But the ego is tricky. It identifies with something—a dream, a cause, a vision—and convinces itself that it's all about that thing when, in reality, it has made that thing an extension of itself by identifying with it!

I don't speak in the abstract. I lived this way for years. In my case, the dream was to be an astronaut—a childhood dream, fueled by hours gazing at the stars and squinting at grainy television coverage of the early manned space flights. The dream was completely sealed in my 7-year-old mind when my dad said to me one day, "You can be an astronaut."

"Really?!" I pop back, trying to absorb that this thrilling experience I'm watching on television could be my own. "Sure!" he says, "You can go into space right now." "Really?!" I say more incredulously, still at that age when I'm not sure just how much my parents can pull off. We have a small closet in our kitchen—a broom closet—that is tall and narrow, vaguely shaped like a rocket, and my parents have taken out the mops and vacuum and dust rags and whatnot, and encourage my sister and me to get in. Boom! The door is closed. We're squished shoulder-to-shoulder in this skinny blackness and my dad starts with the NASA countdown: "TEN...NINE...EIGHT..." I'm so excited I can hardly stand it. "THREE...TWO...ONE...BLAST OFF!" And suddenly a roar emerges, the door starts vibrating, and I say to my sister, "I think we're going somewhere!"

They have pushed the vacuum cleaner up against the door and turned it on. Clever parents! But from that day forward, this is my dream. Not an ordinary, lightweight dream, but an all-consuming, passionate dream that has me writing to NASA at the age of 13, asking which courses I should take in *junior* high school, to best prepare for my life as an astronaut. NASA writes back—a letter I treasure—saying it doesn't much matter, but by the time I get to college, I should be majoring in aeronautical engineering or a physical science. That does it. I start taking every science and math class under the sun, majoring in physics, moving from high-energy physics to biophysics for graduate school, and wouldn't you know it: by the time I graduate, NASA is accepting women into the astronaut program. I submit my application.

I'm overjoyed the day I'm called for an interview. At 29 years old, I trot down to the Johnson Space Center in Houston, Texas, to face the astronaut candidate selection committee and convince them that I'm the perfect human specimen to send into space. Now if you were to ask me in this moment, *Is this all about you or are you all about it?* I would have told you, without a doubt, *I am all about it!* I am all about being an astronaut, exploring space, serving NASA, giving back to people on Earth—all that. And in some sense, all of that would have been true. But it was not the deepest truth. The deeper truth I had to learn the hard way.

So I'm facing the astronaut candidate selection committee and they start asking me questions like, "If you were an animal, what animal would you be?" Am I able to give an authentic, straight-from-who-I-am answer? No, I'm gaming it. Trying to figure out the winning answer. With mental cycles whirring madly, in the space of milliseconds I'm thinking, *Hmmm, animal...since this is a flight job, it should be a flying animal, probably one with a military bearing...* and out pops my answer: "Eagle." Probably the same answer 80 percent of the other candidates give, and maybe for some of them it's true. But if you were in the room that day, you would know, as surely as the committee knew, that this answer does not match *me*.

In addition to the interview, this selection process involves countless questionnaires, some about personality, some about health. And as I'm filling out each one, I keep searching for the "right" answer. *Do you always tell the truth?* asks one of the questions. *Yes, always,* I answer, which is a lie. This is further confirmed when I fill out the health questions and leave out the fierce allergy to cats that turns me into a wheezing, asthmatic mess. I'm gaming the whole thing, my Organizer self trying to be what it thinks is the perfect astronaut candidate. And why am I doing this? *Because this is my dream,* I tell myself, *and this noble end justifies shading a truth here or there. surely everyone else is doing the same, aren't they?*

If this had just gone on for one week, for one astronaut application process, it might not have sunk its teeth into me so deeply. But it went on for years. NASA didn't choose me in that first round, but said I looked interesting enough, so why not take a ground job at the Johnson Space Center to get operational experience? *Absolutely!* I say. And down I go to Houston, Texas, in pursuit of my dream. Who am I concerned with? Myself. And impressing upon every person around me that I am the perfect candidate to send into space. But now it's not a single interview I'm facing, but rather eyes all around. *How do I impress this person? Are my actions on this project going to be viewed favorably by the powers that be? What do you think of me? Am I perfect enough for you?* Day by day, I'm giving away my power, losing any sense of who I am by trying to be all things to all people—not for *their* sake, but for the sake of my dream. For *my* sake.

That's how tricky the ego gets in these matters. For years, I don't realize what a nutty way this is to live. I keep going through the astronaut selection process when it comes up every year or two. I get so close...to the point of being told, "If we had taken one more person, it would have been you." Oh! *Just a little more pushing on this dream and I'll get there*, I think. But meanwhile, my heart is not happy. It starts registering a bit of arrhythmia. Nevermind, push on through. It gets worse with a rapid pulse, which I try to manage with jogging and meditation. *Can't mention* that *on my next astronaut health questionnaire.* I've trained to be a private pilot, and have to pass a routine physical exam to keep flying. My pulse is now so uneven that I fail an ordinary pilot physical. *Can't let NASA find* that *out.* I sit in a bathtub of cool water for 45 minutes before retaking my pilot physical and squeak by.

My heart is going crazy, up one day and down the next, and now a pressure is mounting in my chest. I ignore it; I've been promoted in my Space Station role at NASA and there's so much to do, so much to prove. I awake at 3:27 one morning with my pulse racing over 200 beats per minute and pain shooting down my left arm. I'm 34 years old, having what for all the world feels like a heart attack. Scared, I go to the phone and call the hospital, still not registering that I would need to *go* to the hospital—after all, NASA might find out. "Get in here," they tell me. "Do we need to send an ambulance?" "No, no, no," I assure them, deciding to drive myself, because I don't want to have to lie about an ambulance ride on my next application.

I get to the hospital in fearful denial, to a thankfully empty emergency room, and suddenly it all crashes. *What the hell am I doing!?* As they hook me up to a heart monitor and draw my blood, my thoughts are screaming, *I'm ruining my life! I thought my life was about being an astronaut, but apparently it's not! And here I am giving away my actual life in service of a fiction! Stop! Stop right now!* With utter deflation, my dream slips away. *I guess it's not my life. I need to find what my life is.* A spacious freedom wells up inside. The doctor tells me there's no damage to my heart, and apparently I had a panic attack, not a heart attack. I'm released a couple hours later, and go to work as light as a feather. It may be the first day I do any truly useful work for NASA.

What was my mistake? Was I wrong to follow my dream? No. But I certainly wasn't listening to life. And if I really looked beneath the surface to see what was underneath this dream, I would have seen that it was masking a question of self-worth, a need to prove myself. When this dream formed in my young mind, astronauts were the heroes of the day. *Why, if I could be all that*, I thought, *I would be so far beyond the question of being good enough, smart enough, or making my parents proud enough*—all things that mattered to me. All things that would make me feel better about myself. Even if I could not articulate these thoughts fully as a 7-year-old, there's little surprise that a dream formed at this young stage would essentially be "all about me."

And so it is for much of what drives the "high-need achievers" leaders I work with in every leadership program. There is nothing wrong with the need to achieve—excellence in every area from arts to zoology arises from it, and high performance in business absolutely counts on it. But if what we're fundamentally serving is an inner hunger, we do well to look at that. Acknowledge it. Come to know it. Our awareness of the hunger does not make it go away, any more than awareness of our growling stomach makes the hunger for food go away. But only with awareness can we let this need take its place among all of the needs in our present-moment context. It may still prevail, or it may have to wait just a bit as the situation calls for something different. We may find now is a good time to use our need to achieve to get something done. But without awareness, we blindly serve this need like a hungry ghost, and it is never done eating.

Eat Just Enough

Eating is actually a pretty good metaphor for getting a handle on our needs for the purpose of making this flip to "I'm all about it." It's not that in making this flip our needs go away; we are biological systems, and we will keep getting hungry, we will be cold when it's cold, and we will hunger for love, appreciation, and so forth. But in making this flip, our needs no longer consume us. They are forces we need to tend to and energy we can use.

Part of the message of Maslow's hierarchy is that lower-level needs must be met at some level of sufficiency before we can tend to the needs that rest on them. Physical needs are rock bottom, and eating is certainly one way we meet our physical needs. If we eat just enough, we'll have fuel for our journey, and can get on with meeting other needs. If not much food is available, or we can't afford it, we may become consumed with the need to find enough food. If food is plentiful and we enjoy eating, or we find that it makes us less anxious, we might eat too much, which, according to the Center for Disease Control, nearly two-thirds of Americans do, to the point of being overweight or obese.[4] At this most basic level, we can see our built-in tendency toward greed. And it's not limited to physical needs.

Eating too much or too little both present problems, but eating just enough quiets this physical need without letting it run away with us. We could look at our need for security the same way: Too little security, and we may be in fear for our lives or fearful that we won't have a roof over our heads. But if security is available, we may have a tendency to overdo it, get greedy, and try to make our life so safe that it becomes suffocating. Instead, we want just enough security to take fear off the table so we can get on with other matters.

Likewise with affiliation and personal power: If we're starving for these things, that hunger will be an undercurrent in our every action, and every situation will become another opportunity to get these needs met. But if enough is available, we may still have a tendency to overdo it and want more, more, more. How much approval is enough? How big an office do we need? Just as we don't serve ourselves well by overeating, we do ourselves no favors by over-indulging these needs. We become much smarter in meeting our needs when we can ask, *What's really being served here? Am I really serving other people or simply my own need for affiliation? Is getting this promotion right for me and the company, or is it simply meeting my need for power?* When we can ask questions like this, it's like the pause before dessert when we ask, *Do I really need this, or have I eaten enough?* That pause for awareness gives us a choice. We may not act in service of our need this time, or at least if we do, we don't do it blindly.

Even at the level of self-actualization, we can apply the "just enough" rule to keep our need for achievement in check and allow the self that's actualizing to keep growing. When we jump in and do a task that we're comfortable with, but someone else could be doing, we might ask, *Am I really the right person to do this, or am I doing it only to satisfy my own need for accomplishment?* When we push ourselves too hard and edge toward burnout, we might ask, *Does this situation call for this extreme response, or am I doing this because I'm only happy when I'm achieving?*

The answers to our inquiries won't always be the same, but power comes from asking the question and listening for the answer. One reason that people who need to be high-achievers often get to a place of barely managing is that they keep doing things they know how to do to keep feeding the beast of achievement. If we can pause and ask, *Am I really the best person to do this?* we may sense that this task is a perfect opportunity for someone else to learn, or to partner with another group. When we don't have to be at the center of things, we have much more freedom as leaders in how we get things done. When we don't need credit, the possibilities for collaboration are boundless. When we don't need to be the one achieving, the possibilities for developing others open before us. We start to notice new potential in people. We listen differently in meetings. We focus more energy on the people we're developing and the vision we're realizing. Plus, we create more followership when those we lead sense that we are fundamentally *for* them. Nothing limits a leader more than blindly serving the inner beast.

Pausing to face our needs at any level, and ensuring we're meeting them just enough, and not to the point of greed, we make the flip from compulsively using life to serve our needs into using our needs to effectively serve life. By pulling our needs up to the top of Maslow's hierarchy, where self-actualization keeps giving us room to grow, we use our needs in the smartest way possible.

Making the flip from "it's all about me" to "I'm all about it" inverts our ways of talking and thinking from a self-serving focus to a self that focuses on serving. To revisit some of the faces of "it's all about me," flipping them around might look something like this:

- ☯ Only I can do this. → I'd enjoy doing this, but who else could learn from this?

- ☯ I need to market myself better. → How can I add real and visible value?

- ☯ I'm worried about money. → I can be prudent about money and resourceful about living with just enough if I have to.

- ☯ If our groups get merged, I may be out of a job. → Our groups merging may signal that it's time for a new chapter for me.

- ☯ I need to be heard. → I need to listen more with deep respect to understand how to put my message across to others.

Reading through these lines again, can you feel the spaciousness of flipping them around? Maybe thinking along these lines seems too good or perfect. Forget about being good or perfect! Just experience the joy of it! Joy is that reliable sign that our boundless Zen leader is functioning freely, without the stickiness of ego tugging this way or that. Joy will tell us when we're on the right track. Now it's your turn.

The Zen Leader Flip 8: "It's All About Me" to "I'm All About It"

On the one hand this flip is the same for all of us, as we invert our thinking from "life should serve me" to "I serve life." On the other hand, the compulsive needs we have to untangle in order to do this will be different for every one of us; there is no single formula. Just as you may have resonated with some of the faces of "it's all about me" more than others, so each of us gets stuck at different points in Maslow's hierarchy. Getting unstuck is entirely possible, but it takes some energy, which is why the first step of this flip is to make sure we have some energy to work with. We then move to serving the situation, which may also serve our self-in-our-skin, or be the opposite of what serves our self-in-our-skin, or somewhere in between. We can more easily sense what's appropriate by asking what's being served here, and focus on meeting our own needs just enough, and not with greedy compulsion. And finally, by listening and learning, we let joy flow in and hone our responses for the future.

Manage your energy. It's no coincidence that the behaviors that derail careers surface more under stress, when leaders are tired and their energy is low. It's easier to be at our best when we have plenty of energy. That's why the Three Laws of Energy Management (introduced in Chapter 2) support so many flips, but especially this one. To enter this flip, start with a full charge. Remember:

> ❧ Rhythm, not relentless:
> Find a rhythm in your day
> that stretches and renews,
> including mini-breaks and
> renewing practices.

The Zen Leader

Flip 8

"It's All About Me" to
"I'm All About It"

❧ Manage your energy
❧ Serve the situation
❧ Listen and learn

☙ Down, not up: Center your breath in the lower abdomen; allow it to slow down and stabilize, especially as the pace picks up or emotions arise.

☙ Out, not in: Allow your energy to flow out—through your fingertips, out the top of your spine—releasing tension on the front, flexor side of the body.

As Maslow's hierarchy reminds us, it's hard to make this self-actualizing flip into "I'm all about it" if we're struggling to get basic, physical needs met. But give us a full charge and the idea of eating "just enough" to meet our needs at any level, and we have fuel and freedom for this profound flip.

Serve the situation. Situations unfold moment by moment, and it's not possible or necessary to bring a voiceover of awareness to every moment. But for situations in which you know you've gotten seriously stuck in the past—stuck on your dream, or needing to prove yourself, feel secure, feel loved, whatever—in those moments, ask, *How can I serve the situation? What's best for the whole picture?* Imagine taking yourself out of it and ask, *If I were dead and yet still able to act, what would I do?* Or simply show up, and engage in the spirit of service and trust intuition to guide your actions.

If you start down this line of fully aware inquiry and your inner voice comes roaring back with resistance, as in, "I don't give a damn about all that, I just want [fill in the blank]!" that is your springboard for this flip; you've come to the icy knot that will have to melt to make this flip possible. See if you can name what need is screaming to be met, and get to know it. Shine some awareness on it; it may not melt in the first light, but neither will it get all of you, because the part that's aware is not itself needy. Hear deeply your inner voice of resistance and imagine flipping it. Examples are given in Table 8.1.

Table 8.1

Flipping the Voice of Resistance

Need Level	Voice of resistance is saying...	Flip to...
Physical	I don't have the energy to deal with this. I'm so tired. I'm exhausted. I'm sick.	I have access to more energy now if I breathe deeply and slowly. What's exhausting me that I can let go of? I will recharge and come back to this.
Security	I need more money for family, college, retirement, etc. I need to keep my job no matter what. I'm afraid of what's going to happen to me.	We can be resourceful living with just enough. If I over-indulge myself or my family, the gravity of greed is enormous. No matter what, I can add my best value. I am not separate from life; it doesn't happen *to* me.

Affiliation	I'm afraid if I do this, people won't like me. I need to be included, in the know. I need to keep this person happy.	If this is what the situation calls for, it will eventually be in people's interests. If I keep moving toward the things that are deeply important to me, I'll be included in the right things. I truly don't serve this person by turning him into a bully; what's really right for this person right now?
Personal Power	I have something to prove. I need to be right. I can't stand it that this person has disrespected me. I'll use this person because I can.	Try to prove, and the case is never closed; serve life, and the case never comes up. The more I open up, the bigger "right" gets. What else is right here? Other people act out of their own needs; it has nothing to do with me, and I don't need to make it about me. What's truly in this person's interests?

Self-Actualization	I have so much to do. The work is never done. I'm so busy. I must achieve this dream, vision, or mission. I'm only as good as my last achievement; I need to achieve again.	I don't have to keep achieving to know I'm alive. I can pace myself, and tend to what's essential. This dream, vision, or mission has energized me; I need to keep listening to life for how it might change and how to grow with it. Serve life, and I move beyond the question.

The more you flip around resistant needs, the more you'll understand your own stuck points, the less they'll get all of you, and the less potent they'll become over time. The needs will not go away, but you'll be better able to meet them just enough to get them off the table.

You may start down this line of inquiry or enter a situation in the spirit of service and *still* have no idea what to do. You're not sensing resistance; you're not sensing anything. In that case, wait. Do nothing. Listen. The situation may be best served by staying out of it. Be open to that possibility.

Finally, you may start down this line of inquiry or enter a situation in the spirit of service and find that certain actions suggest themselves. Enter them completely, extend your energy, and serve the situation. You've made the flip.

Listen and learn. As you act, pay attention. Listen to life. Listen for whether your actions come from a place of easy acceptance, or even joy. As we've seen before, these are reliable markers of connectedness. You can also listen for whether your actions get easier or harder, whether they give you energy or drain your energy. You can notice whether you're acting from the best within you, and whether you're feeling a sense of progress. For situations in which influencing others is involved, you can listen for resonance and whether your efforts are catching on with more people.

Not listening was perhaps my biggest mistake in my blind pursuit of the astronaut dream. If I had been listening to life I would have noticed that my actions were not bringing joy, but rather more tension and a sense of living an imposter's life. I would have noticed my heart was worsening. I would have sensed that if this dream was truly right for me, it wouldn't require me to violate my values and hide truths. I wouldn't have had to listen all those hard-to-catch these signals; indeed, I had to virtually plug my ears and go "La, la, la, la, la" to miss life screaming at me. But so it goes.

Learning comes from that bit of reflection that lets us see how we served the situation, figure out what happened, and make any adjustments for the future. The focus on learning is ever so much more productive than a focus on judging—another thing it took me years to learn. As a consummate Organizer, I was always judging myself and wanting to be perfect. I didn't reflect in an easy spirit of learning because it might reveal that I hadn't performed perfectly the first time. But self-judgment is another way to get caught up in our own neediness—meeting our own need to be right, have self-esteem, be safe, whatever. Excessive self-judgment serves us as poorly as does excessive eating.

Flip judgment to learning and the energy turns around from neurotic self-focus to an exploration of our engagement with life. We are both the experiment and the experimenter, and every situation can show us something new.

Putting It to Work: Getting Out of Your Own Way

Throughout this book you've had several chances to reflect on your direction as a leader: your vision and approach, the world you would manifest, and ways to connect, attract, and bring that about. Applying this flip, we pull those thoughts together into the clearest articulation of what it is that you're about right now. Recognizing—as in the case of my dream to be an astronaut—that this "it" can still be laden with self-doubts and personal needs that make it still somehow "all about us," we do well to peel the onion down another layer and see if we can get out of our own way in service of "it." If we're using "it" to serve our needs, at best, it will only add another piece of temporary evidence in the endless lawsuit of self-worth; that is, the endless case we argue against ourselves to prove we're smart enough, good enough, safe enough, or whatever "enough" to settle our fears. If we can get out of our own way, the Zen leader in us serves "it" for the sake of the whole picture. The results are cleaner, and the joy of functioning in this way becomes its own reward.

Perhaps you already have insight, from the reflection at the start of this chapter, into the needs that create the greatest hunger for you. Bring that insight to bear now, as you explore a need you would like to melt, and how that may open up even greater space for the "it" you are about. Grab some paper and give yourself a chance to speak to these questions:

1. When I'm at my best, how do I serve life today? What value do I create? How do I create that value?

2. How do my needs support me in adding this value? How do they get in the way?

   ☯ Physical (need for rest, food, health, energy, sex)

   ☯ Security (need for safety, protection, money)

   ☯ Affiliation (need for friendship, love, approval, warmth)

   ☯ Personal power (need to prove myself, dominate, be recognized, be respected)

☯ Self-actualization (need to achieve, accomplish a mission, create)

3. What need am I most likely to over-indulge? What is a typical thing I tell myself when I'm in blind pursuit of meeting this need?

4. What are three ways to flip around and restate that typical thing I tell myself?

5. If I were to follow this flipped-around advice, how might I create even greater value? If I were to take my needs out of it, how could I be truly "all about it"?

You can run through these questions, not only for the Big "It" you would serve, but also for the practical goals and activities in front of you every day. If you start into these questions and don't know how you serve life, or can't think of the greatest value you could add, come down to a practical level and ask simply, *What am I trying to accomplish right now? And how am I going about it?* Then take a look at how your needs help or hinder. Consider where you get stuck, and what you tell yourself to reinforce that stuckness. Then see how you can flip that around by inverting it, shifting its focus, or assuming the opposite, and see if that approach wouldn't give you more room to pursue your present goals.

Although I didn't ask these questions exactly, they represent the process Glenn—who wanted so much to be promoted—went through in our coaching. Somewhere between the need for personal power and achievement he was stuck on the promotion as a way to eat again at the trough of being affirmed for his achievement and held in high esteem. Things he would typically tell himself ran along the lines of how much *he* had to do, why *he* had to take on this new assignment, and how hard *he* was working. When I asked him how he'd work differently if he suddenly didn't have to worry about the promotion, his first answer was, "I wouldn't do so much myself. I'd get other people to do things."

Hello! Some people might even call that a *definition* of leadership. Why not do that now? "Forget the promotion?" he repeated with fading disbelief. And then new insights started tumbling out of his mouth: Yes, he could forget about being noticed, and enable others. He could forget about who gets credit, and help the right things happen. He could lead the whole context—the entirety of what's happening, rather than one small point or area—and let the chips fall as they may. He'd begun as a case study of how leadership looks small if it gets stuck on validating one's self-in-the-skin, and moments later, his face softened, his shoulders relaxed, and he expressed the possibilities of leadership for the sake of others. Glenn made the flip.

Leadership for the sake of others might sound noble, but forget about being noble—that might be just another trait the ego wants to take credit for. The fact is, when leadership truly *is* for the sake of others, it's a win-win. It's more effective *and* we feel more joy. We feel more joy because we're not stuck. It's more effective because it settles a primal, brainstem question that is always being asked about leaders: "Do I want to follow you?" "Do I trust that in the moment of truth, you won't be in it just for yourself?" If we sense that a leader is still principally building her own case, meeting her own needs, something in us does not want to follow. We don't want to be in the death seat.

Conversely, when we work with a true steward, one who is creating a more valuable world for the sake of others, it brings out the best in us and we get bigger. When a great leader like President Kennedy reminds a nation, "Ask not what your country can do for you; ask what you can do for your country," he pulls people up Maslow's hierarchy toward a greater sense of who they can be in service to others. By contrast, the politician who promises it's all about you, and that he'll go the Capital to "bring back your money," draws people down into angry selfishness. As leaders, we are not only tending to our own hierarchy of needs, but inspiring (or dragging) others up (or down) Maslow's hierarchy as well. As we draw more people up toward their self-actualizing potential, we see more creativity, agility, spontaneity, and broad-based thinking, and less fear.

When we follow a leader who is "all about it," we are larger. We commit more, we engage more, we express that discretionary effort that no one can command from us. When we *are* that leader who is "all about it," "it" manifests more completely through us in the Now, without the footprints of self-doubt or self-glorification; without a legal case for self-worth being fought on the side. Without siphoning off excess energy to feed our self, more energy goes to serving the situation. As our net of concern expands beyond the self-in-our-skin, we become less partial to our own needs and more available to the whole picture.

From partial to whole, from serving our local self to freely actualizing our whole self, we could say this is the ultimate flip of leadership. As we'll see, it is not a new flip altogether, but rather a way of putting together our whole journey.

The Zen Leader

Flip 8 Takeaways

"It's All About Me" to "I'm All About It"

Manage your energy to have fuel for this flip, and keep an awareness of serving your needs "just enough" at any level.

Serve the situation with a question like, *How can I add value here?*

Listen and learn for insight, progress, or joy.

Getting out of your own way:

- ❧ **Take stock.** How do I create value today? How do my needs support that and how do they get in the way?

- ❧ **Target a need.** Which need most gets in my way? What do I tell myself when I go after this need?

- ❧ **Flip it.** What are three ways to restate that need? How would I invert it, let it go, or assume the opposite?

- ❧ **Explore.** What new value could I create if I lived this way?

9

From Local Self to Whole Self

THE DEFINITION OF a "whole leader" is the topic I've posed to a group of executives who have come to a program for Developing the Whole Leader. A grocery list of traits are served up: gets the big picture and the details, drives results, gets it done, is good with people, thinks short-term and long-term, has a clear focus but still listens, balances work and life, can handle ambiguity, works well with diverse people...and so on. Basically, someone who can do a whole lot, whose grocery bag of abilities is stuffed with every possible food group.

From the perspective of the local self, becoming a whole leader can feel like endless (and exhausting!) shopping for new skills—whatever's all the rage in leadership books or business schools this year. Flipping into the perspective of the whole self, there's nothing to acquire; no "becoming" is required, because one already *is*. From this perspective, what's whole about whole leadership is simply being the whole picture.

The skeptics in the Whole Leader program are not convinced. "Sounds too easy," they say. They believe it's easy because they see it as a thought to think, or a claim to make, as in, "I think I'm the whole picture, therefore I am," to mangle Descartes. In truth, it's more akin to, "I am the whole picture, and one of the things I do is think." Seeing this calls for deep work, because at the surface, the only "I" we recognize is our local ego. This self-in-the-skin, this token player on the game board of life, initially consumes our attention, commands that its needs be met, and causes a kind of amnesia in which we forget that we are also the whole picture.

But, as we'll review, several threads of experience point to our intrinsic wholeness whenever we see beyond the boundary of our local self. We'll also see that even the boundary of our local self keeps expanding as we develop. Even with our amnesia, this flip to wholeness can be helped along by imagining we are the whole picture and asking, *How would I handle this situation?* For example, imagine you're implementing a 15-percent cost reduction. If you work it from the perspective of the local self, even if you try to be fair, you will generally serve the local self (including its need to be seen as fair). But if you imagine you're the whole picture—the people who will be laid off, the people who will remain, the customers and community who will be affected, the overall company whose health you want to ensure—you'll act to the best of your abilities to create the best solution for the whole picture.

If we think we are leading something other than ourselves, we're constantly fumbling around in our grocery bag of skills trying to find one that will have the desired effect. But if we know we're the whole picture, we can draw on any aspect of our self, and create shifts in that picture as naturally as if we're working with our own body. That doesn't mean anything goes, just as working with our body doesn't mean we can land a backflip on a balance beam or fix a failing kidney. But it does mean we act in the realization that only one thing is going on, and we're a part of it, which is our functioning as a Zen leader.

This chapter applies the flip of local self to whole self, which ties together our whole flipping journey. We'll explore how the flip to wholeness transforms everyday challenges leaders face, such as cutbacks, growth, or tough performance conversations. You'll find that this flip is a natural extension of a development process that, all along, has been casting a wider net. In the flip from local self to whole self, that net becomes the universe, our whole self is Now, and the change we would lead is manifest through our own transformation.

In the words of Lao Tzu, "Be really whole—the valley of the universe—and all things will come to you."

What "Self" Do You Know?

"Know thyself" is how Plato put it. Plato and Lao Tzu were near contemporaries in different parts of the world, anchoring what came to be Western and Eastern ways of thought. They point to the same truth from opposite directions. We may equate Plato's advice with knowing our strengths and weaknesses, our heritage, our culture, what we stand for, and so on. This kind of self-awareness is important. "The difference between success and failure in leadership," Joseph Badaracco writes, "is not skill, technique, credentials, networking, or even experience. It is the clarity about who one is."[1] But clarity regarding "who one is" goes far beyond the ego's self-appraisal. In the end, to "know thyself" is to know we are the entire universe. But along the way, we see only the partial view, not the whole. When we look at who we are through the lens of the ego, everything we see is another part of ego. It is like looking at the world through a telescope; everything we see fits into a set circle. Thinking we fit into that circle, we miss our boundless nature and think we're far more fixed than we are.

"How many of you think that people can change?" I ask the Whole Leader group, and only a few hands are raised. "Sure, we can change some behaviors," someone offers, "But we're pretty fixed underneath;

we're still our DNA selves." Really? I'm thinking back to biochemistry classes where I learned how mutable DNA is to cosmic rays, how different parts of a gene are expressed under different conditions with radically different results—including cancer. Granted, personality is more enduring than mood, but as I ask the group, "How can we not be changing? Name me one thing in the universe that is not changing." Silence. I pick up a chair and ask, "Is this changing?" Yes, slowly, they acknowledge. How much faster must we be changing with all our biological moving parts, new thoughts by the moment, learning lessons, living life? Okay, we're changing, but still they think there's some core that is "me"—my circle, even though the telescopic scene keeps changing. We might flip the question around, I suggest, and ask, "If something's not changing, what's holding it in place?"

What makes our local self seem static is our frame of reference, which *is* our local self! It's akin to not noticing the Earth is moving because our frame of reference is standing on the Earth. So we make the same mistake in our self-concept as we made in our early astronomy: assuming we're fixed and at the center. But if we look more closely and consider our past, we will notice that our self-image and clarity about who we are has changed every step of the way. You can see this for yourself as you reflect on your own development, a journey we can guide with a great deal of research.[2]

Picture 2-year-old you, with your newly minted ego and two of your first, most mighty words: "Mine!" for everything you wanted and "No!" for everything you didn't want. The emergence of these words comes with the formation of an ego boundary, and pretty strong feelings about what gets to cross that boundary. Your only identification was with the self-in-your-skin. You learned to identify your self with a name: Jean, we'll say. But you couldn't yet reason or empathize. Your narcissistic world was pretty simple and small.

Add a few more years of family relationships and socialization, and your sense of who you are expands to include identification with a certain family, a certain community. In some cultures that are more group-oriented (for example, organized by family, tribe, or caste) this identification with group becomes even more important than who you are as an individual. But even in individualistic societies such as the United States, this sense of belonging surrounds the self-in-one's-skin with a broadened sense of identity. It's not just "Jean" anymore; it's "Jean Jones."

Wait just a minute, individual-you may protest. *Even as we develop a sense of belonging and love for our family, we don't think we are that parent or sister. We're still me-in-my-skin who* has *a parent or sister.* But this is like saying, "I'm still the circle," even though the scene has changed considerably. Look more closely and you'll see that your self-concept has added something new: You're not all alone anymore, isolated and vulnerable. There are people who love you, people you can count on, and your sense of self absorbs this bigger picture; your net is a little wider. If this weren't true, you wouldn't be reading this book: Children who pass through this stage unloved and unconnected to other human beings do not develop normally or become leaders.

Belonging to a group, you learn that it has rules, order, a sense of right and wrong. You learn about consequences as you do (or don't) follow those rules. You begin to think a bit more abstractly; you can count in your head. Your sense of self starts to include more abstract ideas, such as "I'm Jean Jones, and I'm a good girl who makes mommy and daddy proud." A few years ago, you didn't even know what *good* or *proud-making* was, and now you *are* it.

Add some more years, and logic and empathy have a chance to develop. Your self-concept may grow from conforming to rebelling, from being a nobody in school to being "class clown" or "the smart kid." Increasingly, you learn what you're good at and bad at, and what you love and hate, and your self-concept keeps expanding to claim these elements as part of its personality. Looking carefully, you'll notice that your circle of caring, concern, and power also keeps expanding. You can now care about starving children in another part of the world, worry about the future, or join a student protest on campus. You're casting a wider net.

Keep going, and you're adding skills, experience, and titles to your self-concept, some of which make it onto resumes and into job interviews.

It's not just "Jean Jones" anymore; it's Jean Jones, with a degree in pharmacology and a Harvard MBA, who can speak fluent Mandarin, and has 367 followers on Twitter. If you've been promoted in your career, you'll see that each level further expands your net of concerns and sense of who you are. At first you're an individual contributor, concerned with your own performance and building relationships. As a team leader or manager, your concerns widen to the combined performance of a team and the development of its members. You may go on to become a manager of managers, the head of a business unit or a company, with each role, casting a wider net.

Consciousness itself develops through this process, as what you're aware of and might call the "big picture" itself grows bigger. At first you might celebrate only your own success. But after running a team for a while, you might become even more pleased to see others succeed. If you're a district sales manager, your net of concern might be helping your team hit sales targets despite regional downturns. If you're a national sales manager, your net of concern might expand to include the economic conditions of the entire country, and where to make strategic investments.

But again, you may protest that these are just wider concerns that "I" have—*They don't really change "me"; somehow I'm still under here, like a fixed mannequin who has put on more layers of clothes.* Yet read back through these paragraphs: Where was there ever a "you" that wasn't changing? The more you look for this fixed mannequin, the more you see it doesn't exist, can't possibly exist, and that you only thought it existed because you mistook your self for the "circle" of the lens you were looking through.

The Whole Self Revealed

Still, as long as ego is strong and life is busy, amnesia is steadily reinforced and we forget that we are any more than the small circle of our local self. But if you look at people who, for one reason or another, have had the experience of the boundary of local self falling away, what remains, and what they may attempt to express, is their whole self.

For Jill Bolte Taylor, it came quite literally as a stroke of insight,[3] and, as a neuroanatomist, she had unusual insight into her experience. She understood well the differing characteristics of the brain's two hemispheres: the serial-processing left hemisphere, whose functioning is more like Driver-Organizer, I-centered "doing," versus the parallel-processing right hemisphere, more like Collaborator-Visionary, "being." On the left we have a calculating intelligence that thinks in language, which it endlessly chatters in, and "I" am most definitely separate from you. On the right we experience the world kinesthetically, sensing images and interconnected waves of energy comprising a whole.[4]

It was this "I'm in control" left hemisphere that Jill Bolte Taylor lost in a sudden stroke. She describes her experience vividly: "I looked at my arm and couldn't define its boundary...all the molecules ran together, all were energy." She felt completely one with the energy abounding through her, and mind chatter ceased as if someone pressed a mute button. This gorgeous "la la land" was interrupted with the thought, "We have a problem." While one part of her was euphorically shedding 37 years of emotional baggage, another part was registering, "We have to get help."

Not easy to do without being able to discern phone numbers, or speak beyond the garble of "rah RAH rah rah rah." But eventually she succeeded and help arrived. In the ambulance ride to the hospital, she felt "the last bit of air squeezed out of a balloon." Her spirit surrendered and she knew she was no longer in control of her life. Drifting between two planes of reality, she felt "liberated like a genie from her bottle," and that she could "never squeeze the enormity of myself back into this little body." She is shocked to find out later that she *is* still alive. "Is this possible?" she wondered. Is it possible for "people to purposely choose to stand to the right of their left hemispheres?" Bringing the possibility of this insight to people gave her the will to get well. For years she has been sharing her story, perfectly expressing the paradox of human existence: "We are the life power of the universe with manual dexterity."

Brendon Burchard describes a similar experience following a terrible car accident from which he barely emerged, broken and bloody, through what was once the windshield. He looked up and saw a full moon, but no ordinary "I" was seeing. As he recounts it, "...so close, so big and bright, so beautiful. I felt lifted from the wreckage of my life and deeply connected with the heavens and waves of blue streaking across the night sky...a nothingness of silence.... And then, slowly, a feeling of centeredness...I never felt more connected to who I was."[5] He went on to put his "second chance" at life to extraordinary use in helping others share their expertise and becoming quite the Millionaire Messenger himself.

Remarkable as these stories are, they're not unique. They match the experiences of many others who are still conscious near their death as the ego structure dissolves. With the dissolution of ego, so goes the boundary of our "circle" and our usual self-concept. What's left is an all-pervasive, peaceful oneness, variously described in the deathbed utterances of the enlightened mind as "melting into all this beauty."[6]

The third stream of experience in which people see beyond their local selves is that of countless mystics and meditators from every culture and spiritual tradition. Those in whom consciousness unfolds to its fullest all have the same awakening: "I am that," in the words of Gautama Buddha; "Be still and know that I am [God]," in the words of Psalm 46:10. In our ordinary thinking, we interpret the Psalm from the perspective of the local self hearing God "out there." Yet when we dissolve the boundary of the local self, there is no "out there." Such is the experience of oneness, of Being, of mystics through the ages. Note that the Psalm did not suggest, "Run around like a crazy person and know that I am." Like the whirring blades of a fan, the faster we go, the more solid we seem. But when we slow down our local self enough to see through the blades of the fan, the whole view emerges: I am.

Casting a Wider Net

This entire journey of development is not only ours personally, but also the evolutionary story of our species, our societies, and our cultures—a story brilliantly integrated by Ken Wilber[7] and summarized in

Table 9.1. Some of the stages that Wilber and others define have been combined for simplicity in my table, and I've added some examples of how each stage expresses itself in leadership. What's evident through these stages of development is that "I" casts an ever-wider net, starting with the dot of "I" surviving in a dangerous world and culminating in "I am"—one with everything.

Table 9.1
Development of Individuals, Societies, and Leaders

Stage of Development	Focus	Examples	What Leaders Say
Instinctual, animistic	Survival, magical	Primitive tribes, infants, superstition, tooth fairy, blood oaths, make-believe. Collaborator, Visionary (drama, imagination, security through bonding)	"Are you food?" "I bring down the wrath of gods to curse your tribe!"
Power Gods	Dominance, win/lose	Feudal empires, "terrible 2s," teenage rebellion, frontier mentality. Driver (security through fighting)	"Might is right." "Look out for #1." "Crush your enemy."

Mythic Order (pre-modern)	Obedience, right/wrong	Fundamentalism, 4-year-olds, codes of conduct, patriotism, law and order. Organizer (security through obedience)	"I'm right, and if you don't agree with me, you know what that makes you." "Are you with me or against me?" "[Our] God is mighty; death to the infidels."
Rationality (modern)	Logic, achievement	The Enlightenment, capitalism, industrial revolution, Wall Street, materialism, self-reliance. Driver, Organizer (autonomous self)	"I'm right, and I'll bombard you with data until you agree." "Technology is the answer." "Surely all rational minds can agree."

Sensitive Self (post-modern)	Community, relationships	Green movement, networking, collaboration, embracing diversity, animal rights, EQ (emotional intelligence). Collaborator, Visionary (connected self)	"We're all in this together. We need to reach consensus." "Our competitors are also our customers and partners." "We need to consider the long term, and future generations."
Integrative, Holistic	Flex and flow, purpose	Global mindset, recognizing and fostering all stages; spontaneity, unification theories. All energy patterns as needed	"There are multiple right ways that we need to optimize together." "We're all connected." "Fail fast and often, learn and re-launch."
Causal	Unity consciousness	[local] self-transcendence, formless mysticism	"All is one." "I am that." "In non-action we do everything."

That's not to say we all make it through all of these stages—certainly we don't all live to tell about it. As we said with Maslow's hierarchy, we don't scale these stages linearly, once and for all, or all at once. Rather, our progress is halting, back and forth, covering several stages at the same time, and is uneven within our self (for example, our intellectual development may be well ahead of our emotional development). Most adults mostly function in the stages of Mythic Order and Rationality, and these are the dominant levels of consciousness seen in mass movements, be they religious fundamentalism, political demagoguery, or Wall Street capitalism. About 15 percent of the adult population centers in the stage of the Sensitive Self, and less than 2 percent in stages beyond that.[8]

Yet only at these latter stages does a truly global mindset emerge, one that makes the flip from *Or* to *And*, from "it's all about me" to "I'm all about it," and that honors and works with all of the energy patterns and the diversity of humanity at all of its stages. As we've seen, these latter stages—the leading edge of our collective consciousness—is exactly where leadership is most successful in our speedy, complex, interconnected world. The pressure to do more and be more that is felt by the best leaders is exactly the necessity fueling the flips into these stages. Even if we, or the people we lead, don't function here all the time, we can still be pulled up (and pull others up) toward the best within us—as in President Kennedy's call to service—or be pulled down (and pull others down) to our lowest common denominator. *Oh yeah? Up yours.*

Leaders who function at these higher stages of development rarely experience themselves as being whole enough to say, "I am that." But they will frequently say things like, "I care more about my people than myself." Or, "I am committed to doing the right thing for our customers, and the rewards will follow." Expansive statements like these attract people who want to be part of a worthy undertaking or glorious vision. People are drawn to leaders from whom they sense a reciprocal caring; they feel safer with leaders who see the bigger picture and are not afraid to face it. And fear has no room to grow in leaders who feel a part of, not apart from, the whole context in which they lead.

By contrast, the leader about whom others say, "He's only in it for himself," speaks to the fear-producing smallness of a person who leads beyond what he truly cares about, whose self-concept is mostly self-in-the-skin. This mindset wreaks havoc in our world, setting off chain reactions of negative consequences from broke economies to broken trust to burnout. As collective consciousness edges forward, more people—especially the younger generations—can sense that this smallness does not serve, and they want no part of it. Turn that around, let the Zen leader emerge, and one expands to a boundless clarity about who one is, encompassing the entire the world one is creating.

Energy Patterns Show the Way

As noted in Table 9.1, various energy patterns can be identified with each stage of development. That's not to say one pattern is more mature than another; a sage can still use Driver energy. But we can characterize each stage of development as centering on a particular pattern. It's useful to know this connection, for nothing accelerates our development through these stages more than mindfulness in the body, and the patterns can show the way.

As you experienced earlier in flipping from Driver to Visionary energy, Visionary calls for less physical tension. The connection to self-concept is so obvious it's easy to miss: The more tense the body, the more one's sense of self is localized and tightly focused. If you tense your whole body for a moment and burn your eyes into this paper, you'll feel a contraction and density that makes your sense of self solid and separate. Contrast that with the languid expansiveness of the flowing Visionary—go ahead, relax and feel energy flow through your entire being. You'll feel yourself diffusing and expanding generously.

So just as our sense of self changes as we develop, so does it change as we move through the various patterns. For most people, their strongest one or two patterns reflect the sense of self they live in and work from most of the time. Do you recognize yours?

- ☯ **Driver:** A mostly in-the-skin sense of self: an independent agent and self-starter; may be poor at listening to others; likes competing and winning.

- ☯ **Organizer:** An individual sense of self, but oriented by a strong moral compass and conscientious duty to others; relates to others best one person at a time.

- ☯ **Collaborator:** Senses self more in relation to others, and less as an individual; is oriented toward people and groups; builds consensus; engages and empathizes.

- ☯ **Visionary:** Senses self more in context, for example, as a part of society, history, or nature; a fluid sense of self, oriented toward essence, the future, and natural harmony.

To recap our journey in terms of these stages of development, clearly one way to expand one's sense of self, especially coming from the stage of Rationality or a Driver-Organizer mindset, is to move into Collaborator and Visionary. We put this expanded sense of self to good use in the flips from controlling to connecting, from driving results to attracting the future. We've also seen how the patterns support us in our own authentic expression of the paradoxical traits of whole leadership: being steady (Organizer) yet agile (Visionary), shrewd (Driver) yet trustworthy (Organizer-Collaborator), and so on. Being able to strengthen our play by using any pattern as it's called for propels us toward the Integrative stage of development. It's no accident that only when we make peace with and use of these four energies in our self do we embrace the diversity of humanity and honor the patterns and stages of all people. At the Integrative stage and beyond, we can be "all about it," connected with life, and recognize that all possibilities exist within our boundless self.

Leading the Whole Picture of Newark

Geoff Colvin is interviewing Newark, New Jersey's mayor, Cory Booker, for *Fortune* magazine.[9] Booker has recently made headlines, along with Facebook's Mark Zuckerberg, announcing the latter's $100 million pledge to revitalize Newark's schools. "How did you do it?"

Colvin asks Booker about landing this most generous donation. Booker's first response is, "I don't think it was me." He goes on to explain that Zuckerberg had been independently coming to the idea of a major philanthropic act and concludes simply, "...it was two men with the same idea meeting up."

No chest-thumping. No "it's all about me." Whether you like Cory Booker or not, is it not utterly refreshing to hear a political leader pass on taking credit? It instantly inspires a kind of trust as we sense a leader who's bigger than himself-in-his-skin. How ironic that in promoting our local self, we make our self smaller in the eyes of others, and in effacing our local self, others glimpse the bigness within us.

What comes across in the Colvin interview is that Booker has cast a wide net of what he loves and cares about that embraces all of Newark, and he is leading as though he's that whole picture. He describes his Office of Reentry, for example—an innovative support network for men coming out of prison—with empathy, not judgment, for the human beings it serves. "We organized sort of a fraternity...to support our men in reducing their recidivism, but really connecting to their families because the children most likely to go to prison in America are the children of incarcerated adults." The result of this caring? "Our fatherhood program has about a 3 percent recidivism rate," Booker says, compared with the national average of 65 percent.

Booker's net of concerns somehow matches him. His self-image exactly matches his current role. When he's asked about taking on a national role, he says, "I really feel...there's no better place to be than doing what I'm doing right now." When we flip from indulging the local self to serving the whole picture, synchronicity has room to operate, like-minded support coalesces, and the calculus of what's possible is transformed. As Booker goes on to say, "We're taking on the problems people say are impossible to solve, and we're showing that you can create hope and do the improbable, maybe even the impossible." Cory Booker may not experience himself as whole enough to say, "I am that," but he certainly recognizes he can access something greater than his local self. "I'm a strong guy," he says. "But when I join with other people, I feel that we're manifesting some invincibility."

The Zen Leader Flip 9: Local Self to Whole Self

Still, so long as the ego is strong and our lives are busy, we may not experience ourselves as the whole picture. Rather, we're more likely to experience a somewhat fixed self doing a whole lot of things. But we can approach this flip as something of a thought experiment, using our imagination. Casting a wider net of concern, imagining we are that entire picture, we will gain insight that is less partial, more enduring, more whole. The more we practice, even in our imagination, the more we'll notice our sense of self becoming more fluid, less restricted, until imagination becomes reality. As Albert Einstein observed, "Your imagination is your preview of life's coming attractions." In this flip we put that imagination to great use.

Widen the net. If you were to slap yourself in the face—try this at your own risk—you'll notice that you don't actually hurt yourself. Even before your hand strikes your face and triggers your nervous system, there's already an implicit "knowing" that regulates how hard you strike. It's as if your hand knows it's part of a bigger picture that includes your face.

> The Zen Leader
> Flip 9
> Local Self to Whole Self
>
> ☯ Widen the net
> ☯ Imagine what if...
> ☯ Imagination becomes reality

Likewise, we can apply this mindset to daily business challenges and leadership practices by functioning as part of the bigger picture in which we're acting. How big is this picture? It depends on the situation, our sensitivity, and the extent of our imagination, but we can start with knowing it's bigger than our self-in-our-skin, and widen the net.

If we are dealing with a poor-performing employee, we can widen the net to become that person, and sense what is truly in her interests.

If we are part of a team that needs to become more cohesive and high-performing, we can widen the net to include the customers and stakeholders the team serves, the situation it's facing, the team itself as a whole, and each member individually. In view of all of this, we can create progress.

If we are trying to launch or revitalize a business, we can widen the net to include our customers and would-be customers, our competitors and partners, our products and services, and our employees and culture, and sense what serves the whole. The wide net we cast can embrace anything: people and situations, abstract concepts, data from the past, and possibilities from the future.

Whoa! you may be thinking, *That's a lot to hold. How do we ever move forward taking all that into account?* But this is an example of how leaders themselves have to transform to become as big as the situation in which they lead. Consciousness itself has to *expand* to function effectively with expanded responsibilities. That may seem like too much work, but the alternative is worse: if we think small while holding big jobs, we find ourselves continually blindsided and barely managing in a world that seems to be happening to us. When people say of a leader, he or she is "not strategic enough," they're sensing this mismatch between the leader's consciousness and the size of the job.

On the upside, widening the net to be as big as the situations we face is how we find our power to play with them. And it is more of an ongoing *play* than a one-time task. For once we consider a wide net of interests, we will find more than one right way of doing things. We'll have to apply our ability to think in paradox and hold ambiguity. We're never once-and-for-all right, because our net has embraced a system that never stops, in which every action creates a chain reaction. But what we can do is make our best judgment, take our best action, listen, learn, and adjust—the very things we've been practicing through our flips to connecting and attracting the future.

When we widen the net, we do well to "hold" its contents lightly—the way you might "hold" the Internet as a sea of possibility. We cannot hold it literally, any more than we can get to the square root of 2 by counting on our fingers. We need our imagination, which is where the flip to more Visionary energy can help. Even visually, as you move from the Driver's tight, single-point focus (remember sighting down your fingers?) to the expansive (hands at the sides of the head) Visionary, you widen your net. You'll notice that you cannot "hold" the whole picture as tightly as if you zeroed in on just one thing, but you can sense the whole visual context all at once. With practice, you'll come to trust this perspective, not as a way to thread a needle, but as a way to sense connections and large-scale patterns. This simple physical practice will similarly open your mind to cast a wider net and trust the intuition that emerges when consciousness expands beyond the concerns of the local self.

The flip to more Collaborator energy also helps widen the net, as it connects us with all the players in the picture to the point at which we can, like Cory Booker, manifest invincibility with others. A way to use Collaborator energy to widen the net is to get a feel for the stories of the various players in the picture: *What are they passionate about? What are their needs? What is their day like, and how is the situation we're considering playing into that?* You can use your imagination, but when possible, actually experience their reality, and let it inform your empathy and intuition. Feeling into the stories of others, and the stories of the future we would create, we widen the net.

Imagine what if... What if you are that whole picture? With your net cast wide, imagine you are all the players and conditions. As we saw in the flip from "it's all about me" to "I'm all about it," this net is not some kind of separate "it" you would serve; it is *you*. Now how would you serve *you*?

Perhaps your first reaction is confusion: so many conflicting perspectives, needs, desires! So many ways you can't get there from here...it can all seem paralyzing. But this is the anxious thinking of the local self, which is exactly the fuel for this flip, because when we're thinking like our local self, it *is* too much. So let go of the local self. Relax, and enter the Collaborator's sense of play, and the Visionary's ability to hold things loosely. Relax, imagine you are the whole picture, and let intuition operate with your good intentions. You don't have to be perfect, because there is no single "perfect" once multiple agendas come together, but that's okay. Just know you can continue to listen, learn, and adjust as you go. You can do this.

So, for example, say you're handing down a new policy for expense control. You know it's necessary for the health of the company, but you also know it won't be popular. Widen your net and imagine you are the people who will receive it. Thinking as the recipients of this policy, what will be your (in other words, their) first reaction? What are your concerns? What would help you understand why this policy is in your long-term interests? Reflecting on answers to these questions, you might recognize that fairness will be a big issue in people's minds, and they might be wondering if layoffs are next. You'll know to address these concerns when you craft and communicate your message.

Imagining yourself as the whole picture, the needs of the local self will still emerge. You'll still get tired and need to rest. You'll still find yourself falling into coping reactions now and then. This is all part of the whole picture, and having these thoughts is not wrong. Yet if you're able to tend to the needs of the local self just enough, and if you can remind yourself that your greatest need is to be your greatest self—in other words, the whole picture—you will keep pulling yourself up Maslow's hierarchy, up to where whole self-actualization becomes local self-transcendence, up to where you act as the whole picture. Up to leading fearlessly.

Imagination becomes reality. What starts as a thought experiment becomes a habit. What starts as arm's-length understanding becomes deeply informed empathy. What begins as a net that includes one or two others eventually includes multiple stakeholders and complex scenarios. Just as we hone our sensitivity to music by listening to many varieties of it, so we hone our sensitivity to being the whole picture by listening to all of its facets. As we care more about the whole picture, we'll listen more to other people, recognizing that they represent crucial perspectives in the whole. As our sensitivity increases, our imagination and intuition become better informed and more realistic. Even if this flip starts in imagination, as our imagination becomes more realistic, our actions are better tuned, and more resonant within the whole context.

Through this process of flipping to our whole self, our local self is changed. We are changed in what we notice, what we think, and how we act. Because we are changed, a new reality is possible in the Now. As we flip from local self to whole self, we manifest a whole new picture. And eventually, we don't have to imagine *what if* we were the whole picture. We can say with utter clarity, "I am that!"

Putting It to Work: Local Self to Whole Self

What challenging opportunity do you face? You can apply this flip to situations big and little, from growing your business to improving an important work dynamic. To make this flip utterly practical, start by thinking of an utterly practical goal to which you'd like to apply it. It may be a goal that supports the vision you want to attract. It may be a goal about how you can add even greater value, or deal with a current problem. Pick a goal you'd like to put to this flip.

State your goal. Start with the words, *How to...*, and state what it is you're trying to accomplish or bring about.

Write down your current "local self" answer to this question. What are you doing now with respect to this goal?

If you've picked a broad goal, such as "How to grow my business," your answers might be elements of your current strategy; for example:

☯ Deepen current customer relationships.

☯ Advertise more.

☯ Create strategic partnerships.

If you've picked a specific goal, such as "How to coach Sally to help improve her performance," your current local-self answer might be steps you've taken, such as:

- ☯ Monthly meetings.

- ☯ On-the-spot feedback.

- ☯ Showing her how to do things right.

You don't have to be exhaustive; a few answers are enough. You just want to capture your current answers or see how they might change from a wider point of view.

Widen your net. Draw a picture of four concentric circles, as in Figure 9.1.

At the center (Circle 1) is your local self, or "me." In the first circle out (Circle 2), identify the players who are directly connected to your goal. These can be individuals or groups; people whom you consider to be in your "inner circle" related to this goal.

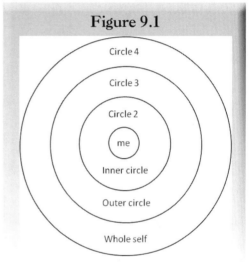

Figure 9.1

Circle 4
Circle 3
Circle 2
me
Inner circle
Outer circle
Whole self

In the next circle out (Circle 3), identify a few other players who are related to your goal, but less directly. They might be future customers, or people who might block or support you; generally those you would consider in your "outer circle" related to this goal.

In the outermost circle (Circle 4), write "whole self" or "all of life."

Figure 9.2 offers examples of what these circles might look like for a goal regarding "How to grow my business" (Figure 9.2a), or a more specific goal such as improving Sally's performance (Figure 9.2b).

Figure 9.2

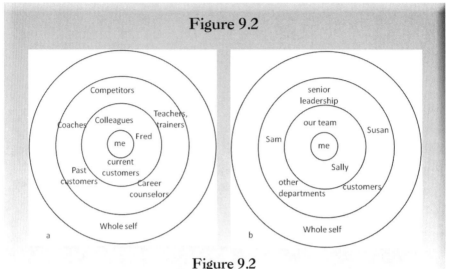

Figure 9.2
Four circles related to (a) growing business or (b) improving Sally's performance.

Imagine what if... Using your pen as an arrow, land on one of the names in Circle 2 or 3 and, speaking in the voice of this person or group, complete the following:

"*Speaking as* [name the person or group you are speaking as],

one of my main issues is [fill in a need of this person/group].

This goal could be in my interests if [fill in how this goal could serve].

My best advice right now would be [fill in best advice for pursuing this goal]."

In the example of how to grow my business, I might land on "current customers," imagine myself as my own customer, and say:

"*Speaking as* your current customer, *one of my main issues is* how to grow my own business in a tough economy. *This goal could be in my interests if* your growth helped me grow. *My best advice right now would be* to spread the wealth and help people learn about me through you."

In the example of Sally's performance, I might land my pen on Sally, and say:

> "*Speaking as* Sally, *one of my main issues is* I don't learn the way you do, and I don't think I can succeed by your standards. *This goal could be in my interests if* you could help me learn my way and be more flexible about what good performance looks like. *My best advice right now would be* let's focus on what you need me to do and let me do it my way."

Pick up your pen and land on a different name in either the inner or outer circle, and repeat, in this new voice, a key need, how this goal could serve, and what would be your best piece of advice right now. Jot down your answers. Repeat several more times and notice how the responses change or reinforce certain themes as you move to different groups or between the inner and outer circle. None of these answers is necessarily more "right" than where you started with your local self, but if you get into the spirit of this exercise, you'll certainly notice they're different, and it may broaden your perspective. Moreover, the advice doesn't have to be for all time. You could repeat this exercise a few months from now and get a different set of perfectly worthy answers.

Finally, land your pen in the outermost Circle 4 and answer in the voice of life itself:

> "*Speaking as the whole picture, one of the needs in this situation is* [fill in from a bird's-eye view].
>
> *This goal could make the world a better place if* [fill in how this goal could serve].
>
> *My best advice right now is* [fill in best advice for pursuing this goal]."

Returning to the "Grow my business" example, speaking as life you might say,

> "*Speaking as the whole picture, one of the needs in this situation is* to show how your product helps your customers be successful. *This goal could make the world a better place if* more people knew how you could help them. *My best advice right now is* to showcase people benefiting from your product."

To coach Sally on improving her performance, your whole self might have this to say:

> *"Speaking as the whole picture, one of the needs in this situation is* to meet Sally where she's at. *This goal could make the world a better place if* you help bring out Sally's greatness without trying to make her into your image. *My best advice right now is* to give Sally a chance to be great at something."

If you compare your answers from the beginning and end of the exercise, you may notice a subtle, even striking shift. Even in the real examples I worked out, you can see how the local-self answers tend to be more tactical ("advertise more"; "monthly meetings") whereas the whole-self answers tend to be more inspirational or strategic ("showcase benefits to others"; "let Sally be great at something"). The whole-self answers don't necessarily contradict those of the local self so much as add new dimensions, or broaden the approach. They may even reveal a better way to state the goal, or an overarching issue that has to be dealt with first.

Because you're reading a book at the moment, this exercise is an act of imagination. But in daily life, you have countless opportunities to engage people in your goal and land on the dot of hearing their perspectives. This exercise has changed the way I listen, especially to feedback or perspectives that my local self doesn't particularly want to hear. For now I know that they represent a dot in the field of possibility somewhere between local "me" and my whole self. The more I understand perspectives I never would have imagined on my own, the more realistic my imagination becomes. And that is the kind of imagination most likely to see, as Einstein would say, life's coming attractions.

So what's the definition of whole leadership? We can return to where we started with perhaps deeper appreciation of the truth behind two answers: On the one hand, it is an expansion of the local self to cast a wider net, engage with empathy, and develop through the various stages that lead from our "terrible 2s" to the wisdom of the sage, with our leadership growing larger and more capable at every turn. On the other hand, it is none of that. It is a flip, a flash of seeing past the local self altogether to the whole self that we are. It is a flip...

- From seeing ourselves as a speck of dust in the universe to seeing the universe expressed through this speck of dust
- From needing to prove one's self to having no self stand apart in need of proof
- From taking care of #1 to becoming one and taking care of the entire picture
- From making the world a better place to transforming one's self to a better place through which a better world manifests
- From a local self barely managing to a whole self leading fearlessly, as nothing stands apart to be afraid

It is a flip similar to the one we make in viewing the classic gestalt drawing of Figure 9.3—the vase and the faces. Perceptually we decide what is figure and what is ground, and that decision constructs our local reality. We might

Figure 9.3

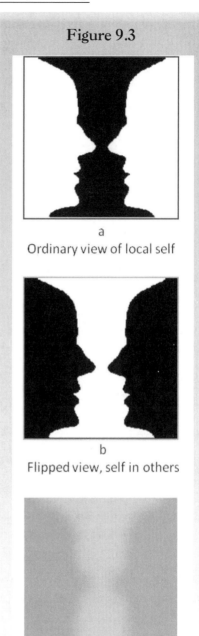

a
Ordinary view of local self

b
Flipped view, self in others

c
Flipped view, whole self

normally regard ourselves as a relatively fixed vase in a sea of faces. Flip that around, become the faces, and we become all about others. At first we may experience this as a sense of serving others or being a steward of something beyond our self. But if we keep imagining our self as the whole picture, we'll notice the boundaries of self become more fluid, and our power to transform seems to go beyond our skin as we manifest invincibility with others. Become the whole picture, and we can use our vase to play a great round of life. This is *really* whole leadership.

If it also sounds like enlightened leadership, that is no accident, for the magnetic pull of awakening has guided our journey all along, and we now close with the final flip.

The Zen Leader
Flip 9 Takeaways
Local Self to Whole Self

Whole leadership is leading as the whole picture.

To approach goals/challenges as your whole self:

- ☯ **Widen the net.** Become all the players and factors in the situation, using empathy and imagination, "holding" them all lightly.

- ☯ **Imagine what if...** You *are* this whole picture; how would you serve it best? Hear or imagine the perspectives around you, including the all-embracing view of your whole self.

- ☯ **Imagination becomes reality.** Keep practicing and eventually no self stands apart: you are that.

10

From Delusion to Awakening

OKAY, YOU CAN stop now. You've explored nine flips that serve better leadership, which is more anyone or any company in the world would ask of you. But if the Zen leader in you is determined to emerge even more clearly, more fully, read on. In a way, our entire journey has been pointing to this flip, and this chapter will give you a chance to see that journey in its totality. But this final flip to awakening is so fundamental and so subtle that you may read these pages and still find it eludes you. Or you may read them now—or come back to them in a few years—and find that something clicks!

That's what happened to me in August 1998. I'm in the women's dorm at Chozen-ji, catching up on some reading while attending a Zen priest seminar. For the past year, Tanouye Roshi has been systematically guiding us through all the "best-selling" sutras. I've read them all (and forgotten much of them), and now I'm reading the Surangama Sutra. *Here we go again.* But as I read, I can't believe my eyes. It's like being back in third grade when you pick up your teacher's arithmetic book and find that it has all the answers in the back! *How can this be?! A book that completely spells out the flip to awakening and how to realize it in your own life!* The Surangama Sutra grabs me by the throat.

And doesn't let go for years. I read it again. And again and again. Until I've completely bored all my friends who ask me what I'm reading: "Still the Surangama Sutra." It's not an easy read. The language and imagery is old, coming from an ancient Sanskrit text.[1] I ask the indulgence of its authors and translators back through time to bring it up to date for you. There are three parts of it I want to share for your final flip; they really did change my life.

Everything Inverted

Imagine we've just entered a large, open room, crowded with people. Students and followers of a great Zen leader have gathered for a Q&A about life, delusion, and awakening. The Leader asks one of the students—we'll call him Joe—a question along the lines of, "Who are you, *really?*"

Joe gives the common-sense answer of being his basic thoughts and moving parts: the eyes that see the Leader, the ears that hear him, and so on. "Hey! That's not who you are!" the Leader thunders. "That's your false thinking, arising from what you think is 'out there.' It has deceived you from the beginning into mistaking a thief for your own son!" He goes on to explain that Joe has everything backwards: What he notices and takes to be himself is not real, and in all that distraction, he misses his true self.

"From the beginning," the Leader continues, "We get caught up in two basic inversions. First, we mistake our clinging mind—our local self—as who we are. Second, because we think we exist as some kind of semi-fixed object, we objectify everything around us and miss its bright essence. We allow ourselves to get turned around by objects when instead, we could turn objects around."

Joe and others are looking confused, as perhaps you are as well. So the Leader tries a metaphor. "If you come to an inn," he asks one of the sages in the room, "would you say the owner is the host or one of the guests?" The sage answers that because the guest comes and goes, the guest could not be the owner, and that the owner would be the host, who has nowhere to go. "Exactly," says the Leader. "And it is the same with us: We have many parts that come and go, be they fleeting thoughts, sensations, or our mortal body, but something notices these things, and that host—that foundational consciousness—has nowhere to go."

And here's where we make the inversion, our crucial mistake: our nervous system clings to movement. It's drawn to shiny objects, and responds to change. We're wired from head to toe to notice what's moving—not what's still. So as we make our unconscious gestalt decision about what's the figure of our life and what's the ground, we assume the figure—the central star of the show—is what's moving! We get it exactly backwards. When we flip to become the background—when awareness becomes aware of itself—only then do we rest in our timeless, boundless self: our host.

The second inversion follows from the first. Because once we exist as a dot of self, we bring all other things into existence. How can we see this? As we explored in the flip from "out there" to "in here," everything we experience from "out there" has "in here" written all over it, from the limitations of our sensors, to the colors we register, and even what catches our attention in the first place. All things exist in relation to "me."

The raw data we take in has one level of "me" written all over it by our sensory limitations. But where this inversion really muddles matters is when it comes to discerning, judging, and making meaning. For the meaning we make has everything to do with our clarity about who we are: guest or host. If we think we are a guest of life, a temporary passer-by in the cycle of birth and death, we are always on the alert for friend or foe or anything that can threaten us. If we know we are the host who has nowhere to go, fear has no toehold.

It's Always About Fear

Now, before you think we've moved into some esoteric realm far removed from your everyday, let's return to the work setting for a moment. You'll see that every boneheaded business decision, every petty office dispute, and every ass-covering or ass-kissing act relates to fear. We may not consciously register that a little fear of death is operating, but in a world of win and lose, gain and loss, hiring and firing, every one of those downsides feels like a little death to a guest. And a guest goes through great gyrations to avoid them. If you've worked in or across a number of organizations, you've seen dozens of stories like these:

The CEO and executive team of a huge but floundering company gather to hear study results from its best and brightest young leaders who were commissioned to find a new future. The young leaders recommend working across organizational silos in teams to create niche products for different customer segments. Their recommendations would radically change the way the company functions and the way people are rewarded. The CEO and the executive team thank them heartily for their outstanding work, and commit to taking action on it. Then nothing happens. Rumor is that the three strongest members of the executive committee who run the three biggest silos won't cooperate. All they see is downside. The CEO, who can't possibly make this year's numbers without them, relents.

All they are is afraid. They probably don't know it, and the ordinary discourse of business will mask their fear with endless data and rational arguments, but these silo-leaders are afraid of loss: of having less power than they once did, less bonus to take home, less certainty about how to operate across the company when they knew perfectly well how to run a silo. What they'll talk about is loss "out there": loss of short-term revenue, loss of what "made us great," which could also happen. Indeed, push them against their will, and a world of loss is what they'll likely create.

Another leader fails to stand up for his team in a tense meeting with senior management when the team's judgment is challenged. He thought his team's judgment was sound, but a Very Important Person has declared that only a moron would agree with the team.

Yet another leader gets an e-mail from a sister division, saying that a promised delivery is going to be three weeks late. She fires off a blaming response, copying two levels of management above her, making clear that any schedule slippage will not be her fault.

All they are is afraid. Afraid for a guest who doesn't want to be dismissed as a moron. Afraid for a guest who doesn't want to be left holding the blame. When the next round of performance reviews (or layoffs!) happen, they don't want to be on the death-side of that calculus.

In one sense, these people are all behaving rationally, doing what seems to be best for the guest, even as they reinforce a rather brutish world of greed and fear. Indeed, the consciousness of our modern age centers on this rational stage of development (recall Table 9.1), where greed and fear operate our markets; our Wall-Street thinking. But even greed is a response to fear, as we want more and more to protect a guest from pain, loss, and eventual destruction.

We are mightily reinforced in this cycle by our own chemistry of emotion. We get a little endorphin jolt when we have an apparent gain, and we're hit with a little corticosteroid bomb by loss.[2] This emotional chemistry is bimodal: it's thumbs up or thumbs down. Our good/bad, life/death responses vary only in degree. There *is* a sense in which a stock market tumble feels like a little death to an investor. Furthermore, emotion seals memory and contributes to learning. We learn to move towards what makes us feel good and away from what makes us feel bad. All of which is perfectly rational. All of which locks our guest into a perfectly rational prison of its own making.

We Are More Than a Guests

Although we certainly live a guest's life in a body that will die, even now, we could be aware of that aspect of our self that is more than a guest—our host self that is not aging, was not born, and will not die. How can we see this? Here's the second scene from our town hall meeting.

Joe has sat down to rest for a bit. A wise and seasoned CEO steps forward—sort of a Warren Buffet type who is widely revered for his great business success and philanthropy. He's getting up in years, and he's aware of his mortality. "I've been taught," he says to the Leader, "that when the body dies, everything just ends. Annihilation. Full stop. Now you talk about something beyond birth and death and I'm not so clear about this."

The Leader asks the CEO, "Tell me, is your body permanent or is it changing?"

"Oh, it's changing, all right," the CEO responds. "It's aging all the time. When I was a child, my face was smooth; now it's all wrinkled. I'm not as strong as I used to be. This body is decaying, no doubt about it. Eventually, like a fire, it will go out."

"You are right that the body is in constant change and, like a fire, will eventually go out," the Leader acknowledges. "But do you know that part of you that is not changing and cannot die?"

"No, I really don't know that part," The CEO admits.

"Think back over your life. Can you recall a scene from your childhood that you still see today?" asks the Leader.

"Sure," says the CEO. "As a child growing up in Michigan, my family would travel to the Upper Peninsula for vacation. I still recall how excited I would be to catch my first glimpse of Lake Superior. And I still travel back to Michigan to see it today."

"Excellent," says the Leader. "And tell me, when you see Lake Superior today, is your seeing of it any 'older' than it was when you were a child?"

"Well, my eyes aren't as good as they used to be. But my seeing of it is the same as always…it always takes me back."

"You note that your face has wrinkles," the Leader continues. "Does this essence of your seeing have wrinkles too?"

The CEO laughs. "Of course not! My eyes are worse for wear, but the essence of my seeing doesn't have any age at all."

"That's right," agrees the Leader. "So why do you concern yourself with annihilation when you're already aware of an aspect of you that is not aging at all? It is like a tornado asking, 'What happens to the wind when I quit spinning?' It is like a wave asking, 'What happens to the ocean when I crest, crash, and recede on the shore?' Know that aspect of you that has nowhere to go."

The CEO in the story is much relieved. But how about you? If you think back to a scene from your childhood that you still see today, can you also sense that the seeing itself has not aged? That bright awareness that allows us to see has no age whatsoever. In fact, it is so boundless and ever-present that it fails to trigger our nervous system in the ordinary way with an edge or a flicker that we register as "something." Because it is not something at all, but rather the vast "nothingness" in which all "somethings" arise, including the moving parts we identify as our self. So even as we sense this boundless awareness that makes every perception, thought, and movement possible, it doesn't interest us. It doesn't grab our attention. Rather, it remains hidden in plain sight; we either fail to see it, or, seeing it, we fail to recognize that it is also us. Our host.

Sustaining the Flip

Joe, too, is skeptical. He's an honest guy, and although the idea of being more than a fleeting phenomenon has great appeal, he knows that he doesn't totally buy it. "Your teaching is wonderful," he says, getting to his feet. "I've heard you say it many times. Right now, I believe it. But a few days from now, I'll be right back to my usual local self. How do I see this through and through?" Here's the third part of the story.

"You're right that knowing something as a temporary thought is different than expressing it through your whole being," the Leader says. "To see it through and through, you must engage your entire body. For that is where the backward learnings of the local self are stored, where all the knots and tension reside, where all the distraction is created, and where the fan blades spin too quickly to see through and through."

"But how do I *do* this?" Joe pleads.

Whereupon the Leader speaks to meditation and invites Joe into a real-time practice of meditating on the "nothingness" out of which all things arise. "As you sit quietly, aware of your breath, aware through all of your senses, as things arise in your awareness, invert them and send them back to their source. You will see that all things come from other things and decay into other things. Your own breath, for example, is supported by lungs, made from tissue, organized by cells, built up from molecules and atoms, made of subatomic particles that are also waves, which are fundamentally empty. Where does the emptiness return to? Rest in that which has nowhere to go."

Joe has an inkling of this experience, but he's still confused, which is natural because integration through the entire body is not the work of a single example or the reading of a single paragraph. Sustaining the flip of awakening takes practice. A good deal of practice. The Leader calls upon other teachers in the room to share their own practices for awakening to their whole nature.

"I used my sense of smell," one teacher offers. "While meditating one day, the smell of sandalwood incense entered my nose. I entered the smell completely, finding it neither sandalwood nor nothing, neither here nor there, neither coming nor going, whereupon my usual knowing vanished, and I reached a state beyond birth or death or any duality."

Another teacher uses sight, and so on. Eventually the Leader calls on the wisest of the teachers to sum up what's been said and offer the best and final piece of advice. This teacher summarizes his advice in memorable verse, concluding roughly as follows:

The ways of practice are many.

Some work better than others,

and some work better for certain people than others.

But if you ask me what works best in general,

I would have to say

Sound.

For sound is ever-present,

And our sense of hearing is ever available to teach us.

To hear your own nature

Invert that faculty used to hear even the wisest words.

Flip your hearing around,

Return all sounds to their source

Until the heard and the hearing have nowhere to go.

Wherever there is motion,

Look to what pulls the strings.

When the puppeteer stops

The puppets have no nature.

Likewise when even one sense stops,

The empty nature of all others is revealed.

Delusion vanishes;

Awakening remains.[3]

Play It Backward

Do you feel as though you just looked at the answer at the back of the book? If my coarse retelling piques your interest, I encourage you to check out the real Surangama Sutra. It recounts an allegorical meeting between Gautama Buddha and his followers. Our Joe is Ananda in the sutra, who speaks the common view of every man or woman. This story is not about a particular belief system; rather, it speaks to the underpinning of human beliefs and experience, which is, to paraphrase Badaracco, clarity about who we are. Unfortunately, what most of us are clear about is backwards. What we take to be real is a dream, and in the distraction of the dream, we miss what's real.

Recounting this ancient story also underscores the fact that awakening to our whole self is not the new-fangled idea of a New Age. It has been part of our collective human experience for more than 2,500 years, and yet ignored by most of us. Why do we ignore it? One reason, as we've said, is that our nervous system is wired to notice the shiny, new object, not the empty essence out of which it arises. It also takes years for us to grow through enough stages of development to think abstractly or sense the essence of something. Similar to what we described earlier with empathy having to edge in alongside narcissism, by the time we mature enough to be able to sense the profundity of the "background," our "figure" is firmly in control. We can make the flip, but we don't do it so long as the dream is pretty much working. If it's a nice, comfortable dream, why wake up? Even if the dream is not working, we come to identify so deeply with our drama that letting it go would end life as we know it: another mini-death.

As a result, this flip only happens when the local self gets good and sick of the dream, and has no other choice for reaching the happiness and fulfillment it senses is possible. In that sense, being in a state of barely managing in our dream serves us well by pushing us to wake up. But by the time the dream isn't working, we may be so entangled in it that we have no idea that awakening is possible, much less how to do it.

I'm reminded of a brilliant movie that came out some years ago: *Memento*. It's a challenging movie to watch because it takes us into the mind of a protagonist, Leonard, who has a memory disorder that causes him to forget things within 15 minutes. So to make our viewing as confusing as Leonard's world, the entire story is told backwards. It starts with the end, at which Leonard has killed a man who had killed Leonard's wife—or did he? We don't know what really happened. Like Leonard, we go by cryptic notes scrawled on Polaroids and clues he has tattooed onto his skin—mementos of people and facts that seem important in this cat-and-mouse game, tracing back to the death of his wife. Who is friend? Who is foe? Clearly people are shooting at him, but why? It's all a confusing mess. As the story backs up further, we piece together Leonard's earlier life and scenes surrounding his wife's murder. Finally, near the end of the movie—which is the beginning of the story—we get to the pivotal scene on which all of this drama will hinge. I suppose I should raise a spoiler alert, but this scene is what makes this movie not only an excellent shoot-em-up thriller, but also a brilliant story about you and me. For at this point Leonard receives a crucial piece of evidence about his wife's death. If he accepts the truth of the evidence, there's nothing to do—no one upon whom to exact revenge. But instead he ignores it, "to have something to live for," and a backward story begins.

Exactly the same thing happens to us: we ignore the truth to have something to live for, and the backward dream of our life ensues, reinforced by a kind of amnesia. I'd read for years that ignorance is the root of delusion and suffering, and mistakenly equated "ignorance" with "stupidity." I thought we just weren't smart enough to get it. Not so; we're plenty smart. The evidence of our boundless, immortal nature is available to us all the time, as the Leader was able to point out to the CEO in the story. But we *ignore* it; we are *ignor*-ant. Our boundless nature doesn't interest us because it doesn't move (though all movement arises within in). It's not a story with a beginning, middle, and dramatic end (though all stories arise within it). We ignore it, and choose a story instead: our story. Me.

Like Leonard, we suffer a sort of amnesia in forgetting who we are. We get too wrapped up to see clearly, and maybe people are shooting at us, metaphorically speaking, or a sense of urgency grabs our attention here—no, there! Like Leonard, many of us live in a world demarked by fear, where only the paranoid survive. Or we get ensnared in coping mode by trying to please, appease, or protect ourselves from powerful others. The pace picks up, resources shrink, deadlines loom: we throw ourselves at it day after day. Once we're in the thick of it—dream or nightmare—it's self-feeding. To flip to awakening, we have to pause the dream and invert our ordinary way of thinking.

We have to run the story backwards to the pivotal point before thought and thinker exist, returning any *thing* to what it comes from until we get to all-abiding awareness that has nowhere to go. We can either accept the truth that this awareness is also our self, or we can ignore it and go back to our dream. But the more we come to this cusp, the more our local self rests in our whole self, and the more we understand we are not two separate parts—a piece and a whole—or warring factions, but rather the entire universe with manual dexterity. This is where *real* clarity about who we are blossoms.

The Zen Leader Flip 10: Delusion to Awakening

So how to get to that cusp? In making the flip to awakening, because we, ourselves are flipped in the making, ordinary tactics will not be up to the job. Instead we have to temporarily stop—hit the pause button on the dream—sit still, breathe, and completely enter the stream of energy flowing through us, and in which we participate. For most people, sound energy is easiest to work with, because many parts of our body (in addition to eardrums) resonate with the frequencies of sound. Dissolving into the stream of sound, boundaries and tension disappear. As thought arises, for example, "a car honking," we flip our normal tendency to think *about* the sound, and simply send the thought, the sound, the vibration back to the emptiness from which it came. Resting in that which has no place to go, guest and host unite.

The Zen Leader
Flip 10
Delusion to Awakening

☯ Slow down...stop
☯ Enter the stream
☯ Rest in that which has no place to go

Slow down...stop. You've seen this step before, as it supports so many flips. Indeed, the meditation practice at the end of Chapter 4 is the best way I know to slow down...

stop. You might review that now, and then become aware of your breathing, allowing your breath, your thoughts, your world to slow down. Sit for maybe 20 minutes and even tension you're not aware of has a chance to fall away.

Enter the stream. While still sitting quietly in meditation, let your senses open fully. Let your eyes take in 180 degrees and nothing in particular. Similarly let your ears hear all frequencies and seize on nothing. Enter the stream of sound completely, as if you were immersed in a beam of sunshine, letting the energy go right through you. Enter this stream of sound with empty, open awareness. Rather than picking out sounds and naming them, feel all sounds as nameless vibration. No discerning judgment required.

Rest in that which has no place to go. Still, judgment will arise, because our minds are busy and we have plenty of language to apply to our perceptions. As judgment arises, as in, "What's that racket out the window?" rather than naming it or reacting to it, return the sound to its basic vibration, and send vibration back to its source, as in "air disturbance, empty waves, out of nothing."

Or if emotion arises, for example, "I hate loud noises," send "I hate loud noises" back to where it came from, as in, "childhood...frightened by sharp noises...danger...before knowledge of danger...unformed, unborn...nothing."

These free-associating sentences are not meant to be logical; this is not an intellectual exercise. This is not *thinking about* sending something back to its source; it is simply *sending* something back to its source—like an instantaneous rewind of a movie. But to give you a feel for it in a book, I have to use clunky, linear words.

Your words and images may differ from mine. This sending back may follow any number of pathways. For example, we can send things back in time to what came from what, as in:

parents, grandparents, ancestors...cave dwellers, animals, plants, single-cell organisms...origin of life, the earth, the universe, the big bang, empty potentiality before the big bang

We can send things back in space in the sense of building blocks:

big things, built from little things, from molecules, atoms, subatomic particles, which are also waves, which are fundamentally empty

We can send things back psychologically:

this issue came from that one, from childhood, to when I made that interpretation, to before I knew, to before any knowing, empty, unborn potential

No matter what pathway we follow, if we go far enough—before subject and object separate, before "I" distills out to mistake thinking as its essence and creates a world "out there"—we end up in the same place of no-thing, emptiness, all-abiding awareness of that which has nowhere to go. Rest in this all-abiding awareness. It is none other than your own Being: boundless emptiness in which all form takes shape. Boundless self in which the impulse to be "I" arises, at which moment, a dream begins.

What's the point to all this sending back or resting in oneness? "I still have to go to work on Monday," you may be thinking. "I still have too much to do. What does it matter if I rest in this stillness for a minute, an hour, or a day?"

Well, first there's the joy. We've almost all experienced this joy in the letting-go moments of our life: from shedding emotional baggage to surrendering to physical pleasure. Almost always we find at that moment of letting go, new space opens up and joy arises. Imagine letting go of all of it! Imagine if we shed our drama altogether or surrendered completely, as Jill Bolte Taylor described that last bit of air squeezed out in the ambulance. Surrendering the local self flips to affirming the whole self—liberated like a genie from a bottle. The self-destruction we feared flips to affirming the self that is beyond destruction! We flip from using life to postpone, preserve, or otherwise protect ourselves to giving life to all things.

The you that re-enters Monday morning is changed, as the Zen leader you are functions fully and freely. You know you are the entire picture:

the game, the maker of the game, and the player on the board. Now don't you think you might live and lead a little more fearlessly?

Nothing stands in your way!

Putting It to Work: Good, Better, and Best Practices

The flip from delusion to awakening is, on the one hand, instantaneous: the insight delivered in an *aha!* moment is wondrous indeed. And then we go back to everyday life, from pressing deadlines to dishes in the sink, and all that *aha!* fades to memory. We might try to call it back, but it's not the same—like remembering a delicious meal: we might recall a pleasant circumstance, but it doesn't provide nutrition.

I used to get so frustrated in my Zen training with this on-again, off-again insight. The intense, week-long training of *sesshin* would invariably invite the connectedness of Samadhi and flashes of seeing my whole self. At the end of *sesshin*, Hosokawa Roshi would always say, "maintain this condition," and I would go back to my everyday life and try to do that, sitting every morning, doing Aikido at night. But I found I couldn't maintain that condition. One time he said "maintain this condition," and it made me so angry, I threw it back at him. "You always say, 'maintain this condition,' and I've tried and tried, but I find it impossible!"

"That's right," he said. "But you have to try."

And that's it. The point is not maintaining some magical state; as dynamic biological systems we don't maintain any state indefinitely. We will always go back and forth between boundless awareness and our local self paying the bills. The point is simply to come back to practice again and again. If you want to flip from delusion to awakening—from amnesia to remembering—you simply have to give yourself a chance to do it again and again.

How you do that and how much you do that is up to you. The local self must be a willing participant in the flip to awakening, as it requires "great doubt, great effort, and great faith."[4] The doubt fuels our motivation. We may experience it as questions, dissatisfaction, barely managing, or work that isn't working. Sometimes I hear people complain about their difficult lives. They're between a rock and a hard place, and so much is going wrong. And yet they have reason after reason why they can't make even the most obvious steps to change. What they don't see is that they're coping with their dissatisfaction—letting the steam out of it, so to speak—rather than using it as fuel for transformation. The greater the doubt or dissatisfaction, the more it can charge up our efforts to resolve it.

The effort is what we make to come back to practice again and again, and, in our practice, to practice sincerely. There are many ways of practice. But if you have found the flips of this book useful, the next section lays out three streams of practice—what we might call good, better, and best—for coming back to them again and again.

Three Streams of Practice

Good
(20–40 mins/day)

A good practice consists of:

1. Mini-breaks, to interrupt the cycle of "busy."

2. A work behavior that lets you practice a desired flip.

3. A physical activity that gives you more energy or the right kind of energy.

4. Reflection, to listen and learn from your experience.

The core practices at the end of Chapters 2, 4, 6, and 7, as well as those online at *www.thezenleader.com* are available to support you.

Mini-breaks. These may be only **2 minutes** long, and are best done **twice a day** to refresh during long stretches of work (for example, mid-morning or mid-afternoon). A great way to use these breaks is to cycle through the flip-supporting breathing exercises (Centering, Invitation to Samadhi, All Patterns at Once).

Work behavior. Apply a desired flip in your work, making a habit of one of the applications we've explored; for example, thinking in paradox (Chapter 3) or practicing influence (Chapter 6). You can move through each flip systematically, spending, say, a month with each. Or look at your life and leadership now and pick a flip that would help you most. Identify a pattern that would support that flip, and then select a work behavior in that pattern from Table 5.1.

Physical activity. Whether it's a workout, a hobby, or a creative pursuit, use a physical activity with awareness to get either more energy or the right pattern of energy. You might consider physical activities that support the flip you're working on (see Table 5.1).

Reflection. Take maybe **15 minutes each week** to listen and learn. You might use this time to revisit reflection exercises in this book, such as your vision (see Chapters 2 and 7) or an important goal (see Chapter 8).

A great reflection practice is to **Look Back, Look Forward.** Look back to the week behind you: Were you able to do what you intended? What worked, what didn't work, and what did you learn? Look to the week ahead: What do you intend? Listen not only to surface answers, but also imagine different perspectives or hear "all of life" speaking (as in Chapter 9).

Better

(40–60 mins/day)

A better practice starts with a good practice and adds 20 minutes a day of **sitting meditation** (see Chapter 4).

In time, try different work behaviors and physical activities as you change and as your needs change; let your expanding awareness guide your practice, in addition to teacher(s) in whom you trust.

Best

(60–80 mins/day)

The best practice builds on the better practice by expanding the sitting meditation to 40 minutes, giving you time to **enter the stream** of sound energy, and **send things back** in the way described in this chapter. Keep returning to rest in that which has nowhere to go.

These streams build on one another, and can be made to fit any life. You'll find ways to tailor them to your own needs and interests. More than anything, you'll find your life, your work, and your leadership re-energized every time you return to practice and remember who you truly are.

The guidance of a teacher is useful along the way, for we'll need help confronting the many tricks, turns, and evasive tactics of the local self. Our local self may be making a sincere effort to practice, but it will also get threatened and want to run away. And that's where great faith or trust comes in. It's not faith in something outside our whole self (where's outside?), but in something greater than the immediate perceptions of our local self. Faith is trusting in the power of practice, even when we don't seem to be making a lick of progress. Faith is knowing it is our nature to reintegrate with our whole self, even as it is in the nature of a flower to turn toward the sun.

The Zen Leader
Flip 10 Takeaways
Delusion to Awakening

I-centered thought is already too small. Find that place of stillness in which "I" and all things arise.

The key in practice is to return again and again:

- ☯ **Good.** Use (a) **mini-breaks**, to interrupt the cycle of "busy," (b) a **work behavior** that lets you practice a desired flip, (c) a **physical activity** to get more energy, or the right kind of energy, and (d) **reflection** to listen and learn.

- ☯ **Better.** Build on a good practice and add 20 minutes a day of sitting **meditation**. Find trustworthy teacher(s).

- ☯ **Best.** Expand your meditation to 40 minutes to enter the stream of sound and send things back to emptiness, **resting in that which has nowhere to go.**

Moved by great doubt to make great effort, supported by great faith, the flip to awakening becomes our own experience. A journey that began with barely managing culminates in the fearless leading of one who has nowhere to be lost to, and nothing to prove. All that we feared might destroy us flips to setting us free! Whereupon we can flip around and play back our entire journey, chapter by chapter:

NINE—Whole self and local self mutually interweave; not a single act fails to serve the whole picture.

EIGHT—It is no longer a matter of generosity to be "all about it" so much as boundless self-expression; why on earth would we make the infinite "all about the finite"? Rather, we use our "manual dexterity" while we have it.

SEVEN—Naturally we attract the future, because we no longer ignore what's real, and our sensitivity is far-reaching.

SIX—Connected as waves are to water—a part *of*, not apart *from*—we no longer wrestle to control life like a foreign object.

FIVE—We have a healthy awareness of our personality, but we are not a prisoner of it; we can strengthen our play using any kind of energy.

FOUR—Transcending the boundary between "in here" and "out there," we own and transform our reactions and fears, and our capacity grows.

THREE—We're no longer confined by the limits of this *Or* that; we play in the power of *And*, transcending the duality of opposites.

TWO—Including the duality of life and death, which no longer holds us in the tension of its grip, we are free to extend our energy in all directions, according the myriad changes.

ONE—Which is the transforming freedom of the Zen leader in us.

Blast off!

Notes

Introduction

1. "Internet 2009 in Numbers," Royal Pingdom, January 22, 2010. *http://royal.pingdom.com/2010/01/22/internet-2009-in-numbers/* (accessed January 27, 2012).

2. Marlin Company Poll, "Attributes in the American Workplace," 2004–2008, Gallup Poll research on employee engagement, 2007.

3. American Psychological Association Survey of Workplace Stress, 2004.

Chapter 1

1. Cashman, K., *Leadership from the Inside Out* (Provo, Utah: Executive Excellence Publishing, 2000).

2. Tolle, E., *A New Earth* (New York: Plume Penguin, 2005).

Chapter 2

1. Dotlich, David, and Peter Cairo, *Why CEO's Fail* (San Francisco: Jossey Bass, 2003).

2. Simpson, John, *When Simpson Met Mandela* (High Life Magazine, June 2010).

3. Loehr, Jim, and Tony Schwartz, *The Power of Full Engagement* (New York: Simon & Schuster, 2003).

4. Ibid.

5. I thank Wayne Honda Roshi for sharing this method.

6. The "front–back" designation for legs is somewhat reversed, as the back of the knee is the flexor side, akin to the crook of the arm.

Chapter 3

1. Johnson, Barry, *Polarity Management: Identifying and Managing Unsolvable Problems* (Amherst, Mass.: HRD Press, 1992).

Chapter 4

1. Schutz, Will, *The Truth Option* (Berkeley, Calif.: Ten Speed Press, 1984).

2. Loehr, James, *The Power of Story* (New York: Free Press, 2007).

3. Edwards, Betty, *Drawing on the Right Side of the Brain* (New York: Tarcher/Putnam, 1999).

4. Benoit, H., *Zen and the Psychology of Transformation* (Rochester, Vt.: Pantheon, 1955).

5. O'Brien, Michael, and Larry Shook, *Quicksilver* (Spokane, Wa.: Sombrero Press, 2010).

Chapter 5

1. Horney, K. *Our Inner Conflicts* (New York: Norton, 1945).

2. Briggs Myers, I., *Introduction to Type* (Palo Alto, Calif.: Consulting Psychologist Press, 1998).

3. Costa, P., and R. McRae, *The NEO Personality Inventory* (Odessa, Fl.: Psychological Assessment Resources, 1985).

4. Hogan, R., *Hogan Development Survey, Personality Inventory, Motive, Value and Preference Inventory* (Tulsa, Okla.: Hogan Assessment Systems, 1997, 1999).

5. Herrmann, N., *The Creative Brain* (Lake Lure, N.C.: The Ned Herrmann Group, 1989).

6. Rathbone, J., *Residual Neuromuscular Hypertension* (New York: Columbia University Press, 1936).

7. Hunt, V., and M. Weber, "Validation of the Rathbone Manual Tension Test for Muscular Activity," *Archives of Physical Medicine and Rehabilitation* 45:525–529.

8. Coordination Patterns™ is a trademark of Betsy Wetzig.

9. Whitelaw, G., and B. Wetzig, *Move to Greatness* (Boston: Nicholas Brealey, 2008).

10. FEBI is a registered trademark of Focus Leadership, LLC.

11. Anthony Attan led much of this validation research, along with Bob Caron, and great support from our Performance Programs partner, Paul Connelly. For more information on research behind the FEBI, or the FEBI itself, visit *www.focusleadership.com.*

12. For more ways to develop access to patterns, see *Move to Greatness.*

Chapter 6

1. Wood, J., *Leaving Microsoft to Change the World* (New York: HarperCollins, 2006).

2. Dwyer, C., *The Shifting Sources of Power and Influence* (CITY: ACPE Publication, 1992).

3. These steps are adapted from Cohen, A., and D. Bradford, *Influence without Authority* (New York: John Wiley, 1991); and Fisher, R., and W. Ury, *Getting to Yes* (New York: Penguin, 1991).

4. These breathing exercises are adapted from *hara* development exercises taught at Chozen-ji and from Lisa Sarasohn's exercises in *The Woman's Belly Book* (Novato, Calif.:, New World Library, 2006), used with permission. I gratefully acknowledge these sources.

Chapter 7

1. See, for example, Lutz, A., L. Greischar, N. Rawlings, M. Ricard, M., and R. Davidson, "Long-term meditators self-induce high-amplitude gamma synchrony during mental practice," *The Proceedings of the National Academy of Sciences USA* 101.46 (2004): 16369–16373.

2. Tolle, E., *A New Earth* (New York : Plume Penguin, 2005).

Chapter 8

1. Maslow, A.H., "A Theory of Human Motivation," *Psychological Review* 50.4(1943): 370–396.

2. PFC Ross McGinnis was awarded the Medal of Honor for his self-sacrificing service. See *http://cmohs.org/recipient-detail/3459/mcginnis-ross-a.php*.

3. CNN Staff, "Mother Teresa: A Profile," retrieved from CNN Online, May 30, 2007.

4. See the CDC's Website, *http://www.cdc.gov/obesity/data/trends.html*, for data on obesity in America.

Chapter 9

1. Badaracco, J R., Jr., *Defining Moments* (Cambridge: Harvard Business School Press, 1997).

2. See, for example, Kohlberg, L., *The Philosophy of Moral Development: Moral Stages and the Idea of Justice* (New York: Harper & Row, 1981); Beck, D., and C. Cowan, *Spiral Dynamics* (Cambridge: Blackwell Publishers, 1995); Wilber, K., *A Theory of Everything* (Boston: Shambala, 2000); Wilber, K., *A Brief History of Everything* (Boston: Shambala, 1996).

3. Bolte Taylor, Jill, *My Stroke of Insight* (New York: Penguin, 2008). The quote is from an online video by the same name.

4. This mapping to the patterns is accurate in terms of so-called left- and right-brain thinking. But the energy patterns, like actual thoughts, involve both hemispheres, even if one is primary. Whereas each pattern has a different ego-concept, it is not the case that the more right-brain patterns of Collaborator and Visionary are ego-free. Indeed, the ego is expressed in all of the patterns, appropriate to its stage of development (for example, teenager vs. sage).

5. Burchard, B., *The Millionaire Messenger* (New York: Morgan James, 2011).

6. See, for example, Singh, Kathleen, *The Grace in Dying* (San Francisco: HarperCollins, 1998).

7. Wilber, K., *A Theory of Everything* (Boston: Shambala, 2000); Wilber, K., *A Brief History of Everything* (Boston: Shambala, 1996).

8. Wilber, K., *A Theory of Everything*, pp 9–13.

9. Colvin, G., *Newark Mayor Cory Booker*, interview in *Fortune*, November 15, 2010.

Chapter 10

1. See *The Surangama Sutra*, translated by Charles Luk (New Delhi: Munshiram Manoharlal Publishers, 2001).

2. Pert, C., *The Molecules of Emotion* (New York: Touchstone, 1999).

3. Adapted from "Majusri's Gatha Teaching the Appropriate Method for Human Beings," in *The Surangama Sutra*.

4. As articulated by the great Zen master, Dogen.

Index

About the Author

DR. GINNY WHITELAW didn't dream she'd become an innovator in leadership development. She dreamt of being an astronaut, and wrote NASA at the age of 13 to ask about the courses she should take in junior high school to best prepare. Treasuring the letter they sent back, she followed its advice to study science, which led to three years in a high-energy physics lab, a doctorate in biophysics, and a lifelong interest in energy and the human body.

Along the way she also started intense physical training, first in martial arts, and then in Zen, which led to a 5th-degree black belt in Aikido and her becoming a roshi (Zen Master) in the Chozen-ji line of Rinzai Zen. She also found her way to NASA. There, she went into management, not space, eventually becoming the Deputy Manager for integrating the Space Station program, and receiving

NASA's Exceptional Service Medal for her efforts. All of this came together in a new way, however, when she attended her first NASA leadership program and discovered, to her own surprise, *this* was her work. She continued to learn everything she could about leadership development and combine it with everything she knew about Zen, biophysics, and the human body.

For the past 16 years, Dr. Whitelaw has brought this rich background to the service of leaders all over the world. She cofounded Focus Leadership with a mind-body integrated approach to developing transformational leaders and their teams. Together with Mark Kiefaber, she developed the FEBI (Focus Energy Balance Indicator) to measure the energy patterns of personality, and she trains practitioners all over the world in how to apply the FEBI in their work. She has also led, coached, and taught in countless programs for Global1000 leaders, in part through her affiliation with Oliver Wyman Leadership Development, and as adjunct faculty to Columbia University's Senior Executive Program. She is the co-author of *Move to Greatness* (with Betsy Wetzig, 2008), and continues to teach Zen applications to leadership, in which the ideas of *The Zen Leader* have met with such enthusiasm, they needed to be written down.